LISTENING, COMMUNITY ENGAGEMENT, AND PEACEBUILDING

& gratitude

Zenebe

Zenebe Beyene
08/09/23
Oxford, MS

This book explores the role of listening in community engagement and peacebuilding efforts, bridging academic research in communication and practical applications for individual and social change.

For all their differences, community engagement and peacebuilding efforts share much in common: the need to establish and agree on achievable and measurable goals, the importance of trust, and the need for conflict management, to name but a few. This book presents listening – considered as a multi-disciplinary concept related to but distinct from civility, civic participation, and other social processes – as a primary mechanism for accomplishing these tasks. Individual chapters explore these themes in an array of international contexts, examining topics such as conflict resolution, restorative justice, environmental justice, migrants and refugees, and trauma-informed peacebuilding. The book includes contemporary literature reviews and theoretical insights covering the role of listening as related to individual, social, and governmental efforts to better engage communities and build, maintain, or establish peace in an increasingly divided world.

This collection provides invaluable insight to researchers, students, educators, and practitioners in intercultural and international communication, conflict management, peacebuilding, community engagement, and international studies.

Graham D. Bodie is Professor of Integrated Marketing Communication in the School of Journalism and New Media at The University of Mississippi, USA.

Debra L. Worthington is Professor of Communication and Director of the School of Communication & Journalism at Auburn University, USA.

Zenebe Beyene is Associate Professor and Coordinator of International Programs in the School of Journalism and New Media at The University of Mississippi, USA.

LISTENING, COMMUNITY ENGAGEMENT, AND PEACEBUILDING

International Perspectives

*Edited by Graham D. Bodie,
Debra L. Worthington, and
Zenebe Beyene*

Routledge
Taylor & Francis Group

NEW YORK AND LONDON

Designed cover image: © Moncherie / Getty Images

First published 2023
by Routledge
605 Third Avenue, New York, NY 10158

and by Routledge
4 Park Square, Milton Park, Abingdon, Oxon, OX14 4RN

Routledge is an imprint of the Taylor & Francis Group, an informa business

Library of Congress Cataloguing-in-Publication Data
Names: Bodie, Graham, editor. | Worthington, Debra L., editor. |
Beyene, Zenebe, editor.
Title: Listening, community engagement, and peacebuilding : international
perspectives / Edited by Graham D. Bodie, Debra L. Worthington,
Zenebe Beyene.
Description: New York, NY : Routledge, 2023. | Includes bibliographical
references and index.
Identifiers: LCCN 2022058374 | ISBN 9781032102610 (hardback) |
ISBN 9781032079233 (paperback) | ISBN 9781003214465 (ebook)
Subjects: LCSH: Peace-building--Cross-cultural studies. |
Listening--Social aspects--Cross-cultural studies. |
Conflict management--Cross-cultural studies.
Classification: LCC JZ5538 .L57 2023 | DDC 303.6/9--dc23/eng/
20230302
LC record available at https://lccn.loc.gov/2022058374

ISBN: 978-1-032-10261-0 (hbk)
ISBN: 978-1-032-07923-3 (pbk)
ISBN: 978-1-003-21446-5 (ebk)

DOI: 10.4324/9781003214465

Typeset in Bembo
by MPS Limited, Dehradun

CONTENTS

CONTRIBUTORS

Nichole Argo is Director of Research and Field Advancement at Over Zero, an organization that works to build resilience to identity-based violence and other forms of group-targeted harm. A social psychologist by training, Nichole has also done extensive field research in conflict zones within Africa and the Middle East. Her research on intergroup dynamics and participation in violence has been published in top psychology and security journals. Her research at Over Zero seeks to advance the fields of atrocity prevention and democracy by focusing on sacred values (arguing that polls/surveys must not just identify what positions the public holds, but how deeply they hold them, and why) and the essential but overlooked concept of belonging (demonstrating the relationship between lack of belonging in the United States and social ills in health, intergroup dynamics, and democracy). Long interested in the intersection of science and practice, Nichole co-founded the Interdisciplinary Center on Political Violence at The Center for International Studies at MIT, co-directed "The Project on Radicalization: A Neuroscientific Approach" at the Center for Counterterrorism at Tufts University, and is a current co-Founder/Director of two local democracy initiatives: The Lived Experiences Project and the Needham Resilience Network. She has consulted with governments, media groups, and policy think tanks, and her work has been profiled by major media outlets, such as Chicago National Public Radio and Fox News. Dr. Argo holds degrees from Stanford, MIT, and the New School for Social Research. Her forthcoming book is titled *Human Bombs: Social Identity and Sacrifice in a Divided World* (2024).

Ambar Basu is Professor in the Department of Communication at the University of South Florida. His scholarship locates health inequities in the context of cultural, political, economic, geopolitical, and development agendas in marginalized spaces.

Zenebe Beyene specializes in media in conflict and post-conflict societies. He has taught, researched, or provided training in Ethiopia, Kenya, Rwanda, Uganda, and the United States. Dr. Beyene has served as a consultant for InterNews Network, US Agency for International Development, United Nations Development Program, Voice of America, Pennsylvania University/Carnegie Foundation, Oxford University, and Oxford University/UK Embassy in Ethiopia and Aadland Consult/IDEA International. Dr. Beyene has published or co-published work about building peace through listening, the role of the Ethiopian diaspora in political affairs of the homeland, tolerance and online debate in Ethiopia, the role of TeleCourt in changing conceptions of justice and authority in Ethiopia, the role of ICT in peacebuilding in Africa, media use and abuse in Ethiopia, *From an Emperor to the Derg and Beyond: Examining the Intersection of Music and Politics in Ethiopia*. Framing Contesting Nationalisms, Resistance, and Triumph in Ethiopian Popular Music, and International Peace Journalism (PJ) Practice: Comparing the levels of PJ awareness among Bangladeshi and Ethiopian journalists.

Graham D. Bodie is Professor of Integrated Marketing Communication in the School of Journalism and New Media at The University of Mississippi. He is recognized as an international expert on listening and the social cognitive underpinnings of human communicative behavior, having authored over 90 published papers in outlets such as *Human Communication Research, Communication Monographs, Communication Research, Communication Yearbook*, and the *International Journal of Listening* and two other co-edited books: *The Sourcebook of Listening Research: Methods and Measures* and *The Handbook of Listening*. His productivity has placed him in the top 1% of published Communication Studies scholars. Dr. Bodie's research has been funded by the National Science Foundation and US Army, and he regularly appears in local and national media outlets on issues relevant to listening in close relationships. He currently serves as Chief Listening Officer for Listen First Project, a non-profit dedicated to bringing people into conversation despite differences.

Rachel Brown is Founder and Executive Director of Over Zero, an organization that works to build resilience to identity-based violence and other forms of group-targeted harm. She is a recognized expert on confronting hateful and dangerous rhetoric, and her work for the past decade has focused on using communication to prevent violent conflict around the world. Rachel authored *Defusing Hate: A Strategic Communication Guide to Counteract Dangerous Speech* and was a Fellow at the U.S. Holocaust Memorial Museum's Simon Skjodt Center for Prevention of Genocide. She also founded and was the CEO of Sisi ni Amani-Kenya (SNA-K), an internationally recognized organization that pioneered new strategies to build local capacity for violence prevention and civic engagement in Kenya. Rachel has provided training and strategy support to organizations and programs in the United States, Europe, Asia, and Africa and consulted for organizations including the World Bank, DAI, and Internews. Her work has been profiled at conferences, events, and publications globally, including CBS, PopTech, the United States Institute for Peace, United States Airforce Academy, UN Department of Political and Peacebuilding Affairs, universities across the United States, and the Stavros Niarchos Foundation International Conference on Philanthropy.

Joske Bunders-Aelen is Chair Professor of Transdisciplinarity for Sustainable Development at World Peace University in Pune, India, and Visiting Professor at the Athena Institute for Innovation and Communication in the Health and Life Sciences, Vrije Universiteit Amsterdam. She is the founder and was director (until 2019) of the Athena Institute. Her research focuses on understanding and addressing system change in the field of biotechnology, mental health, and agriculture. Specific topics are the role of complexity, social entrepreneurship, leadership, and co-production of knowledge through the facilitation of stakeholder processes, especially in community engagement.

Ekemini Ekpo is Research Associate at Over Zero. Her previous work has included research on the intersections of race, gender, and gun violence in affiliation with the Harvard Chan School of Public Health and an examination of the internet as a space for white nationalist identity formation. She holds an A.B. in Sociology from Harvard University.

Iginio Gagliardone is Associate Professor in Media and Communication at the University of the Witwatersrand and Associate Research Fellow in New Media and Human Rights at the University of Oxford (Programme in Comparative Media Law and Policy). He is the author of *The Politics of Technology in Africa* and *China, Africa, and the Future of the Internet*.

Mary Jo Harwood, LSW, DNCCM, has spent over 30 years addressing the impacts of unrecognized and unresolved trauma on communities and individuals experiencing prolonged violence. She has trained nationally and internationally on the impact of trauma. Her experience with incidents of mass casualty and sexual assault survivors provides the expertise necessary to remove trauma as a barrier to sustainable peace and community cohesion. A member of Mediators Beyond Borders International since 2007, she has applied her expertise through work with child soldiers in Liberia, Pastoralists in Kenya, women and youth in South Sudan, and consulted with teams in Northern Nigeria and Kenya to address the intersection of trauma and peacebuilding through the application of conflict and trauma sensitive programming. She is a member and recognized Diplomat of the American Academy of Experts in Traumatic Stress and the National Center for Crisis Management. Currently, Mary Jo works for the Traumatic Stress Institute fostering the transformation of organizations and service systems to trauma-informed care.

Andrew Cessna Jones is Assistant Professor in the Communication Department and Interim Director of the Morrison-Novakovic Center for Faith and Public Policy at Davis & Elkins College. He also serves as affiliate faculty with LCC International University in Klaipeda, Lithuania. Dr. Jones was the first recipient of the Hinderliter Endowed Faculty Fellowship, a recipient of the European Consortium of Liberal Arts and Sciences (ECOLAS) Julie Johnson Kidd Research Fellowship, and a regular participant in the ERASMUS+ and COSTaction schemes. Dr. Jones is a frequent presenter at international conferences in rhetoric and communication in Europe and the United States. His publications include research in political communication, presidential rhetoric in Eastern Europe, and rhetoric in popular culture.

María E. Len-Ríos, PhD (Missouri), is Professor of Strategic Communication and Associate Director at the Hubbard School of Journalism and Mass Communication at the University of Minnesota. She conducts research in the areas of public relations, health, and diversity. Her research addresses the Latino publics and their engagement with media and politics and its effect on health. She also studies the work of journalists in producing health news stories, covering issues of difference, and public relations professionals' role in influencing news content. She is co-editor of the textbook *Cross-cultural Journalism and Strategic Communication: Storytelling and Diversity*. Her research has appeared in *Science Communication, Journal of Communication, Journalism & Mass Communication Quarterly, Public Relations Review, Journalism Studies, Health Communication*, the *Howard Journal of Communications*, among others. She is a board member-at-large and co-Chair of the IDEA (Inclusion, Diversity, Equity, and Access) Standing Committee of the International Communication Association.

Michael McDowell's research interests include performance ethnography, popular music, critical pedagogy, and democracy.

Chris McRae works at the intersections of performance studies and critical pedagogy in the consideration of the communicative and cultural acts of listening, music performance, and pedagogy.

Berhanu Mengistu, PhD, is Emeritus Professor of Public Policy and Administration at Old Dominion University in Norfolk, Virginia, USA. Among his favorite courses to teach are Alternative Dispute Resolution (ADR), Change Management and Transformation, Public Finance & Budgeting, Logic of Social Inquiry, and Leadership and Organization Theory and Behavior. He frequently offers workshops in the areas of conflict resolution, negotiation and mediation, peacemaking and peacebuilding, inter-faith dialogue for peacemaking, shared leadership, and other soft skills including communication styles, managing emotional intelligence, holding crucial conversations, and bridging differences for consensus-building. He has been a Fulbright Scholar in the Republic of South Africa, Ethiopia, and Ukraine. Currently, he is the winner of The Ambassador for

Distinguished Scholar Program. He serves as the Chair of the Ethiopian Forum for Constructive Engagement (www.Ethioselam.com) and serves as the Vice President of the Consortium for International Management, Policy, and Development (WWW.CIMPAD.ORG).

Ginny Morrison, JD, is a founding member and served in various leadership roles for Mediators Beyond Borders International, and leads Collaboration Specialists. For more than two decades, she has conducted assessments and designed and co-led multi-year projects involving reconciliation, dialogue, and trauma resilience throughout West Africa and East Africa, as well as Iraq, Myanmar, and Bosnia and Hercegovina. Her fieldwork of longest-standing integrated former child soldiers and sex slaves into post-conflict Liberian communities, mentored local NGOs developing interfaith coexistence and trauma resilience in Nigerian communities devastated by Boko Haram and farmer-herder violence, and advanced healing and reconciliation in Rwandan communities. Ms. Morrison holds a law degree from the University of California at Berkeley, and a Conflict Transformation certificate from Eastern Mennonite University's Center for Justice and Peacebuilding. She has also completed executive coursework through the Harvard School of Public Health, American University, and the United States Institute of Peace.

Patricia Moy, PhD (Wisconsin), is Christy Cressey Professor of Communication, adjunct professor of political science, and Associate Vice Provost of Academic and Student Affairs at the University of Washington. Her research examines the processes by which mediated and interpersonal communication can shape public opinion, political behavior, and public life. Currently editor of *Oxford Bibliographies in Communication*, she is a former editor of *Public Opinion Quarterly* and sits on the editorial board of leading journals such as *Journal of Communication*, *Communication Research*, and *Political Communication*. Moy is a former president of the American Association for Public Opinion Research, World Association for Public Opinion Research, and the International Communication Association, where she is an elected fellow.

Peter John Mugume, PhD, holds several positions at the University of Rwanda (UR) including lecturer of peace and development at the Centre for Conflict Management (CCM), where he also coordinates postgraduate programs; lecturer in the School of Governance; and Coordinator of the Social and Military Sciences program. Dr. Mugume focuses his teaching, research, and community service on enhancing the process of regional integration and contributing to regional and international peace, stability, and cooperation. He is the Team leader of the Peace, Conflict, and Security subprogram at the University of Rwanda and Sweden's Cooperation for Research, Higher Education and Institutional Advancement and the Co-PI of the Social Sciences for Severe Stigmatised Skin Conditions (5S-Project) for Rwanda. Dr. Mugume has been involved in different research activities in Rwanda as well as research on peace and security in the Central Africa Region.

Josephine Mukabera holds a PhD in Interdisciplinary Gender Studies from Seoul National University/South Korea, an MA degree in Development Studies from Ireland, and an Advanced Diploma in Mental Health Nursing from Kigali Health Institute (University of Rwanda). She has 15 years of work experience in trauma counseling and community development and 13 years of teaching in higher learning institutions of Rwanda. Dr. Mukabera is currently a lecturer at University of Rwanda.

Parameswari Mukherjee, MA (University of Cincinnati), is a doctoral student at the Department of Communication, University of South Florida. She locates her research at the intersection of health communication and organizational communication studying the neoliberal health discourses and health program organizing. Her research on culture-centered approaches to communication explores the blind spots in the mainstream cultural articulations of human illness and well-being in under-resourced communities that are marked by inaccess to material resources and discursive platforms. Her work on how a host of international, regional, and local stakeholders construct the environmental health problem of arsenic poisoning in a postcolonial context has been recently published in *Health Communication.* As a Graduate Teaching Associate at University of South Florida, Parameswari takes a postcolonial pedagogical approach in teaching Public Speaking that engages in critical listening to understand alternative articulations challenging the status quo. She anticipates completing her PhD in 2023.

Aubrey Helene Neumann is Assistant Professor of Theatre at Davis & Elkins College. She earned her doctorate from The Ohio State University where she received the honor of Distinguished University Fellowship and completed her dissertation centering applied theatre with rural youth. In addition to her formal education, Dr. Neumann has performed regionally and trained with SITI Company, Albany Park Theatre Project, the Shakespeare Theatre of New Jersey, and the Gaiety School of Acting in Dublin. Her works have been published in *Youth Theatre Journal, Texas Theatre Journal,* and *New England Theatre Journal.*

Barbara Regeer, PhD, is Associate Professor of Transdisciplinary Strategies for Sustainable Development and System Transformation at the Athena Institute for Innovation and Communication in the Health and Life Sciences, Vrije Universiteit Amsterdam. Her research interests are in emerging innovative strategies for (sustainable) development, with a specific focus on the facilitation of multi-stakeholder processes, knowledge co-creation, social change, and mutual learning between all actors involved, in such areas as sustainable food systems, integrated rural development, mental health care, child and youth care, and disability mainstreaming. Besides publications in the mentioned areas in international peer-reviewed journals, she has (co)authored books on approaches for knowledge co-creation for sustainable development. She coordinates, and teaches in, various courses on (transdisciplinary) research methodology, science communication, policy processes, and (social) innovation. She is the director of the Graduate School for Transdisciplinary PhD Education at Athena Institute.

Eike Mark Rinke, PhD (Mannheim), is Lecturer in Politics and Media at the University of Leeds. His research examines empirical and normative aspects of political communication on the individual and societal level, including the democratic quality of journalism and citizen behavior during election campaigns, social protest events, and in everyday life. His work has been published in *Journal of Communication, Political Communication, International Journal of Press/Politics,* and *Communication Methods and Measures,* among others. He currently serves as Associate Editor of *Political Communication* and is a former editor of the ICA and APSA Political Communication Divisions' newsletter, the *Political Communication Report* (2014–2016).

Larry Schooler is an award-winning journalist turned mediator, facilitator, public engagement consultant, and educator. He teaches conflict resolution, the history of conflict, and facilitative leadership at the University of Texas at Austin, and he is a Senior Director for Kearns & West, where he works with agencies around the world to resolve disputes, build consensus, and involve the public and stakeholders in decisions that will affect them. Dr. Schooler established the first public engagement division for the City of Austin, Texas, one of the first of its kind nationally, where he designed innovative and award-winning tools for involving the public in decision-making like Conversation Corps and "A View From You," a televised "reverse town hall" focused on input from the audience. His work has been recognized by (among others) the National League of Cities, the National Conference of State Legislatures, and the Harvard School of Government. Dr. Schooler served as President of the International Association for Public Participation (US affiliate) and is a senior fellow at the National Civic League and the Annette Strauss Institute for Civic Life at the University of Texas at Austin. He is also a member of the Board of Directors for the National Coalition for Dialogue and Deliberation. Dr. Schooler holds a bachelor's degree in history from Yale and a doctoral degree in conflict resolution from Nova Southeastern University. He is the author of a manual entitled *Keys to an Effective Public Meeting* and a forthcoming book on truth and reconciliation commissions. He lives in Austin with his wife and two children.

Prabha Sankaranarayan is a conflict transformation practitioner who has mediated, facilitated, and trained in Europe, Asia, Africa, and the United States. Her public and private sector work includes conflict analysis for public/private partnerships, consultation & assessment for industrial development zones, design and implementation of trainings for multinational corporations; interfaith dialogues as well as facilitation of multi-stakeholder mediations. Prabha is actively involved in regional, national and international civic activities focused on civil liberties, sexual violence prevention, conflict mitigation & mediation, and the recovery and rehabilitation of trauma survivors. She is Adjunct Professor at Washington and Jefferson College. She designs programs and interventions, trains and delivers presentations (nationally and internationally) on the impact of family and community violence, the intersection of trauma and peace-building, restorative justice, conflict resolution, mediation, and transitional justice. She speaks English, Tamil, and Hindi.

Luis Carlos Sotelo Castro is Associate Professor in the Department of Theatre at Concordia University, Montreal (Quebec, Canada). He is a core member of Concordia's Centre for Oral History and Digital Storytelling. In 2018, he founded at Concordia the Acts of Listening Lab, a hub for research-creation on the transformative power of listening to painful narratives, with particular reference to testimonies by exiles from sites of conflict. His latest publications explore listening in the context of post-conflict performances of memory. For instance, see "Facilitating voicing and listening in the context of post-conflict performances of memory. The Colombian scenario." In: De Nardi, S., Orange, H., et al. *Routledge Handbook of Memoryscapes* (Routledge, 2019), and his article "Not being able to speak is torture: Performing listening to painful narratives." *International Journal of Transitional Justice, Special Issue Creative Approaches to Transitional Justice: Contributions of Arts and Culture* (March, 2020).

Henrik Syse (b. 1966) is Research Professor at the Peace Research Institute Oslo (PRIO), Professor of Peace and Conflict Studies at Bjørknes University College, and a much-used public speaker. He also teaches regularly at the Norwegian Defense University College, the University of Oslo, and other institutions of higher learning, and he is Chief Editor (with James Cook) of the *Journal of Military Ethics*. From 2005 to 2007, Henrik was Head of Corporate Governance for Norges Bank Investment Management (NBIM) which manages Europe's largest sovereign wealth fund, and he continued, until 2009, as an advisor and consultant on social issues for NBIM. He was also a member of the Norwegian Press Complaints Commission from 2002 to 2016, has been a Member of the Norwegian Academy of Language and Literature since 2010, and served a full six-year term from 2015 to 2020 as a member of the Norwegian Nobel Committee, which awards the Nobel Peace Prize, serving as its Vice Chair 2017–2020. He was nominated as a Young Global Leader by the World Economic Forum in Davos in 2007. Henrik has written and edited approximately 20 books as well as many articles and essays. His publications span the fields of philosophy, politics, business, religion, and ethics. He is often used as a commentator on social and ethical issues by the media. He holds a Master of Arts degree in political philosophy from Boston College (USA) and a

Dr.Art. (Ph.D.) degree in moral philosophy from the University of Oslo. He is also a Sunday School teacher – and a specialist on The Beatles.

Jane Umutoni holds a Master's degree in Gender and Development Studies and a Bachelor's in Business Studies. She is currently Assistant Lecturer and Researcher at the UR-CASS Centre for Gender Studies. Over time, Ms. Umutoni has gained valuable experience in teaching within higher education, conducted research, managed and participated in research projects as well as served as a consultant. She has co-authored scholarly articles and reports on various topics mainly around the following areas: Peacebuilding and Social Cohesion in Post-conflict Contexts, Women's Entrepreneurship, Gender and Forced Migration, Gender and Education, Children in Consensual Unions, and Disability Rights, among a few others. Jane is a strong advocate for girls' rights, especially their right to education. She is equally passionate about women's socio-economic empowerment as well as promoting positive masculinity.

Debra L. Worthington, Professor of Communication at Auburn University, has published numerous articles on listening, particularly as related to measurement and individual listening style. She is the lead author of one of the principal textbooks in listening, *Listening: Processes, Functions, and Competency* and co-editor of *The Sourcebook of Listening Research: Methods and Measures* and *The Handbook of Listening*. She has received multiple top paper and panel awards, including the Ralph G. Nichols Listening Award and the Burton Award for Legal Achievement. Her research has been recognized by organizations such as the American Society of Trial Consultants, the European Communication Research and Education Association, as well as by multiple divisions of the National Communication Association, the Eastern Communication Association, and the Southern Communication Association. In 2017, she was inducted into the International Listening Association's Hall of Fame and received the 2017 ILA Listening Researcher Award. She has received multiple research contracts and grants from public and private organizations and is a past president of the International Listening Association.

Bobby Zachariah is a social worker and practitioner of SALT (Support/Appreciate/Listen/Team) in organizational approaches to community competence building, psychosocial support, and city-wide collective action. He has led organizations dealing in development needs, post-disaster challenges, public health, suicides, and youth livelihood.

1

LISTENING, COMMUNITY ENGAGEMENT, AND PEACEBUILDING

Defining terms and setting the stage

Graham D. Bodie[1], Debra L. Worthington[2], and Zenebe Beyene[1]

[1]SCHOOL OF JOURNALISM AND NEW MEDIA, UNIVERSITY OF MISSISSIPPI, UNITED STATES
[2]SCHOOL OF COMMUNICATION AND JOURNALISM, AUBURN UNIVERSITY, UNITED STATES

How can communities, especially those with myriad markers of diversity and populations that have contradictory needs and values, ensure all voices are heard? Which voices should be prioritized in decisions that affect all members of a community? When and to what extent should elected officials invite participation among community members and on whom should they focus their attention? Is it reasonable to assume that opening space for the most vulnerable in a population will necessarily lead to solving intractable conflicts or addressing problems such as poverty, health disparities, systemic racism, or uneven distribution of resources? In the midst of violent conflict, what role do dialogue, deliberation, conversation, negotiation, and related forms of community engagement play? Is it always possible to encourage listening during efforts to build or sustain peace?

Clearly, there are no easy answers to questions like these. By bringing together a diverse set of scholars whose work has transformed communities and nations across the globe, we hope this book can begin to stitch together a reasonable narrative and provide insight and guidance to others who work in the areas of community engagement and peacebuilding. At the center of that narrative is the role and function of listening. While there are individual articles and chapters that focus on the role of listening within community engagement (e.g., Hendriks et al., 2019; Moore & Elliott, 2016; Rowan & Cavallaro, 2019) and peacebuilding efforts (e.g., Beyene, 2020; Johansson, 2017), there is no encompassing text serving students, academics, practitioners, and others with interests in these topics. Although the importance of listening to these areas is recognized, there is also clear evidence that those involved in community engagement and peacebuilding efforts, despite their best intentions, often fall short (Johansson, 2017).

DOI: 10.4324/9781003214465-1

The goal of this text is to provide contemporary insights into the role that listening—as related to individual, social, and governmental efforts—can better engage communities and build, maintain, or establish peace in an increasingly divided world.

This chapter focuses on defining the central term of this book, listening. We begin by acknowledging the many uses (and misuses) of the term and then move to a discussion of how interpersonal forms of listening, with their focus on comprehension and understanding, capture some but not all of the complexity of listening at scale. Both community engagement and peacebuilding work necessarily move beyond listening to a single story or providing space for a single individual to feel heard; they both represent opportunities for large-scale listening, something that is often overlooked or ignored by the organizations responsible for encouraging participation from multiple stakeholders. Scholars and practitioners engaged in community engagement and peacebuilding often champion various forms of engagement, participation, empowerment, conflict resolution, and reconciliation. Whatever term is used, it is typically imbued with notions of "creating space to listen." Our goal is in this book to both explore and begin to unpack what exactly they mean by that.

What is listening?

Listening is an action, ideally an ethical one, undertaken with a spirit of mutual respect void of goals to marginalize or otherwise suppress competing voices. When engaged properly, it entails genuine presence in the service of others and leads to awareness, understanding, trust, and more productive and peaceful communities. Unfortunately, the term listening is also used to describe individual actions and public-facing initiatives that fall short of these ideals. Political listening tours and social media listening tools, for instance, often do little more than uncover new ways to tailor messages and provide politicians or corporations strategies to better sell their constituents (see Macnamara, 2016). Local partners working with international, non-governmental organizations (NGOs) in peacebuilding efforts sometimes feel they are not being listened to, despite working with practitioners who claim to be foregrounding local voices (Anderson et al., 2012; Johansson, 2017). Large-scale surveys and other data collection efforts branded as listening to external or internal stakeholders often fail to fully capture individual voices mainly because they are designed to gather information at a more aggregate level. Indeed, "[merely] creating channels for publics or employees to have 'voice' is inadequate. Voice that is unheard is useless to both the speaker and the audience" (Lewis, 2020, p. xiii).

The difference between genuine listening and attempts only labeled as such, therefore, does not rest merely on whether the speaker *feels* heard. To be sure, from the perspective of the speaker, the act of (truly) listening signals that their voice has value, that they are valued, and that their perspective has merit and meaning. All of these outcomes are important, perhaps imperative, in both community engagement and peacebuilding efforts. As such, attempts to increase opportunities for people to "speak up," "have voice," or otherwise participate and engage are essential to organizations and society, particularly to democratic forms of participation (e.g., Bickford, 1996; Dobson, 2014).

While it is true that listening will not (and perhaps should not) always result in agreement, compromise, justice, peace, or reconciliation, and might result in undesirable outcomes for some (e.g., re-triggering a trauma response), successful listening cannot simply rely on the impression that it has happened. Rather, genuine listening is an active, two-way, and symmetrical process that ultimately results in change. Sometimes the change that results from listening is internal to the listener who gains added perspective or understanding and thinks about an issue somewhat differently. Other times, internal change is insufficient. It must go beyond the individual or interpersonal level if it is to (re)shape decision making and begin to dismantle the structures that make problems feel intractable in the first place.

Part of the reason listening is ill-defined within community engagement and peacebuilding scholarship is because the term is largely conceptualized as a personal practice enacted within interpersonal interactions. Traditionally, listening has been conceptualized as a set of affective, behavioral, and/or cognitive processes enacted in the service of enjoying, responding to, and/or making sense of aural information, produced by others (Worthington & Bodie, 2018). Most models begin with the reception of sound, often labeled hearing, then suggest humans go through various stages of (selective) attention, comprehension, interpretation, evaluating, and responding, to name a few of the more common processes (Worthington, 2018). Within this framework, then, the paradigmatic case of "good" listening is when a single individual fully understands what another single individual has attempted to communicate and, as a result, effectuates a deeper relational dynamic (Burleson, 2011). To be sure, practitioners must be skilled in asking questions, expressing understanding, and paraphrasing; they also benefit from training in various models of dialogue, such as appreciative inquiry (Cooperrider et al., 2000), that stress shared discovery and mutual problem-solving. As we will see in the section that follows, however, such interpersonal forms of listening are not easily translated at scale.

From interpersonal to large-scale listening

The earliest research on listening was conducted to uncover strategies students use in classroom settings while listening to lectures (see review by Beard & Bodie, 2014). Throughout the 1950s and continuing until the late 1980s, several research programs were launched to develop tests capable of measuring *listening comprehension*. Although these tests differed in some important ways, each was designed to capture how humans are able to understand (i.e., make sense of) spoken language and use that understanding to respond appropriately (Ridge, 1993).

Starting in the 1980s, research on listening took a distinctly relational turn. Much of this work was published by communication scientists who drew heavily from the therapeutic literature (e.g., Rogers, 1957); in this context, a main goal of listening is the formation, maintenance, and transformation of close relationships (e.g., friendships, romantic relationships; Bodie & Denham, 2017). Particularly important in the context of close, personal relationships is the type of understanding marked less by mere comprehension or even evaluation of information and more by related abilities often labeled empathy, sympathy, or compassion.[1] We listen to the news of a building's collapse, a friend tells us of trouble with their child, or a family member describes recent financial problems, and we respond with compassion or sympathy. Indeed, research finds that more sophisticated attempts to comfort a distressed person move beyond a focus on the route details of an event, focusing instead on explicitly acknowledging and validating the perspectives and feelings of the distressed (Bodie et al., 2016; Burleson, 2003).

The shift from situating listening as an individual phenomenon to an interpersonal-level one, resulted in a change of focus. Instead of emphasizing understanding, comprehending and making sense of messages for the purposes of learning, researchers focused on an other-oriented, feeling-centered, empathic form of attention. From a psychophysiological perspective, empathy involves *feeling as* the other, meaning specific neural processes are activated as we experience the same (or at least a similar) emotional response as the other person (Lamm et al., 2019). Empathy provides a closer identification with the other and a closer sharing of a mental state. Here, listening both drives and is affected by our empathic response. Thus, our empathic response to another person's situation may lead us to engage in the kind of listening that centers the other person's perspective and feelings, and that shared affective and cognitive response may lead us to listen more closely, carefully, and for a longer period of time than perhaps we would otherwise.

Consideration of the thoughts, feelings, perspectives, conditions, and circumstances of others is at the heart of human engagement in all its forms, including efforts to build community and peace. Perhaps most important for this chapter (and for this book more generally), however, is the following: While there are clear examples of when an other-oriented and feeling-centered form of listening can be beneficial, such as in the context of dialogues seeking to bring communities together across difference (see Bodie & Godwin, 2022), this type of listening does little to change anything about systems or structures that cause pain and anxiety in particular communities, neighborhoods, or across specific classes of people (Dobson, 2014). In other words, the type of change elicited when we are listening interpersonally, often colloquially referred to as changing hearts and minds, might be necessary but is certainly insufficient (e.g., Dickson, 2009). The power of listening, if it is to be truly transformative at scale, must extend beyond some finite set of individual outcomes such as better understanding or increased empathy, as important as those outcomes are for a fully functioning society

(Freinacht, 2017). As Cohen (2019) put it, dialogue "cannot solve all problems or bridge all gaps. Calling for coexistence without seriously addressing the issues that underlie polarization can become a shallow call for peace with no justice" (¶11).

It is true that listening enables individuals and institutions to gather relevant information about others' mental states and perspectives and the complex contexts within which they are situated. Thus, community development and peacebuilding practitioners should be trained in skills that allow for better comprehension and understanding. Although we are imperfect mind-readers, "failing to consider the mind of another and running the risk of treating him or her like a relatively mindless animal or object ... are at the heart of dehumanization" (Epley, 2014, p. xiv). Importantly, dehumanization is a strong predictor of intergroup hostility (Beyond Conflict, 2019; Giner-Sorolla & Russell, 2019), suggesting that creating spaces for seeing others' humanity is important beyond just the interpersonal realm (e.g., Wilmer, 2018). At the same time, it is true that simply feeling heard is inadequate when moving beyond the interpersonal. Situations involving the unequal distribution of power and conflict rooted in racism or other forms of hatred, for instance, at minimum raise questions regarding ideals of "open-mindedness" or the need for creating space for all voices and perspectives (e.g., Wahl, 2019). Indeed, each of us (the authors of this chapter) has heard critiques of the work we do as being naive and idealistic, quixotic in fact. Thus, as we expand our understanding of listening beyond the interpersonal to what Macnamara (2016) has called "large-scale listening" (p. 4), we must consider not only the outcomes of listening in broader (e.g., organizational, societal, and cultural) contexts but also the elements that make this sort of listening possible.

Making large-scale listening possible

What we know from research exploring listening in close relationships and from the work of dialogue practitioners who encourage conversations across differences is the importance of *creating space* for people to interact in supportive, welcoming, and inclusive environments free from judgment. Such spaces are needed if people are to feel heard. Thus, providing opportunities for people to voice their real, honest, and raw opinions; react to current policies that affect their lives; and participate in shared decision making are essential ingredients for effective community engagement and peacebuilding efforts. The creation of space for large-scale listening was coined by Macnamara (2015) as "an architecture of listening" that can help counterbalance "the policies, systems, structures, resources, and technologies devoted to speaking" (p. 47). In contrast to much (perhaps even a majority in some cases) of the work done by NGOs, governments, international aid organizations, and the like, which involves speaking to stakeholders (e.g., holding informational forums, putting together one-pagers for people to understand how to take control of their health), an architecture of listening requires a shift in thinking. Fundamental to this shift, according to Macnamara (2020), are elements "required to supplement inter-personal communication and aid human interpretation of the large volume of information and feedback received in the form of structured and unstructured data" (p. 391). These elements include a *culture* of listening, *policies* for listening, the *politics* of listening, *structures* and *processes* for listening, *technologies* for listening, *resources* for listening, *skills* for listening, and the *articulation* of listening to decision making.

As used in the context of community development and peacebuilding, culture refers to the general and often taken-for-granted norms, beliefs, "best practices," and customs of an organization, work team, program, intervention, or other systems of practice. We believe listening is a central norm shared across community engagement and peacebuilding efforts, often manifested in the idea that outside agents and local partners are equals; it seems axiomatic that outside actors should genuinely listen to and implement the perspectives and advice offered by those most affected by the decisions being made. This norm is grounded in a consensus, albeit not one that has always existed, that outside entities cannot "bring" change or peace with them; rather, community engagement and peacebuilding are long term, comprehensive approaches that require understanding and honestly addressing the root causes of conflict within a given area. In an extensive study of over 6,000 recipients of international aid, for instance, Anderson et al. (2012, p. 83) reported

> wide agreement that outside aid providers should work through existing institutions where they are strong and support them, if weak, to help them gain experience and resources for bettering their societies. Receivers and providers of aid together recognize that international donors are only temporary actors in recipient societies and that governments and local organizations know their contexts better than outsiders do.

And, yet, as this team reported, recipients of aid often comment that they are uninformed, uninvolved, and unheard.[2] Indeed, a lack of attention to "the voice of the people" is an often-cited reason for the failure of all kinds of community engagement and involvement efforts, including those centered on conflict resolution and peace.

How participants' voices are included in the decision-making process is most readily captured by various models of participation. Quite popular among these models is the five stances Wilcox (1994) presented based on the work of Sherry Arnstein. At the very lowest level is *information* or simply telling people what is planned. Clearly, simply providing an open forum where community members are told what is planned hardly constitutes a genuine attempt to hear different perspectives. Any community engagement or peacebuilding efforts built on a culture that only embraces an information approach cannot be said to constitute

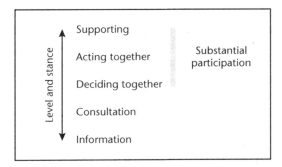

FIGURE 1.1   Five stances for community engagement projects (Wilcox, 1994)

Source: With permission under the Creative Commons license.

any effort to actually listen. In Macnamara's language, these efforts are built on an architecture of speaking (in other words, they do not have a culture of listening). As one ascends the Wilcox ladder, control moves from initiators to community members (see Figure 1.1), thus creating different listening cultures.

Even in these higher rungs, however, listening can still become a catchphrase rather than an embedded practice that involves earnestly seeking to understand multiple perspectives. For instance, Wilcox noted that when engaging in *consultation*, community members may be offered a variety of options, which then requires listening to the feedback provided about each option. But as we have already suggested, simply providing space to hear feedback does little to ensure that feedback is actually utilized in decision making. Consultation, therefore, seems more about allowing people to feel heard than about employing genuine listening. Similarly, when *deciding together,* although there is greater engagement when choosing among possible solutions, unless sufficient time and resources are devoted to developing actual processes of listening, this rung can look much more like consultation than a new form of participation.

Regardless of the type of participation utilized in a given project, community engagement and peacebuilding practitioners should make their listening culture more explicit. As one notable example, in their *Participation, Leadership, and Civic Engagement* (PLACE) report, the County Board of Arlington, VA (2012) provided clear acknowledgment of how they envisioned community participation in their stated values of inclusiveness, individual activism, long-range planning, respect for process, level playing field for all, personal connections, reach the individual, responsive, no predetermined outcomes, volunteerism, and progressive nature of Arlington. Moreover, they expressed a commitment to "listen to all concerns" because "good ideas can come from anywhere" (p. 11).

When explicit statements about listening are not available, culture can be gleaned from the policies already in place as well as internal and external politics enabling and constraining different levels of listening practice. Policies for listening are more than vague philosophies; they include specific directives and guidelines to relevant departments, units, and agencies on who is to be listened to and how listening is to be conducted. Even if the PLACE document did not have explicit value statements, for instance, we could glean their listening culture from various documents such as the *Six-Step Public Engagement Guide for Capital Projects* which outlines engagement policies that articulate how to, for instance, define the scope of a project, identify relevant stakeholders, and determine how much engagement is appropriate (Arlington County Office of Communications and Public Engagement, 2018). Within this document, we find several explicit directives to "work with stakeholders in a cooperative and collaborative way" and "ensure public notice and engagement is based on building trust and seeking to involve all stakeholders and range of perspectives, without predetermined outcomes." We also find, however, examples that, on the surface, seem reasonable but that nevertheless may be grounded in internal or external political pressure. For instance, several "activities [that] do not require an engagement plan" are listed including "water service line maintenance" and "pothole and patching." To repair a water service line or fill a pothole seems apolitical, though which lines to repair or potholes to prioritize for filling can be quite political. Who decides which of these issues are most salient to a community? What internal (e.g., inter-agency) and external (e.g., social or cultural milieu) politics helps to decide (oftentimes unconsciously) which projects are most important or get funded? Does the public have a voice in determining project priority, budget allocation, or the schedule and timing of meetings? More generally, prioritization and issue salience are likely governed (or at least dictated) by specific policies and politics, in which case there are also likely available structures/processes, technologies, and resources (including skill development opportunities for leaders and community members) that assist in decision making and project implementation.

Efforts by community engagement and peacebuilding initiatives to invite input, address critics, and monitor social media conversations should also include explicit processes and training in the skills that enable leaders and community members to make sense of the vast diversity within the public commentary. At a basic level, decisions must be made on who is delegated these responsibilities, including which units, departments, agencies, and people within these entities are responsible for listening. What processes are in place that enable the highest likelihood that multiple perspectives are not only invited but actually heard? Within job descriptions used to hire practitioners or decide on contractors, how often do words that signal a listening culture (e.g., communication, engagement, consultation, collaboration) appear?

Within the budgets of those units, departments, and agencies responsible for opening spaces for public engagement, what technologies and other resources (e.g., human resources, time, financial) are available to enable greater listening? And what opportunities to learn new listening-related skills (e.g., relationship building, two-way dialogue, validating emotions) are made available? Functions such as research and processing public correspondence (e.g., emails, letters, voicemail) seem, on the surface, dedicated to some form of listening, though as we mentioned at the start of this chapter, those processes can leave important voices out of the larger conversation if enough attention is not paid to how information is collected and analyzed.

The final element of Macnamara's concept of an architecture of listening is how departments or teams focused on attending and responding to public comments (like research or public relations) are held accountable for acting on the information they hear. What gets sent to decision makers and ultimately gets reported in public-facing documents? Who decides how best to discuss "sensitive issues" or "critical commentary" with those in decision-making positions? And how do community engagement and peacebuilding teams decide when not to act on minority or majority opinions expressed in open forums, private emails, or other non-public-facing documents (letters, voicemails, surveys, interviews, etc.)?

Summary

Although listening is most readily conceptualized as an individual (intrapersonal) or interpersonal act, organizations, including those with community engagement or peacebuilding missions, also take a stance on the importance and role of listening in their work. It is important to note that the systems created to enable genuine listening at scale do not replace human listeners, though they can help "facilitate communication that is delegated, mediated, and asynchronous" (Macnamara, 2020, p. 391). Moreover, they cannot simply be add-ons or afterthoughts but rather must be built into the very fabric of any large-scale listening endeavor (i.e., an architecture of listening). The "open culture, policies, resources, technologies, and skills to facilitate listening" (p. 393) as well as the way in which units responsible for attending to myriad perspectives are held accountable should be accepted as essential by all involved – from executive-level leadership who likely plan or orchestrate listening events to the practitioners doing the work. Moreover, these elements can be used as a check to the infrastructure and practices used in the field. In general, the necessity of scaling a concept such as listening means that we take those activities and ideas developed and shown to work in interpersonal settings, with the goal of meeting the needs of the masses. It does not mean, however, that we extrapolate all elements of interpersonal listening, as our discussion on empathy and "changing hearts and minds" above indicated. It does mean that we can utilize specific methods of listening at scale, some of the more popular of which we summarize below.

Methods for large-scale listening

While recognizing there are important differences (as well as the wide variety of approaches and frameworks within each), community engagement and peacebuilding efforts have much in common – the need to establish and agree on achievable and measurable goals, the importance of trust, and the need for conflict resolution and management to name but a few. Efforts to listen to, amplify voices of, or otherwise include multiple perspectives in decision making go by various names such as community involvement, collaboration, public consultation, public forums, dialogue, and deliberation (see Schooler, Chapter 2). And, there are iterations found in practices such as participatory budgeting, public planning (urban development), democracy building, and citizen panels.

Importantly, any one of these ways to engage or invite relevant stakeholders into the decision-making process can be developed and administered with more or less attention to actual participation (and, as we raised above, more or less likelihood that genuine listening will occur). Moreover, community engagement and peacebuilding practitioners can utilize various methods for listening to match their goal(s) based on the time and other resources available to actually implement genuine listening. Next, we chart several standard methods for listening used in community engagement and peacebuilding efforts with a focus on those methods that reflect our notion that successful listening must move beyond the mere impression that it happened.

Participatory action research

Administering a survey or conducting a set of town halls (or a more formal listening tour) is often little more than a nod to inviting genuine participation. If, however, these methods are situated within models of Participatory Action Research (PAR) or Community-based PAR (CBPAR), then they begin to look less like one-way, asymmetrical research designs and more like true two-way, symmetrical listening-based designs that place relationships at their core (Ferguson, 2018). The problem with most approaches that attempt to use research as a form of honest community participation is that community members are rarely consulted in its design, analysis, or interpretation. PAR and CBPAR, on the other hand, are built on "a set of principles and practices for originating, designing, conducting, analysing and acting on a piece of research" distinguished by the following characteristics (Pain et al., 2011, p. 2):

- Driven by participants (a group of people who have a stake in the environmental issue being researched), rather than an outside sponsor, funder, or academic (although they may be invited to help);
- Offers a democratic model of who can produce, own and use knowledge;
- Collaborative at every stage, involving discussion, pooling skills and working together; and
- Intended to result in some action, change, or improvement on the issue being researched.

As a model, PAR emphasizes listening to and across participants as part of the questioning process. For example, PAR encourages participation and recognizes the importance of hearing from those who have been ignored or unheard. Learning is reversed as community members become the source of local information. As a result, critical thinking and listening are key elements of the questioning process of the PAR approach. While Fine (2006) and others (e.g., Manzo & Brightbill, 2007) suggest that listening is both an ethical component of PAR and a necessary element when engaging in PAR activities, Krueger-Henney (2016) has argued for the inclusion of intentional social listening as "PAR is full of these ambiguous and in-between spaces that are packed with uncertainties and that can blur visions of constructing counter-hegemonic, anti-racist, and decolonial inquiries" (p. 57). Patel (2016) contended that a greater understanding of the nature and role of listening within PAR processes is needed as it is through listening that co-researchers can address those "social, physical, and ethical locations, which profoundly compromise the potential for transformational change" (p. 5).

Asset based community development

Similar to PAR, Asset Based Community Development (ABCD) begins with the assumption that local people have the capacity to build strong communities (Kretzmann, 2010; Kretzmann & McKnight, 1993; Mathie & Cunningham, 2003). While traditional models of community engagement begin with "needs assessments," that is surveys designed by "experts" that assess the problems faced within a community, ABCD centers on a community's assets and strengths. This change is important as it allows individuals to emphasize abilities and possibilities of a community, rather than problems or other negative framings. As a community-driven model, professionals act as facilitators, not experts, drawing on co-created local assets. This emphasis recognizes that change is community driven and that the members of a community are both the agents and the drivers of change (Mathie & Cunningham, 2003; Mathie et al., 2017). Thus, central to this approach is the relationship building that occurs when community members interact with one another as active citizens rather than as clients receiving a service from an institution or agency (Mathie & Cunningham, 2003).

One technique that follows the principles of ABCD is the charrette, most often used in community planning and urban development wherein there is known or heightened potential for confrontation between developers and residents (Lennertz & Lutzenhiser, 2017). While a charrette can be adapted to a variety of project types, it typically focuses on design-related projects. As a part of this process, a team of stakeholders (e.g., government officials, citizens, developers) work together to develop and implement a plan centered on a specific goal or project. The basic charrette design involves short, intensive meetings encompassing as many stakeholders as possible, who collaborate to identify possible problems and debate potential solutions. Notably, the charrette planning process has, over time, been compressed into a short period of time (i.e., hours or days), though it was originally devised as an intense and weeks-long process that brings together the greatest number of stakeholders, promotes feelings that all parties are being heard, heightens creativity and collaboration, and builds a shared vision.

Listening circles

Listening Circles (LCs), or Councils, are perhaps the large-scale listening method most closely aligned with how listening is conceptualized in the interpersonal domain. LCs use storytelling as a means of promoting empathy, building emotional connections, and fostering mutual understanding (Higgins, 2011). They consist of 10–25 members facing one another in a circle, typically with 1–2 trained facilitators, who brief participants on the rules: everyone participates via speaking and/or listening; only one person at a time can speak, although speaking is not mandatory; and speaking turns are often signaled by holding an object (e.g., stick, ball), which is passed from person to person or placed in the middle of the circle to be picked up by another group member (Itzchakov & Kluger, 2017). As Itzchakov and Kluger (2017) described, facilitators "invite the participants to consider four 'intentions' when they participate: to listen from the heart, to talk from the heart, to talk succinctly, and to talk with spontaneity" (p. 664). While neutral expressions of support are encouraged (e.g., "Oh" or "Amen"), circle members are asked to avoid providing positive or negative feedback. Following several practice sessions, facilitators identify a topic of discussion.

The LC model is at the heart of a practice utilized by the *Alluvial Collective* (2021; AC; formerly the William Winter Institute of Racial Reconciliation). Since 1999, the AC has hosted a series of events they call *The Welcome Table* ("Table") which highlight the importance of "listening, storytelling, and relationship building as prerequisites for producing real and measurable change" (see *The Welcome Table*). To date, the AC has made measurable change in communities and school districts across Mississippi. For instance, the AC convened a set of Tables between 2015 and 2016 in Lafayette County, Mississippi, from which grew an ongoing and developing project around lynching memorialization (Lafayette County Remembrance Project, 2021). Members of these Tables were invited, as were other members of the community, to an April 2017 presentation by a Northeastern Law School student who was conducting research on lynching. By November 2017, a formal steering committee was formed to research the feasibility of placing markers around the county. The first marker memorialized Elwood Higginbottom and was unveiled in an October 2018 ceremony that drew over 500 people. One additional marker has been placed on the grounds of the county courthouse to memorialize the seven known lynching victims in the county, including Mr. Higginbottom. Although the *Welcome Table* is not the only part of the AC's important work, it opens a space for honest conversation, founded on the principle that participants listen first to understand. More importantly, such listening can lead to further action and notable change that is community driven and sustainable. Of course, *can* is the operative word in that last sentence as systemic change does not necessarily follow individual shifts in attitudes, mindsets, or opinions.

Reconciliation

Reconciliation is, according to Forsberg (2001), "the process of developing a mutual conciliatory accommodation between formerly antagonistic groups" (p. 63). This definition assumes the commitment of all parties in conflict to ending hostility and creating a conducive environment for lasting peace, a process that requires acknowledgment of the past so "that it will cease to poison the present and instead become simply the past" (Shriver, 2001, p. 259). Such acknowledgment is typically described in terms of four elements that facilitate reconciliation: truth-telling, forgiveness, justice, and peace (Pruitt & Kim, 1983, p. 225).[3]

Within truth-telling, there is an honest accounting of past injustices, allowing perpetrators to confess to wrongdoings and/or crimes and clarifying account-ability. When done well, perpetrators express sincere remorse and repentance so that victims forgive their perpetrators, and victims are provided a platform to tell their stories. In most cases, post-traumatic experiences tend to be more painful when victims are not heard and supported (see Sankaranarayan et al., Chapter 9). When societies fail to provide platforms for victims to tell their stories and share their pains, it harvests bitterness, which can contribute to a spiral of violence. In contrast, creating an infrastructure in which victims narrate their suffering and perpetrators express sincere remorse is a step in the right direction. The combination of the two, perpetrators' confession and victims' narration, can enable victims to regain their dignity, and regaining one's dignity is vital in the reconciliation process; however, it may not bring complete closure (Shriver, 2001), and some have argued that forgiveness, or what Ledrach (1997) labeled mercy, "alone is superficial. It covers up. It moves on too quickly" (p. 28).

In *Listening for Democracy*, Andrew Dobson (2014) tells the story of Jo Berry, the daughter of Sir Anthony Berry who died in a 1984 bombing of the Grand Hotel in Brighton (UK), and Patrick Magee, the man imprisoned for planting the bomb. After Magee's release from prison in 2000, he and Berry began a series of conversations that involved what Dr. Scherto Gill of the Guerrand-Hermes Foundation for Peace called "deep listening" (that mirrors in many ways restorative justice practices; Johnston & Van Ness, 2011, Sotelo Castro, Chapter 10). Consistent with what we (above) suggested about genuine listening, Berry reflected that the point of her conversations with Magee was not to (p. 24)

> reach an end state such as reconciliation or forgiveness, but to focus on the process. And a key part of the process is listening … [What] is more important … is being interested in listening to the other perspective and trying to understand it, even if you are not willing to agree with it.

Similarly, Magee was quoted as referring "to listening when asked what he has learnt from his meetings with Berry: Slowing the dialogue down to ensure you hear properly and explain adequately may be the best means of engaging with someone you have hurt" (p. 24).

Because the reconciliation between Berry and Magee was primarily personal in nature (rather than systemic), their mode of compassionate listening seemed not only reasonable but perhaps ideal. When it comes to social polarization, intractable conflict, or larger-scale injustices, however, compassionate listening may fall on deaf ears. As we have already noted, it is largely void of action and does little about the systems and structures that perpetuate the violence that has led to a need for reconciliation. Thus, although both Berry and Magee gained insight from their conversations, it is unclear that these conversations did much to solve deep-seated structural issues that were the ultimate reason Magee staged his attack.

Therefore, the power of listening (and the larger process of reconciliation), if it is to be truly transformative, must include justice; that is, societies must create mechanisms to deal with wrongdoings so that injustices do not occur again. The question is not whether justice is important, but what is the best course of action that would not undermine the reconciliation? How, in the language of Pankhurst (1999, p. 244) can we get the balance (between justice and reconciliation) right? Goldstone (2000) best summarized the importance of justice in this way: "It is my belief that when nations ignore victims' calls for justice, they are condemning their people to the terrible consequences of ongoing hatred and revenge" (p. 60). Furthermore, ignoring victims' calls for justice can also create a vicious cycle of violence and revenge. Justice comes in many forms, of course. Some might opt for vengeful justice in order to gain instant gratification or, in some cases, short-term solutions. However, that form of justice tends to be "an-eye-for-an-eye [which] makes the whole world blind."[4]

To extend this metaphor, what reconciliation ultimately attempts is an eye-opening, but not one that focuses on the past. While the first three elements (truth-telling, forgiveness, and justice) involve looking back, peace is forward-looking. Understanding and learning from the past lays the foundation for charting a new path. That is what countries such as Ireland, South Africa, and Rwanda (see Mugume et al., Chapter 12) have done. Peace cannot be achieved until the past has been confronted and effectively dealt with. By tackling past injustices and committing to peace, perpetrators and victims can create conditions for future harmony, unity, cooperation, and security (Pruitt & Kim, 1983). As Lederach argued (1997, p. 28):

> with peace came images of harmony, unity, well-being. It is the feeling and prevalence of respect and security. But, it was observed, peace is not just for a few, and if it is preserved for the benefit of some and not others it represents a farce.

Of course, depending on the magnitude and severity of past misdeeds, the pain and trauma endured might be too severe to forgive. As was observed during the South African Truth and Reconciliation deliberations, some preferred a formal judicial process to handle some cases. However, there was a dilemma: When an entire group is implicated in past injustices and crimes as occurred in South Africa and Rwanda, how could one help a society move beyond its tragic past and herald a new era? One answer is to achieve a "balance between forgiveness and justice. Without justice, apology and forgiveness are hollow. Without forgiveness, a demand for justice is harsh. Both extremes are likely to derail the reconciliation process" (Pruitt & Kim, 1983, p. 223).

Summary

Reconciliation and the larger project of peacebuilding in a particular region should not be considered individual operations, and neither exists outside of a dynamic of community engagement and citizen participation. Each method we have discussed (and those that follow in the chapters of this book) are endeavors undertaken at the community level. The whole point of a book focused on the role of listening in building communities and peace is that we are human *through* (not in spite of) others, connected through our shared humanity. And yet, as Tutu observed, "You can only be human in a humane society. If you live with hatred and revenge in your heart, you dehumanize not only yourself, but your community" (as quoted in Krog, 1999, p. 143). A minimum requirement, thus, appears to be that parties should be willing to listen to each other with respect and without judgment. Those opportunities should, ideally, be built by the very people with the most at stake. And while a single event cannot resolve or heal problems in a community much less "bring" peace to a region marked by decades of intractable conflict, what they can do is "give people a voice and allow them to choose how to understand themselves and their relation to others and, especially, to live with difference" (Cleven et al., 2018, p. 55).

How to read this book

This book takes seriously the idea that listening is fundamental to engaging diverse others in meaningful change. What we want to highlight is the importance community engagement and peacebuilding scholars place on listening, and yet how this term is also often treated as a catchphrase rather than one deserving of close scrutiny. Communities "being served" by urban planning initiatives, community members "invited" to civic engagement initiatives, voters "attending" political listening tours, and stakeholders with competing interests asked to "engage" with peacebuilding efforts, may or may not actually be allowed "a voice" in the decision-making process, especially those who live on the margins; those voices are not, in fact, often heard. We hope this book will enable practitioners to develop the ability to construct genuine listening moments and increase their awareness of how to successfully engage and empower "the people."

We have divided this book into two units, not because community engagement and peacebuilding are two distinctly different lines of scholarship, but because it allows us to provide an overview and multiple examples of each (to strike a balance between these related fields if you will). Each unit opens with a chapter that provides definitions of key terms and phrases and reviews past research at an aggregate level. Those chapters that follow these unit openers can be thought of as case studies of sorts, though not all authors provide in-depth exploration of a single method or project. What each chapter author does do, however, is provide practical guides for implementing their methods of practice. Finally, the astute reader has likely noticed we did not provide explicit definitions of community engagement or peacebuilding. We have done this intentionally, allowing each author to wrestle with those terms as they see fit.

Notes

1 Although a full review of what constitutes empathy is beyond the scope of this chapter, it is instructive to note the varied uses of this term as well as the conflation of empathy with other prosocial behaviors (e.g., Batson, 2009). Most notable is the distinction several make between empathy and sympathy, but also terms such as compassion, open-mindedness, intellectual humility, and moral sensitivity (see Mower, 2020). Regardless of the specific term used, from this perspective, competence in listening is one's ability to open space for someone to share personally sensitive information without fear of judgment, leading to enhanced understanding of one's emotions, thoughts, and feelings as well as emotional improvement and other markers of well-being (Jones, 2011).
2 Even the idea that someone merely "receives" aid suggests that past and perhaps current practices of international aid (and perhaps, as an extension, the community engagement and peacebuilding efforts often tied to these efforts) are grounded in a less-than-ideal culture of listening. As Johansson (2017) pointed out, "in peacekeeping research, even the terminology used indicates a tendency to downplay local perspectives, despite what is said" using as an example the work of Fortna and Howard who referred to "internationals … as active subjects [while] the local population is treated as passive and called the 'peacekept'" (p. 15). Although culture is more than language, how we talk about and reference the "objects" of our work provides one perspective on how we might view listening as something fully participatory or not.
3 When these differences involve understanding language and cultural differences (e.g., nuances and meaning that can shade interpretations even when people are from the same region or country and seemingly speak the same language), some process of intercultural mediation (IM) may be necessary (Katan, 2013).
4 This quote is attributed most often to Mahatma Gandhi.

References

Anderson, M., Brown, D., & Jean, I. (2012). *Time to listen: Hearing people on the receiving end of international aid*. Cambridge: CDA Collaborative Learning Projects.
Arlington County Office of Communications and Public Engagement. (2018, March 19). *A six-step public engagement guide for capital projects*. https://arlingtonva.s3.dualstack.

us-east-1.amazonaws.com/wp-content/uploads/sites/21/2018/03/Six-Step-Public-Engagement-Guide-for-Capital-Projects.pdf

Batson, C. D. (2009). These things called empathy: Eight related but distinct phenomena. In J. Decety & W. Ickes (Eds.), *The social neuroscience of empathy* (pp. 3–15). MIT Press. 10.7551/mitpress/9780262012973.003.0002

Beard, D., & Bodie, G. D. (2014). Listening research in the communication discipline. In P. J. Gehrke & W. M. Keith (Eds.), *The unfinished conversation: 100 years of communication studies.* Routledge.

Beyene, Z. (2020). Building peace through listening. In D. L. Worthington & G. D. Bodie (Eds.), *The handbook of listening* (pp. 419–426). John Wiley & Sons.

Beyond Conflict (2019, May). *Decoding dehumanization: Policy brief for policymakers and practitioners.* https://beyondconflictint.org/wp-content/uploads/2020/06/Decoding-Dehumanization-Policy-Brief-2019.pdf

Bickford, S. (1996). *The dissonance of democracy: Listening, conflict, and citizenship.* Ithaca: Cornell University Press.

Bodie, G. D., & Denham, J. P. (2017). Listening in(to) close relationships. In M. Stoltz, K. P. Sodowsky, & C. M. Cates (Eds.), *Listening across lives* (pp. 41–61). Kendall Hunt.

Bodie, G. D., Cannava, K., & Vickery, A. J. (2016). Supportive communication and the adequate paraphrase. *Communication Research Reports, 33,* 166–172. doi: 10.1080/08824 096.2016.1154839

Bodie, G. D., & Godwin, P. (2022). On the limits of listening for bridging divides and cross-cultural understanding. In L. Chao & C. Wang (Eds.), *Communication across differences: Negotiating identity, privilege, and marginalization in the 21st century* (pp. 225–243). Cognella.

Burleson, B. R. (2003). Emotional support skill. In J. O. Greene & B. R. Burleson (Eds.), *Handbook of communication and social interaction skills* (pp. 551–594). Erlbaum.

Burleson, B. R. (2011). A constructivist approach to listening. *International Journal of Listening, 25*(1–2), 27–46. 10.1080/10904018.2011.536470

Cleven, E., Bush, R. A. B., & Saul, J. A. (2018). Living with no: Political polarization and transformative dialogue. *Journal of Dispute Resolution, 2018*(1), 53–63. https://scholarship.law.missouri.edu/jdr/vol2018/iss1/7

Cohen, J. S. (2019, December 3). In a polarized world, dialogue is a radical act. America: The Jesuit Review. https://www.americamagazine.org/politics-society/2019/12/03/polarized-world-dialogue-radical-act

Cooperrider, D., Sorensen, P. F., Whitney, D., & Yaeger, T. F. (Eds.). (2000). *Appreciative inquiry: Rethinking human organization toward a positive theory of change.* Stripes.

County Board of Arlington, VA. (2012, December). *Participation, leadership and civic engagement (PLACE): Report to the county board.* https://topics.arlingtonva.us/wp-content/uploads/sites/21/2014/11/PLACE-Report-FinalWithPageNo.pdf

Dickson, E. (2009, August 22). A bright shining slogan: How "hearts and minds" came to be. *Foreign Policy Magazine.* https://foreignpolicy.com/2009/08/22/a-bright-shining-slogan/

Dobson, A. (2014). *Listening for democracy.* Oxford University Press.

Epley, N. (2014). *Mindwise: Why we misunderstand what others think, believe, feel, and want.* Vintage Books.

Ferguson, M. A. (2018). Building theory in public relations: Interorganizational relationships as a public relations paradigm. *Journal of Public Relations Research, 30*(4), 164–178. https://doi-org.umiss.idm.oclc.org/10.1080/1062726X.2018.1514810

Fine, M. (2006). Bearing witness: Methods for researching oppression and resistance – A textbook for critical research. *Social Justice Research, 19*(1), 83–108. 10.1007/s11211-006-0001-0

Forsberg, T. (2001). The philosophy and practice of dealing with the past: Some conceptual and normative issues. In N. Biggar (Ed.), *Burying the past* (pp. 65–84). Georgetown University Press.

Freinacht, H. (2017). *The listening society.* Metamoderna.

Giner-Sorolla, R., & Russell, P. S. (2019). Not just disgust: Fear and anger also relate to intergroup dehumanization. *Collabra: Psychology, 5*(1), 56. 10.1525/collabra.211https://link.gale.com/apps/doc/A610206515/AONE?u=anon~4f7fd666&sid=googleScholar&xid=57aac226

Goldstone, R. J. (2000). *For humanity: Reflections of a war crimes investigator.* Yale University Press.

Hendriks, C. M., Ercan, S. A., & Duus, S. (2019). Listening in polarised controversies: A study of listening practices in the public sphere. *Policy Sciences, 52*(2), 137–151. 10.1007/s11077-018-9343-3

Higgins, J. W. (2011). Peacebuilding through listening, digital storytelling, and community media in Cyprus. *Global Media Journal: Mediterranean Edition, 6.* https://www.academia.edu/8458982/Peacebuilding_Through_Listening_Digital_Storytelling_and_Community_Media_in_Cyprus

Itzchakov, G., & Kluger, A. N. (2017). Can holding a stick improve listening at work? The effect of Listening Circles on employees' emotions and cognitions. *European Journal of Work and Organizational Psychology, 26*(5), 663–676. 10.1080/1359432X.2017.1351429

Johansson, P. (2017, May 17). Feeling for the game: How emotions shape listening in peacebuilding partnerships. *E-International Relations.* https://www.e-ir.info/2017/05/17/feeling-for-the-game-how-emotions-shape-listening-in-peacebuilding-partnerships/

Johnston, G., & Van Ness, D. W. (Eds.). (2011). *Handbook of restorative justice.* Routledge.

Jones, S. M. (2011). Supportive listening. *International Journal of Listening, 25*(1–2), 85–103. 10.1080/10904018.2011.536475.

Katan, D. (2013). Intercultural mediation. In Y. Gambier & L. V. Doorslaer (Eds.), *Handbook of translation studies* (Vol. 4; pp. 84–91). John Benjamins. 10.1075/hts.4.int5

Kretzmann, J. P. (2010). Asset-based strategies for building resilient communities. In J. W. Reich, A. Zautra & J. S. Hall (Eds.), *Handbook of adult resilience* (pp. 484–495). Guilford Press.

Kretzmann, J. P., & McKnight, J. L. (1993). *Building communities from the inside out: A path toward finding and mobilizing a community's assets.* Center for Urban Affairs and Policy Research, Northwestern University.

Krog, A. (1999). *Country of my skull: Guilt, sorrow, and the limits of forgiveness in the new South Africa.* Random House.

Krueger-Henney, P. (2016). What are we listening for? (Participatory Action) Research and embodied social listening to the permanence of anti-black racism in education. *Journal of Critical Pedagogy, 7*(3), 49–65. http://libjournal.uncg.edu/ijcp/article/view/1326

Lafayette County Remembrance Project. (2021, February 8). A show of strength: Facing and telling the truth about lynchings in Lafayette County. *Mississippi Free Press.* https://www.mississippifreepress.org/9096/a-show-of-strength-facing-and-telling-the-truth-about-lynchings-in-lafayette-county/

Lamm, C. R., Rütgen, M., & Wagner, I. C. (2019). Imaging empathy and prosocial emotions. *Neuroscience Letters*, *693*(1), 49–53. 10.1016/j.neulet.2017.06.054

Lederach, J. P. (1997). *Sustainable reconciliation in divided societies*. United States Institute of Peace Press.

Ledrach, J. P. (1997). *Building peace: Sustainable reconciliation in divided societies*. United States Institute of Peace.

Lennertz, B., & Lutzenhiser, A. (2017). *The charrette handbook* (2nd ed.). Routledge.

Lewis, L. (2020). *The power of strategic listening in contemporary organizations*. Rowman & Littlefield Publishers.

Macnamara, J. (2015). *Creating an "Architecture of Listening" in organizations: The basis of engagement, trust, healthy democracy, social equity, and business sustainability*. University of Technology Sydney. uts.edu.au/sites/default/files/fass-organizational-listening-report.pdf

Macnamara, J. (2016). *Organizational listening: The missing essential in public communication*. Peter Lang.

Macnamara, J. (2020). Listening for healthy democracy. In D. L. Worthington & G. D. Bodie (Eds.), *The handbook of listening* (pp. 385–396). Wiley.

Manzo, L. C., & Brightbill, N. (2007). Toward a participatory ethics. In S. Kindon, R. Pain & M. Kesby (Eds.), *Participatory action research approaches and methods: Connecting people, participation and place* (pp. 33–40). Routledge.

Mathie, A., Cameron, J., & Gibson, K. (2017). Asset-based and citizen-led development: Using a diffracted power lens to analyze the possibilities and challenges. *Progress in Development Studies*, *17*(1), 1–13. 10.1177/1464993416674302

Mathie, A., & Cunningham, G. (2003). From clients to citizens: Asset-based community development as a strategy for community-driven development. *Development in Practice*, *13*(5), 474–486. 10.1080/0961452032000125857

Moore, K. R., & Elliott, T. J. (2016). From participatory design to a listening infrastructure: A case of urban planning and participation. *Journal of Business and Technical Communication*, *30*(1), 59–84. 10.1177/1050651915602294

Mower, D. S. (2020). Philosophy. In D. L. Worthington & G. D. Bodie (Eds.), *The handbook of listening* (pp. 217–232). Wiley.

Pain, R., Whitman, G., Milledge, D., & Lune Rivers Trust. (2011). Participatory Action Research toolkit: An introduction to using PART as an approach to learning, research and action. Durham University. http://communitylearningpartnership.org/wp-content/uploads/2017/01/PARtoolkit.pdf

Pankhurst, D. (1999). Issues of justice and reconciliation in complex political emergencies: Conceptualizing reconciliation, justice, and peace. *Third World Quarterly*, *20*(1), 239–256. https://www.jstor.org/stable/3993193

Patel, L. (2016). *Decolonizing educational research: From ownership to answerability*. Routledge.

Pruitt, D. G., & Kim, S. H. (1983). *Social conflict: Escalation, stalemate, and settlement* (3rd ed.). McGraw Hill.

Ridge, A. (1993). A perspective on listening skills. In A. D. Wolvin & C. G. Coakley (Eds.), *Perspectives on listening* (pp. 1–14). Ablex.

Rogers, C. R. (1957). The necessary and sufficient conditions of therapeutic personality change. *Journal of Consulting Psychology*, *21*(2), 95–103. 10.1037/h0045357

Rowan, K., & Cavallaro, A. (2019). Toward a model for preparatory community listening. *Community Literacy Journal*, *13*(1), 23–36. doi:10.25148/clj.13.1.009088

Shriver, D. (2001). Where and when in political life is justice served by forgiveness? In N. Biggar (Ed.), *Burying the past* (pp. 25–43). Georgetown University Press.

The Alluvial Collective. (2021). *The welcome table.* https://alluvialcollective.org/community-building/the-welcome-table/

Wahl, R. (2019). On the ethics of open-mindedness in the age of Trump. *Educational Theory, 69*, 455–472. 10.1111/edth.12379

Wilcox, D. (1994). *The guide to effective participation.* Joseph Rowntree Foundation.

Wilmer, F. (2018). Empathy as political action: Can empathic engagement disrupt narratives of conflict. *Journal of Social Science Research, 13*, 2860–2870. 10.24297/jssr.v13i0.7934

Worthington, D. L. (2018). Modeling and measuring cognitive components of listening. In D. L. Worthington & G. D. Bodie (Eds.), *The sourcebook of listening research: Methodology and measures* (pp. 70–96). John Wiley & Sons.

Worthington, D. L., & Bodie, G. D. (2018). Defining listening: A historical, theoretical and pragmatic assessment. In D. L. Worthington & G. D. Bodie (Eds.), *The sourcebook of listening research: Methodology and measures* (pp. 3–17). John Wiley & Sons.

2

BEYOND THE TOWN HALL

From chaos to collaboration in community listening

Larry Schooler

MOODY COLLEGE OF COMMUNICATION, DEPARTMENT OF
COMMUNICATION STUDIES, UNIVERSITY OF TEXAS AT AUSTIN

"I called your office and was told I would have the mic to speak!" bellowed the unnamed, thickly accented Pennsylvanian, a constituent of the late Senator Arlen Specter, during public meetings on the Affordable Care Act in 2010. He continued,

> And then I was lied to, because I came prepared to speak, and instead, you wouldn't let anybody speak! You handed out, what, thirty cards?! Well, I've got news for you, that you and your cronies in the government do this kind of stuff all the time. Well, I don't care *(applause)* I don't care how damn crooked you are. I'm not a lobbyist with all kinds of money to stuff in your pocket so you can cheat the citizens of this country. So, I'll leave. And you can do whatever the hell you want to do … I'm leaving. *(exits)*

As the man exited, the camera followed him, then panned back to Senator Specter who declared, "Ok, ok, ok. We've just had a, we've just had a demonstration of democracy, okay?"[1]

In approximately two-and-a-half minutes, this exchange revealed both a yawning gap between (a) the expectations of an exasperated constituent and one of their key federal representatives, and (b) an implicit definition of democracy at odds with conventional wisdom. To begin, the convener of the meeting labeled it a "town hall," disregarding that it took place in a hotel ballroom and has little in common with the Town Meetings of New England. Although a full history is beyond the scope of this chapter, it is important to note that, in contrast to the shouting match that this and other so-called "town hall meetings" often become, true town meetings are meant as pure democratic spaces (Field, 2019). They often include a facilitator hired from a professional network of neutral, third-party

DOI: 10.4324/9781003214465-2

moderators who utilize structured agendas and prescribed protocol for participants to debate, deliberate, discuss, and decide on issues important to the community (Clark & Bryan, 2005). Whereas the "town hall meetings" of today largely serve a perfunctory role in defense of a preordained position (Field, 2019), true town meetings give registered residents of a given municipality a direct say and vote in budgetary and other matters before they become law or policy. Indeed, journalists (Rosenberg, 2019), commentators (Healy, 2017), scholars (e.g., Bryan, 2003), and other public intellectuals alike have decried the rapid rise of "faux" town halls over the past few decades and continue to ask what demonstrations like the one in Lebanon, PA mean for community engagement more generally.

Particularly important for a chapter within a collection of essays on "listening" is the disconnect between the aims of the speaker and the listener. In the exchange with Senator Specter, the speaker disrupted the "town hall meeting" with what he and others felt was a legitimate complaint because, as they articulated, Senator Specter did not "sanction" their voices to be heard. The essence of the complaint lies with the processes the conveners used for the public to have a say, without ever really having a say. For instance, while the event provided for public input, that input was limited to the first 30 people who filled out an interest card, a number that seems inadequate given over 1,000 people were attempting to secure a seat in a space that held only 250. It was clear even before that evening, of course, that the issue under discussion, healthcare, would likely draw passionate voices across multiple perspectives. It was 2009, and the partisan rancor over so-called Obamacare was already at a fever pitch by the time August rolled around. Just that April, Specter announced a switch in party affiliation from Republican to Democrat, leading conservative activist and lobbying groups to begin mobilizing in light of this new filibuster-proof (60-seat majority) Senate.

Indeed, this gentleman claimed he was encouraged to "come prepared to speak" by Spector's office, and when he realized that promise would be broken, he charged up so close to the Senator that police and Secret Service officers surrounded him (Glass, 2009).[2] Fox News broke away to cover it live. People in the audience both applauded and shouted "time" to signal the speaker should yield the floor to others. Yet, the Senator's reaction is puzzling – does the man's interruption, justified or not, demonstrate "democracy"? He may have, of course, been exercising his constitutionally protected right to speak without fear of imprisonment (and he stated with confirmation from Specter several times he was "free to leave"), but the idea that his participation (either in a legitimate way if he had been able to fill out a card or in the way he ultimately decided to participate) would play any meaningful role in the decisions made by Specter or the government more generally seems far-fetched. Thus, while it might be appropriate to assert this man participated in a justified act of civil disobedience, to say we witnessed democracy in action seems a stretch.

As unfortunate as the proliferation of faux town meetings may be, especially considering rising concerns over acts of violence (Kleinfeld, 2022), numerous governments, from the local to state to the national level, have begun experimenting with, and even institutionalizing, an entirely different form of "democratic listening." Known by various terms including deliberative democracy, public participation, public engagement, public consultation (which is more common in Canada and Europe), or civic engagement, this paradigm offers participants entirely different listening and speaking (i.e., participatory) roles than the one given to attendees of town hall meetings like the one convened by Specter. As articulated by groups like the International Association for Public Participation (IAP2) and the National Coalition for Dialogue and Deliberation (NCDD), this kind of democratic listening is meant to ensure that "those who are affected by a decision have a right to be involved in the decision-making process" (IAP2, n.d.). If this appears, on the surface, like a return to the direct democracy of ancient Athens, Greece, and early formulations of a "true" town hall, that is deliberate. Indeed, the purpose of this chapter is to provide a guide to this slow and steady revolution in American democracy and in democratic listening. From a reset in the values underpinning democratic participation to innovative tools and strategies for involving the public in decision-making, I will attempt to show how many governmental institutions have begun to improve and strengthen their capacity to listen to their constituents, and how much more work remains.

Increasing trust through transparency and two-way communication

> For various sad reasons, the faith in representative government is deteriorating. Not everywhere. Denmark has got pretty strong faith in its representative government. So, it's not absolutely intrinsic to representative government that it's, that it's kind of screwed up and is going to make people lose faith in it. But people are losing faith in representative government and looking for alternatives. (J. Mansbridge, personal communication, 10 April 2020)

This outlook, offered by Jane Mansbridge of Harvard's Kennedy School of Government, is backed by data gathered from nationally representative samples of US adults. According to the Pew Research Center (PEW, 2022), for instance, "Since the 2007–2008 financial crisis, no more than about a quarter of Americans have expressed trust in the federal government to do what is right all or most of the time." Their 2022 data showed "only two in ten Americans say they trust the government in Washington to do what is right just about always (2%) or most of the time (19%)." Similarly, Edelman's (2021) trust barometer report continues to show global decreases in trust for a variety of institutions including government, NGOs, and media; business was conferred more trust than government in 18 of 27 countries. More significantly, Pew researchers (Wike & Fetterolf, 2021, ¶ 3) found that for many, democracy is not delivering; people like democracy, but their commitment to it is often not very strong; political and social divisions are amplifying the challenges of contemporary democracy; and people want a stronger public voice in politics and policymaking.

Unfortunately, that stronger public voice is often reflected merely in volume of the person's voice – shouting at a public meeting, for example, or rallying large numbers of protestors to disrupt democratic deliberations.

The notion of being heard – such an integral component to the resolution of any conflict – does not suffice in today's world. To an extent, a member of the public or a coalition may raise its voice loudly enough – either by decibels or by the number of speakers – to affect change, be it the recall or removal of elected officials or the repeal of long-established policy. That said, for most citizens in a democracy, the notion of using strident rhetoric in a public speech holds little sway and places added demand on members of the public, most of whom have chosen not to take on the task.

Harvard's Jane Mansbridge spoke to numerous New England Town Meeting attendees and found:

> that there were people who'd never spoken at town meeting and never would speak at town meetings. I began to get a clue as to the dynamics when I talked to one man who I asked would you be likely to speak up at town meeting? And he was one of the many who said that he was not likely to get to speak up at town meeting. He said, but if I got mad enough, I would. So that tells us that one of the dynamics going on is that people don't kind of screw up the courage to speak, unless they're already kind of quite emotionally driven from inside. (J. Mansbridge, personal communication, 10 April 2020)

Mansbridge also concluded that anyone who has summoned the courage to speak, due in part to an intolerable level of anger, may then create their own echo chamber. Once convinced they are right, she argued, they are less likely to listen to someone else who challenges their now firmly held assertions. That, in turn, can create wider gulfs between people of differing views – if they cannot even hear what the "other side" thinks, they fill the vacuum of information about that other side with worst case scenarios, stereotypes, over-generalizations, and even conspiracy theories (e.g., Bail, 2021; Yudkin et al., 2019). Having done that, a government agency often faces a near impossible task of discerning the public good amidst two opposite viewpoints.

Seeking influence and impact

Beyond the anecdotal evidence, one can merely look around any meeting conducted by a city council, county commissioners court, or state legislative committee, where a member of the public could theoretically speak. For most items up for consideration, including the appropriation of millions of dollars in a single vote, few if any speakers come to the podium. When a larger group of speakers emerges, the governing body often limits speaking time and excludes many who have waited hours for a few minutes of speaking time. That show of rhetorical force, with speakers interrupted by applause or catcalls, can often paint a highly misleading picture of public opinion. Only those with disposable time, not to mention the fortitude to risk ridicule, step forward in most of these sessions, not the silent majority. Such public hearings – an ironic moniker if, in fact, many who seek to be heard are not – often occur only as a bill is being considered and after numerous closed-door meetings, during which participants (again, usually only elected officials with variable access to public opinion) can meaningfully affect the direction of a public policy. Hearings may also occur late into the evening after dozens of other measures are considered, or during daytime business hours when a much smaller audience can even attend – in either case, can an elected official or public administrator be expected to listen as carefully when exhausted or about to decide? It is nearly impossible to schedule a single hearing at a time convenient to all those impacted by a public policy decision. Accordingly, the choice to limit public input to such hearings is both short-sighted and exclusionary, if not discriminatory. It deprives the decision-makers of access to a broad cross-section of community sentiment, and it gives only certain members of the public a meaningful opportunity to be heard.

From public "hearings" to democratic "listening"

To establish a much stronger link between the governing and the governed, we must consider the differentiation between public "hearings" and democratic "listening." In public hearings, one can certainly argue that a member of the public speaks while government officials listen, but in the absence of a space for meaningful conversation, and at the 11th hour of a decision-making process, it could feel to the speaker as if they are speaking to an inanimate object. When we speak passionately about a topic, we usually seek some sort of reaction from our listening audience – empathy, understanding, support, or perhaps even clarification or a counterpoint, some demonstration of "active listening." In public hearings, we may find the biological function of hearing present but not the higher-order skill of active listening.

Democratic "listening," then, suggests that the speaker and the listener share common goals – to understand one another, to learn from one another, to help each other see aspects of an issue they had not seen or comprehended before. It implies that the physical space for that listening must consequently be configured not as a theatre, worship space, or courtroom, with government officials physically raised above their constituents on a dais and all eyes fixed on the political show in front of them. Instead, both speaker and listener (whose roles might switch during the process) need seating on the same level, ideally with some closeness, in a smaller group, where one is more likely to speak at a conversational volume, with eye contact, and with the chance to clarify or explain their views.

To understand the significance of a paradigm shift from public hearings to democratic listening, it is instructive to return to the original notion of representative democracy in the United States. In Article 1 of the US Constitution, language describes a House of Representatives composed of "Members chosen every second Year by the People of the several states," with apportionment of representatives based on population and a single representative representing a subset of the entire state's population. While debates have raged for centuries as to the relative strength of a delegate or a trustee model of representation, some state legislatures continue to use the "house of delegates" nomenclature. Such nomenclature suggests that while senators may take on the role of trustee and use their own knowledge and experience to make decisions, representatives (or delegates) are meant to provide a voice to their constituents. While the partisan process many states use for drawing congressional and legislative districts may produce lopsided election results disconnected from a state's broader political leanings, the elected representative maintains a certain obligation to, in fact, represent the views of their district.

Of course, one of the great challenges associated with representing a district of thousands lies with the older methods of gauging public sentiment. Macnamara (2016, p. 9) and others (see Argo & Brown, Chapter 8) have argued that to listen "at scale" requires more than sophisticated technology but also requires:

> A *culture* that is open to listening; *Policies* for listening; Addressing the *politics* of listening such as recognizing voices that are marginalized; *systems* that are open and interactive; … *skills* for listening; and *articulation* of the voice of stakeholders and publics to policy making and decision making.

Much of these conditions are lacking in the more traditional forms of public hearings discussed earlier. To wit, the "town hall meetings" discussed earlier clearly do not appeal to most voters, or even non-voters. Attendees of such meetings may never speak or otherwise express their views if an earlier speaker earns scorn for a similar viewpoint or cheers for the opposite one. Few among us would willingly choose to engage with someone who makes us feel unsafe for taking a particular point of view; as such, we will retreat to a safer space (say, a political party or a social media feed made up of only the viewpoints we support), all of which act to increase toxic polarization (Burgess et al., 2022). That polarization, in turns, makes it that much more difficult to help holders of differing viewpoints learn from one another and craft consensus. The polarization process may have convinced them that anyone with a dissenting point of view, or of a different political party, cannot understand views other than their own, much less consider embracing them. It is a vicious cycle, indeed.

Nevertheless, as unappealing as today's "town meetings" may be, any member of the public can contact an elected official by phone, letter, or social media; those seeking a direct, in-person audience may find their requests ignored in the absence of an influential friend of, or financial contributor to, the elected official's campaign. While a face-to-face meeting, particularly conducted in private, might give the impression of authentic listening on the elected official's part, it is a communication medium closed to many (or most) constituents and thus cannot deliver the voice of the people at large. While even the most dedicated elected official could not likely meet with all their constituents, in theory, a decision-maker could absorb a sizable number of tweets, mailed letters, or telephone calls and be influenced by those communications before making a decision (e.g., Irons, 2021). That said, the inability to trace whether writers or callers are constituents or even human (e.g., tweets produced by bots, automated messages), coupled with minimal transparency around how many constituents communicate a given position, makes such methods inadequate to meet the broader needs of listening to a constituency.

The silver lining in all this is that, in recent years, numerous governmental agencies around the world have diversified their democratic listening portfolios. Even modifications to the usual format of a town hall meeting have made a difference. Many governments, particularly at the local level, for instance, have converted such meetings into workshops or "community conversations" (Cornett et al., 2016; Power, 2016; Wertheim, 2020). Of particular significance is the use of facilitated discussion in small groups, often composed of people who have not previously met and/or hold differing positions. At a smaller roundtable with strategically and thoughtfully written discussion prompts and a neutral facilitator to maximize inclusion, such workshops have attracted a far more diverse audience of participants. More importantly, where a public hearing might only include the voices of a dozen, a workshop or community conversation (particularly when repeated at various times of day and week and in different neighborhoods) yields hundreds, if not thousands, of voices heard.

Despite their success, however, such public forums still present difficulties for those seeking to be heard. The need for childcare or supervised children's activities at meetings conducted after school; the limitations of an English-only meeting for a community whose first language is otherwise; mobility challenges in getting to, or into, a venue; and the anxiety of sharing personal views in front of strangers can all become insurmountable obstacles. That has helped produce other innovations in face-to-face democratic listening, such as a "meeting in a box" (or bag or another container; e.g., NJTPA, n.d.). Such portable meetings, which often include materials for hosts and participants that replicate a public workshop, afford attendees some greater comfort by occurring in already existing groups – families, neighbors, work colleagues, members of a community organization, etc. – at a time and place familiar and convenient to all. While a government agency may trade off some forms of "quality control" in the reporting of what was heard, relying on volunteers to share a nuanced and comprehensive account, the boxes can expand the reach of a government's ears and efficiently and effectively leverage a community's social capital (Claxton et al., 2015).

Still other governments have utilized forms of "pop-up" engagement, positioning themselves at community gatherings like festivals and gathering places like shopping areas or parks and devising visually compelling activities to entice passersby (e.g., see Gregor, 2010, for a description of "Speak Week"). Some provide jars corresponding to different modes of transportation and encourage participants to share their priorities using poker chips that represent tax dollars. Others utilize "dot stickers" to allow residents to pinpoint areas of greatest need or adhesive notepads to share opinions or agree with others. Still others simply treat such mobile stations as a place for listening – ala "The Doctor Is In" from the Peanuts cartoons or office hours in an academic setting – to give constituents an audience with governmental listeners. Some elected officials embark on walks or bike rides with a similar purpose. Some communities have even developed programs that train community members to become facilitators and join a "conversation corps" to catalyze civic dialogue across a community, rather than just in official public meetings. In all such cases, the size of the population heard (listened to) by government has increased exponentially from those who speak at public hearings (Young et al., 1993). Importantly, government can then produce a clearer understanding of public sentiment inclusive of viewpoints across the political spectrum and public policy more reflective of the public good.

One such process, undertaken on behalf of the City of Austin's *Imagine Austin Comprehensive Plan* (IACP), yielded some 15,000 participants at in-person forums alone. These forums took on different purposes and functions throughout the three-year process of developing the plan. Some events focused on dialogue, an exchange of views to increase understanding among participants without the need for group members to unearth areas of agreement or make any decisions. Concurrently and subsequently, a Citizens Advisory Task Force (and other bodies like the Planning Commission) convened for deliberation, evaluating a manageable set of growth scenarios, and discovering a consensus scenario to guide the IACP. Community members could participate alongside the Task Force through both public events where they could learn about and discuss the scenarios in small groups, as well as through rented "meetings in a box" that enhanced the convenience and accessibility of the process. "Speak Week" events allowed even those unaware of the process to encounter staff and volunteers at busy intersections, gathering places, and events to provide their input, with guidance on how to participate in a deeper way. Across the entire planning process, online tools enabled those less inclined to attend meetings to have their own perspectives heard – via multiple choice surveys, "click and drag" prioritization exercises, and threaded and moderated discussion boards. Most importantly, City staff worked with Citizens Advisory Task Force members to review all comments made by the public and identify how those comments might be incorporated, or a justification for excluding them. While the City of Austin certainly received criticism for having lower participation from some parts of the community, the Imagine Austin process did engage a remarkable array of Austinites in dialogue and deliberation. That, in turn, likely provided the Council the confidence to endorse the plan unanimously.

The "scale" of listening

Typical of scholarship on efforts to engage the public is a focus on "numbers served" or other quantitative markers of success (e.g., amount of commentary, number of sessions held, surveys collected). That is certainly the tone I have taken so far in this chapter, and these markers of success are reasonable benchmarks against which public consultation professionals can judge their impact. At the same time, an interesting set of alternatives exists in a variety of face-to-face engagement and listening tools that actually shrink the participant population, but may, in turn, enlarge its ability to represent the public. Notable among these are deliberative polling (Fishkin, 2018) and the citizen jury (Smith & Wales, 2000). In both, members of the public apply to participate and are chosen in such a way as to produce demographic and even political representations of the affected population. Both processes emphasize the need for dialogue and deliberation, rather than the production of public input. While participants may be polled at the outset to understand their perspectives and ensure a variety of viewpoints are represented, the aim of the exercise is to present information from multiple perspectives to a diverse group, which can then discuss and arrive at more reasoned judgment. Naturally, such methods have their critics (e.g., Kenyon, 2005; Merkle, 1996), and these can be organized primarily around the limitations on participation associated with the size of the participant population (in the dozens or hundreds) and the requirements to participate (often multiple, elongated sessions). Nevertheless, the two models build upon the subdivision of a town hall meeting's audience into smaller group conversations to include deeper deliberation and a chance for more active listening.

Of course, with so much dialogue occurring using technology, it behooves governments to incorporate multiple media in its effort to listen. Such technologically assisted listening has taken on new meaning in the wake of a global pandemic, during which time face-to-face meetings came to a complete halt across much of the world, and governmental agencies were permitted to conduct official business via videoconference or other means. But even prior to this time, governments began harnessing the power of older and newer technologies to help hear the people's voices. For example, a newer application of older technology has taken hold in communities and legislative districts across the USA – the "telephone town hall" (Congressional Management Foundation, n.d.). While retaining some of the limitations associated with in-person "town hall" meetings in requiring audience members to queue up for a short speaking opportunity, the technology does bring with it additional assets. For one thing, the system dials out to an audience in the thousands or even tens of thousands, and while many will receive and decline the call, those who accept the call often come from under-represented communities or have never otherwise taken advantage of opportunities for public comment.[3] The system also allows for real-time polling via a touch-tone phone, enabling the government to listen to more than just a caller's brief comments. Some forms of the technology have even evolved to include real-time interpretation in a second or third language, with messages rendered from the other language to English for moderators to incorporate into the English-language session. In an age where one out of every four homes, according to Pew Research Center (2021), still lack high-speed Internet access, the use of a telephone remains a powerful ear for government.

So, too, does text messaging, a widely available and embraced medium worldwide. Already utilized extensively by retailers and businesses hoping for new customers, governments have begun piloting a variety of synchronous and asynchronous uses of SMS to communicate with constituents (2015 Mongolian Referendum, 2020; Participatory Budgeting, 2017). Platforms such as "Poll Everywhere" have allowed for real-time responses to both multiple-choice and open-ended questions, irrespective of where a person is sitting in proximity to a computer (in contrast to frequently used "clickers"). The often-anonymized responses can create greater safety for participants wary of being shouted down at the podium, while the variety of question types and answer displays (including instant word clouds) help read a room more quickly and effectively than a show of hands. "Text, Talk, Engage" and its predecessor "Text, Talk, Act" allow for asynchronous discussion driven by a series of prompts received over SMS.[4] After a participant opts into a discussion, a question is posed that an individual or group can answer via text, leading to follow up questions. It can take on the qualities of a meeting in a box, sans box, where several participants discuss their answers and a shared response goes into a text reply; or, it can function more like a survey for those unable or less likely to visit or find a web-based questionnaire. The tool lacks a real-time human facilitator and functions based on an automated "question tree," where an initial question may help the user identify their perspective (student, teacher, parent), geography, or other demographic characteristic, or a specific subtopic of interest and receive customized questions to discuss (with or without peers). Answers are then compiled and coded to allow the organization using the service to gauge sentiments across large populations.

The use of text messaging as a tool to foster dialogue and deliberation holds special significance, in part, due to the near ubiquitous presence of text messaging among citizens of all ages – particularly younger adults, who often eschew in-person meetings and phone calls to communicate more quickly through technology (Smith, 2015). Text messaging also does not require an Internet connection of any kind, and while some messages may include a cost, they are often far less expensive than a monthly Internet subscription or data plan.

Of course, no listening strategy can exclude the incredible reach the Internet can provide. Though susceptible to many limitations including the cost of access and the dangers associated with Internet trolls, carefully crafted online spaces can afford huge audiences a chance to be heard, both by the convening government and by their neighbors or fellow citizens. A web-based survey can, of course, help collect input more quickly and cheaply than a paper survey, though often without assurances that one person completed only one survey. More sophisticated platforms have begun to experiment with required registration to participate (e.g., Social Pinpoint); some even require a user to authenticate that they live in each jurisdiction or district or are a registered voter (e.g., Polco). More importantly, the tools available for democratic listening have evolved beyond a unilateral survey with limited question types. Multiple platforms have now instituted moderated fora, in which an open-ended question prompts discussion and replies from a plethora of respondents (e.g., Social Pinpoint). Still other platforms have incorporated maps and icons allowing a participant to indicate precisely where the government should focus its attention, investment, or policy (e.g., Metroquest). Newer platforms have tackled the notion of tradeoffs in public spending. A visitor to a site like "Balancing Act" will encounter a depiction of a budget or spending plan that they can understand more readily than by reading the budget itself. They can then make either generalized judgments (e.g., cut parks spending and use the savings for policing) or make more finely grained comments (e.g., move funding from one recreation center to another). Unlike many other forms of listening-at-scale, such tools help place the public into the shoes of public administrators and elected officials more squarely. In other contexts, the public may clamor for a widely supported measure to be adopted, such as needed fixes to a beloved public pool, but then revolt at the notion that such a move necessitates either a sizable tax increase or the closure of another facility. Like deliberative polling or citizens juries, these tools allow for deeper listening. That is, listening beyond a person's initial reaction and toward a greater understanding of what is at stake.

The future: unanswered questions for democratic listening

With all this innovation, it is reasonable to ask what it will mean in the future to listen in a civic or public space. Although it may not be the first innovation, discussions of space- and place-based dialogue and deliberation will inevitably raise possibilities afforded by the advent of virtual and augmented reality (Miller & Bailenson, 2020). These advances in how we connect across space and time may lead governments to consider more than just meetings conducted via video conference or phone and, instead, an immersive experience whereby a participant examines a public issue directly, as a government official would, before sharing their perspective (Copeland, 2015). Similarly, drones and other technology allowing for a bird's eye view of a scene could give an entirely new vantage point. If trends around urban and center city migration, for instance, continue, one can imagine interesting developments in street-based dialogue. Street-based dialogues may be less formal as in a demonstration, or more formal as in roundtables in streets such as those seen in places like the Mideast, or "longest table" events pioneered by organizers in Tallahassee, FL (e.g., Anderson, 2019). As we offer people "a seat at the table" (whether that table is proverbial, literal, physical, virtual, or otherwise), various technological innovations will help push the old "town hall meeting" model into a new century.

In terms of scale, the sudden ubiquity of livestreaming, making virtually anyone with an Internet connection capable of broadcasting, creates the potential for many more conversations on a single topic to occur at the same time, whether convened by government or not, whether heard by government or not. A resurgence, or revolution, in public expressions of rage may yet demand different means through which to capture sentiments of both the loud(er) and the silent. In other words, greater opportunities for large-scale speaking require similar advancements in large-scale listening like that afforded by organizations such as Cortico and their public conversation network known as Local Voices Network (LVN).[5]

In his talk organized for FWD50, *Listening at Scale: From Cacophony to the Will of the People,* Adams (2022) made the following claim: "governments' power to influence, understand, engage with, and inspire their populations is fading, particularly relative to technology. And this trend is inexorable unless the people watching this talk learn to harness the power of social technologies." Along with the declining trust people around the world place in major institutions that I cited earlier in this chapter, Adams raised the strange imbalance we see between inefficiencies in how governments interact with their constituents and the efficiencies of interaction afforded by technologies such as Facebook. And, yet, we are presently given too few opportunities to honestly, openly, and meaningfully interact with others online about important issues, especially with those with whom we disagree. Perhaps the most relevant question Adams asked, at least for purposes of concluding this chapter, is this: "if … the founders of so many democratic countries were designing governments today, would they rely on [such outdated modes of] communication" like "sending representatives from across the land" to engage in "'real' deliberation, face-to-face"? To believe that we must rely on the traditional "town hall meeting" or other "in-person" approaches to dialogue, deliberation, and other modes of democratic participation (e.g., voting) seems outdated at best and perhaps works against creating sustainable and resilient democracies at worst. As stated in the YouTube notes for this talk,

> With demonstrations of emerging civic technologies, Adams shows how we are entering an era when large-scale, intricate analysis of public information, and web-based mass collaboration, will allow all of us to better listen, deliberate, and cooperate at scale.

Regardless of the exact form these changes may take, it seems inevitable that the world will witness a significant expansion of democratic expression and demand to be heard. Whether, and how, governments will listen remains to be seen.

Notes

1 This exchange occurred during a "health care town hall" meeting in Lebanon, PA, featuring Senator Arlen Specter on 11 August 2009. Clips of the exchange have been archived by various news sources including the Associated Press and Fox News.
2 It should be noted that Senator Specter began traveling to town hall meetings with support from US Capitol Hill Police around the time he switched parties. Although he acknowledged that demonstrations were largely "civil" and rhetoric "within acceptable limits," he also pointed to "fights breaking out and people hospitalized" as justifications for a heightened focus on safety.
3 The author has designed and facilitated telephone town hall meetings across the country and compared demographic data shared by participants, as well as comments made by participants, with attendees to public comment sessions. While these data and resulting reports remain proprietary, interested readers are invited to reach out via email for further information (larry.schooler@austin.utexas.edu).
4 https://texttalkact.com/
5 https://cortico.ai/platform/

References

2015 Mongolian Referendum via Text Message. (2020, January 17). In *Participedia*. https://participedia.net/case/5685

Adams, N. B. (2022, June 14). *Listening at scale: From cacophony to the will of the people*. YouTube. https://www.youtube.com/watch?v=5aYwZVavhG4

Anderson, R. (2019, November 6). *The Longest Table now a local tradition*. The Famuan. http://www.thefamuanonline.com/2019/11/06/the-longest-table-now-a-local-tradition/

Bail, C. (2021). *Breaking the social media prism: How to make our platforms less polarizing*. Princeton University Press.

Bryan. F. M. (2003). *Real democracy: The New England Town Meeting and how it works*. The University of Chicago Press.

Burgess, G., Burgess, H., & Kaufman, S. (2022). Applying conflict resolution insights to the hyper-polarized, society-wide conflicts threatening liberal democracies. *Conflict Resolution Quarterly*, *39*(4), 355–369. doi:10.1002/crq.21334

Clark, S., & Bryan, F. (2005). *All those in favor: Rediscovering the secrets of town meeting and community*. (10th anniversary ed.). RavenMark.

Claxton, G., Dugan, M., & Schooler, L. (2015). Planning the city in the new economy: Comprehensive planning in Austin, TX. *Carolina Planning Journal*, *40*(2). https://carolinaplanning.unc.edu/volume-40-2/

Congressional Management Foundation. (n.d.). *Telephone town hall meetings*. https://www.congressfoundation.org/office-toolkit-home/telephone-town-hall-meetings-home

Copeland, E. (2015, June 29). *Could virtual reality improve civic engagement in policy making?* Democratic Audit UK. https://www.democraticaudit.com/2015/06/29/could-virtual-reality-improve-civic-engagement-in-policy-making/

Cornett, M., Landrieu, M. J., Benjamin, S. K., & Cochran, T. (2016, August 10). *Community conversations and other efforts to strengthen police-community relations in 49 cities*.

The United States Conference of Mayors. https://www.usmayors.org/2016/08/10/community-conversations-and-other-efforts-to-strengthen-police-community-relations-in-49-cities/

Edelman. (2021). *Edelman Trust Barometer 2021*. https://www.edelman.com/sites/g/files/aatuss191/files/2021-03/2021%20Edelman%20Trust%20Barometer.pdf

Field, J. B. (2019). *Town hall meetings and the death of deliberation*. University of Minnesota Press.

Fishkin, J. (2018). Deliberative polling. In A. Bächtiger, J. S. Dryzek, J. Mansbridge & M. Warren (Eds.), *The Oxford handbook of deliberative democracy* (pp. 315–328). Oxford University Press. doi:10.1093/oxfordhb/9780198747369.013.10

Glass, E. (2009, August 11). *Specter gets special police protection*. CNN. https://politicalticker.blogs.cnn.com/2009/08/11/specter-gets-special-police-protection/

Gregor, K. (2010, April 2). Comprehensive plan coming to you. (Naked City: News briefs from Austin, the region, and nowhere else). *Austin Chronicle*. https://www.austinchronicle.com/news/2010-04-02/988310/

Healy, J. (2017, May 11). Midwestern manners a memory at one Iowa Republican's town halls. *The New York Times*. https://www.nytimes.com/2017/05/11/us/iowa-voter-anger-rod-blum.html

International Association for Public Participation (IAP2). (n.d.). *IAP2 core values*. https://www.iap2.org/page/corevalues

Irons, M. E. (2021, August 24). MIT's 'Real Talk' campaign gives likely voters voice in Boston's race for mayor. Researchers enlist activists to engage "invisible" residents about the future of the city. *Boston Globe*. https://www.bostonglobe.com/2021/08/24/metro/mits-real-talk-campaign-gives-likely-voters-voice-bostons-race-mayor/?event=event25

Kenyon, W. (2005). A critical review of citizens' juries: How useful are they in facilitating public participation in the EU water framework directive? *Journal of Environmental Planning and Management, 48*(3), 431–443. doi:10.1080/09640560500067558

Kleinfeld, R. (2022, March 31). *The rise of political violence in the United States and damage to our democracy*. [Congressional Testimony: Select Committee to investigate the January 6th attack on the United States Capitol]. Carnegie Endowment of International Peace. https://carnegieendowment.org/2022/03/31/rise-in-political-violence-in-united-states-and-damage-to-our-democracy-pub-87584

Macnamara, J. (2016). Illuminating and addressing two 'black holes' in public communication. *PRism 13*(1). https://www.prismjournal.org/uploads/1/2/5/6/125661607/v13-no1-a1.pdf

Merkle, D. M. (1996). The polls-review: The National Issues Convention deliberative poll. *The Public Opinion Quarterly, 60*(4), 588–619. https://www.jstor.org/stable/2749637

Miller, M. R., & Bailenson, J. N. (2020). Augmented reality. In D. L. Worthington & G. D. Bodie (Eds.), *The Handbook of Listening* (pp. 409–418). Wiley.

North Jersey Transportation Planning Authority (NJTPA). (n.d.). *Innovations in public involvement tips and best practices: "Meeting in a Box."* https://www.njtpa.org/NJTPA/media/Documents/Get-Involved/Public-Involvement/Public-Engagement-Toolkit/Tips%20for%20Planning%20and%20How%20To/Meeting-in-a-Box.pdf

Participatory budgeting with SMS (Jarabacoa, Dominican Republic). (2017, June 25). In *Participedia*. https://participedia.net/case/652#

Pew Research Center (PEW). (2021, April 7). *Internet/Broadband fact sheet*. https://www.pewresearch.org/internet/fact-sheet/internet-broadband/

Pew Research Center (PEW). (2022, June). *Americans' views of government: Decades of distrust, enduring support for its role.* https://www.pewresearch.org/politics/2022/06/06/americans-views-of-government-decades-of-distrust-enduring-support-for-its-role/

Power, P. (2016, April 14). Take part in a community conversation. *Livingston Daily.* https://www.livingstondaily.com/story/opinion/columnists/2016/04/14/take-part-community-conversation/82989468/v

Rosenberg, P. (2019, December 15). From ancient Athens to the town hall: Can a new wave of deliberative democracy save the world? "Citizens' assemblies" and similar forms of ground-level democracy are suddenly everywhere. Can we all get along? *Salon.* https://www.salon.com/2019/12/15/from-ancient-athens-to-the-town-hall-can-a-new-wave-of-deliberative-democracy-save-the-world/

Smith, A. (2015, April 1). *U.S. smartphone use in 2015.* Pew Research Center. https://www.pewresearch.org/internet/2015/04/01/us-smartphone-use-in-2015/

Smith, G., & Wales, C. (2000). Citizens' juries and deliberative democracy. *Political Studies, 48*(1), 51–65. doi:10.1111/1467-9248.00250

Wertheim, C. (2020, July 2). Community conversation stresses mask use: Glenwood listening session covers coronavirus and the economy. *Post Independent.* https://www.postindependent.com/news/community-conversation-stresses-mask-use/

Wike, R., & Fetterolf, J. (2021, December 7). *Global public opinion in an era of democratic anxiety.* Pew Research Center. https://www.pewresearch.org/global/2021/12/07/global-public-opinion-in-an-era-of-democratic-anxiety/

Young, C., Williams, G., & Goldberg, M. (1993). *Evaluating the effectiveness of public meetings and workshops: A new approach for improving DOE public involvement.* United States Department of Energy Office of Scientific and Technical Information. doi:10.2172/10182527

Yudkin, D., Hawkins, S., & Dixon, T. (2019). *The perception gap: How false impressions are pulling Americans apart.* More in Common. https://perceptiongap.us/

3

PERFORMATIVE LISTENING AND SOLIDARITY

Critical intercultural communication and community engagement at the margins

Chris McRae, Ambar Basu, Parameswari Mukherjee, and Michael McDowell

DEPARTMENT OF COMMUNICATION, UNIVERSITY OF SOUTH FLORIDA

The study of intercultural communication in the last decade or so has witnessed a shift from a post-positivist and interpretivist interpretation of communication across and between cultures to a more critical orientation. This paradigm shift has seen a move away from considering cultures as boxes; it has also led to a change in the study of intercultural communication to one that involves developing skill sets to be an efficient communicator across and between these culturally-separate and constitutively homogenous boxes. We have and are witnessing more scholarship on critical intercultural communication – where the emphasis is on understanding that communication and culture are inherently political phenomena, and that intercultural communication needs to account for differences in power, knowledge, and control in a global milieu.

In the introductory chapter of the *Handbook of Critical Intercultural Communication*, Halualani and Nakayama (2010) reasserted a call to continue to forge new imaginaries wherein intercultural communication and community relations are situated within the realms of institutions, histories, ideologies, and absences. Sorrells (2010) attended to this call by theorizing intercultural communication in the context of global inequities, advocating for "[grounding] the study and practice of intercultural communication in critical engagement, democratic participation, and social justice" (p. 177). Further, Sorrells promoted positioning and dialogue as fundamental bases for such a critical grounding. Our project aims to extend this line of theorizing. We argue that understanding and practicing solidarity is central to critical intercultural communication and community engagement, particularly in contexts of historical inequity and silencing of marginalized voices. Additionally, we argue that listening, specifically

DOI: 10.4324/9781003214465-3

performative listening, is foundational to this ideation and practice of solidarity. We claim that listening in a performative sense (McRae, 2020; McRae, 2015b) is crucial to practicing solidarity, which in turn is crucial to practicing intercultural community engagement at the interstices of marginalization and inequity.

Performative listening (McRae, 2020; McRae, 2015b) works to engage others through critical acknowledgement and consideration of the ways differences mark and constitute relationships. Engaging others, particularly those in marginalized global spaces, in a way that matters to the dominant discourse, encompasses the art and practice of solidarity (Dutta & Pal, 2010). The coming together of performative listening and solidarity, we believe, is novel and important to forging new imaginaries in intercultural communication and community engagement. In this chapter, we first present literature that examines the basic tenets of critical intercultural communication. Then, we bring together ideas of intercultural communication, community engagement, listening, and solidarity. In the last section of the chapter, we propose a fresh imaginary that foregrounds performative listening as critical to solidarity in critical intercultural communication and community engagement.

Critical intercultural communication

Arasaratnam (2015) presented a thematic analysis of the major strands of intercultural communication research published in three major intercultural communication/research/relations journals between 2003 and 2013. They are:

- identity, acculturation, and global migration;
- communication dynamics, intercultural competence, theories, models, scales, and frameworks;
- perception, prejudice, stereotypes, and discrimination;
- cross-cultural differences; and
- intercultural education, training, and study abroad.

A careful reading of these themes demonstrates that the study of intercultural communication has not ventured too far from constructing scales and models that measure communication competence across national-level cultural articulations. In fact, toward the end of the piece, Arasaratnam highlighted a need to challenge and extend national-level comparisons that may have been legitimate means of studying cultural differences among homogenous populations at one time. Arasaratnam also pointed to a more nuanced study of intercultural identities, particularly from a communication perspective.

Moon (2010) similarly stated that dominant intercultural communication research from the mid-eighties is either grounded in a variable analytic tradition in which culture is defined in terms of national citizenship or in terms of the individualism/collectivism framework; further, in this line of research, "little attention is given to structural influences or power dynamics" (p. 37), and the focus is primarily on dichotomies such as individualism-collectivism, low-context/high-context, and "interpersonal processes, intercultural competence, and adaptation" (p. 37).

Within this disciplinary context, there emerged a critical perspective, one that brought into question the linear formulations of culture and communication. Culture and communication came to be positioned as political and hence contested spaces and processes, each constituting the other and contextualized in the interstices of power, control, and resistance. This line of thinking about intercultural communication produced scholarship that spoke to issues such as "the relationship between and among culture, communication, and politics, in terms of situated power interests, historical contextualization, global shifts and economic conditions, and different politicized identities in terms of race, ethnicity, gender, sexuality, region, socioeconomic class, generation, and diasporic positions" (Halualani & Nakayama, 2010, p. 3). The corollaries of making meaning – communicating – across and between cultures became important to the study of intercultural communication, as did ideas of justice and equity.

Thus, in the context of global cultural and communication transactions, intercultural communication scholarship shifted from a focus on how to make these communication transactions more efficient, which by extension supported profit and capital. Instead, it became important to understand and theorize how and why meaning making happened, as it occurred in particular historical moments, rooted in local-global communication linkages. Studying how intercultural communication was contributing to, while also helping to resist globalization forces, was crucial to this new imaginary in intercultural communication.

Sorrells (2010) put forth a call to visualize a critical intercultural communication practice that is grounded in global democratic participation and social justice. Positioning culture as a history that is continuously being made and unmade through a communicative network operating simultaneously at multiple levels, Sorrells (p. 182) stated:

> A central goal in critical approaches to intercultural communication includes challenging systems of domination, critiquing hierarchies of power and confronting discrimination to create a more equitable world.

This chapter follows Sorrells's lead and makes an effort to connect critical intercultural communication and its social justice impetus with concepts related to community engagement, dialogue, and solidarity with the margins.

Dialogue, community engagement, positionality, and solidarity

Extending this central goal of fostering justice in a global world of increasing inequities calls for a dialogic dimension of intercultural communication. This means that intercultural communication practitioners must understand that knowledge and communicative practices are created in mutually reinforcing dialogic spaces created by the dominant order and spaces at the margins. This approach suggests a fundamental shift in the role of the researcher from (a) an interventionist who imparts knowledge and skills to cultural participants to (b) a listener and a co-participant who engages in dialogue with cultural participants. Such a dialogic approach also asks that researchers/practitioners rethink the schema of engaging with the community for the purposes of redistributive social justice.

Following Freire's (1970) position that dialogue entails the fusion of identities among the participants based on the absence of subject-object distinctions, community engagement to create more just socio-cultural spaces necessitates imagining a sense of the self and the world as one developed through the interactions among participants in dialogue. The very process of engaging in dialogue introduces key ideas into the discursive spaces that have typically been omitted or taken for granted; the voices of cultural participants in a community become a part of the discursive space through this process of dialogue. The emphasis of this form of community engagement geared towards social justice is on the meanings that are created and applied in the discursive spaces of community members, and not in the transmission of the meanings from outside agents to participant spaces.

Community engagement for social and redistributive justice can be conceptualized as a critical intercultural communication approach that seeks to narrate local stories and achieve social change by the very introduction of these localo-centric voices (Basu, 2022) into the dominant discursive spaces. A similar approach to peacebuilding and community engagement is found in Broome and Collier (2012) who identified three dimensions: 1) personal, 2) relational, and 3) structural, all of which are filtered through communication, cultures, and context (pp. 251–3). Broome and Collier presented an ethic of community engagement that considers history, culture, intersectionality, and power dynamics "that contribute to conflict transformation, relationships that are equitable, inclusive, enhance justice, and the work of intercultural alliances" (p. 252). The authors thus forward an understanding of community engagement that centers dialogue and localized stories.

We engage in this ethic of transformation, equity, inclusivity, and justice in the pages that follow. We argue that this ethic is extended and enriched by the theoretical implications of performative listening that are informed by an ethos of dialogic performance. Conquergood (1985) situated dialogic performance as inherently interwoven and embodied in communities, stating: "Instead of speaking about them one speaks to and with them" (p. 10). Dialogue here is understood as both collaborative and reflexive, a way to situate one's positionality with the community. Madison (2006) forwarded a dialogic performative that does not "perpetuate ideologues of Otherness or assembly line clones of co-performative practitioners," but rather, "to clear more space for Others to enter and ride" (p. 321). Here, the boundary between community and researcher becomes less rigid. This dialogic performative does not eliminate the need for identifying stakeholders and understanding needs within the community; rather, Madison situated the researcher's presence within the conversation as a reflexive move that implicates the researcher/practitioner in the community. This ethic not only embraces what Broome and Collier (2012) identified as the nuanced, often contradictory, and deeply contextual factors that comprise a community, but forwards a framework of a dynamic community that is in constant conversation, being made and remade.

This making and remaking of meanings is a political and performative process, one where the everyday performance of meaning/discourse (in other words, communication) is (understood as) constantly challenged and remade. Butler (1988) offered a paradigm for performativity that understands it as citational, as both a "stylized repetition of acts" (p. 519) and a site of "constituted social temporality" (p. 520). The attention to repetition offers potential for change in processes, identities, relations, and structures that constitute communities and individuals within them. In the context of intercultural communication, performativity is the potential for agency in and among communities. The political potential for performativity and community engagement is a politics of transformation, of constituting and rearranging structures on the community's terms. We offer performative listening as a step toward taking this commitment further. By fostering dialogue contingent on listening to and with communities, performative listening re-centers the community as the site of agency in the conversation.

This form of community dialogue, Sorrells (2016, p. 22) wrote, offers a critical entry point for intercultural praxis inviting us to:

> stretch ourselves—to reach across—to imagine experiences, and creatively engage with points of view, ways of thinking and being, and beliefs different from our own while accepting that we may not fully understand or come to a common agreement or position.

In addition to an entry point, the space of engagement created by such a dialogic impetus is also a reflexive space for the researcher/practitioner, where they are able to locate their ideals, beliefs, practices, and convictions with respect to the interactions that take place across communities. Madison (2005), drawing from Conquergood, stated that dialogic engagement in this sense resists conclusions and is committed to keeping the conversations in intercultural spaces open and ongoing; open and ongoing in the sense that there is a tacit understanding that these conversations are a product of the history and geography of the communicative act and are, hence, predicated on the always unequal distribution and interplay of power and knowledge. Critical intercultural communication can thus be thought of as a stance from which it is salient to account for a researcher/practitioner's politics in the meanings made in intercultural encounters. This sense of accountability offers possibilities of solidarity with communities at the margins of society.

If critical intercultural communication and community engagement are positioned to contribute to social justice, one important function and aim of such a practice should be to exist in solidarity with those across the globe that face the brunt of socio-politico-cultural inequities. To quote de Oliveira (2014, p. 77):

> solidarity in this sense is to share the struggle of trying to escape various forms of oppression. It is a manifestation of support and existential posture and policy. To share the fight against the oppression of the other is to join the other in achieving social justice.

Hence, solidarity recognizes the marginalized in a way that advocates a commitment to social justice and a more just distribution of material and discursive resources in our world. It finds validation through engagement with communities at the margins, but in a format that accounts for the power divide and seeks to alter it by being prepared to listen to those at the margins talking back and resisting the content and frames that constitute the engagement/dialogue. It materializes through a readiness to formalize and engage in a manner that disrupts our "high-minded discourse of ethical benevolence and epistemological privilege, especially at those moments when that discourse claims to speak for the other" (Beverly, 2004/1999, p. 40). In other words, a critical intercultural stance that constitutes solidarity invokes methods of engaging with communities at the margins of society through a readiness to participate in a struggle to listen to voices that are traditionally drummed out of the dominant. This act of solidarity is not so much an attempt to speak for or represent these marginalized articulations objectively; rather, it is more about being complicit—with one's biases and prejudices—in creating, interpreting, and documenting them. Hence, the stance of solidarity in critical intercultural community engagement creates a space for listening to voices against inequity in ways that not only signify the conditions of inequity, but also in ways that communicate and enact the potential of such listening to transform structures and cultural conditions of marginality.

Intercultural communication and listening

Listening research in intercultural communication tends to work from a definition of listening as a skill that might be taught and improved in and across cultural differences. Beall's (2010) review of intercultural listening indicates a continued emphasis on listening research that attends to and analyzes listening effectiveness and cultural differences that are characterized by behaviors, nonverbal actions, and values (pp. 225–236). For example, Thomlison's (1991) definition of intercultural listening centers on improving listening effectiveness and reducing communication uncertainty between participants from two different cultural groups (pp. 89–90). This approach draws attention to the impact of cultural differences on individual communication practices and emphasizes the importance of openness when engaging with and listening to others across communities (pp. 130–131).

Much of the listening research that considers intercultural communication focuses on the ways cultural differences shape listening practices. For example, Dillon and McKenzie (1998) examined listening and communication competence in terms of ethnic differences in the classroom context. Pence and James (2015) analyzed the impact of biological sex and personality on, what they refer to as, active-empathic listening. Similarly, Sargent and Weaver (2003) considered the impact of sex differences on the practice of listening. Schnapp (2008) noted the role of intercultural differences in shaping listening practices and behaviors in religious and spiritual contexts. In these examples, patterns of engagement with communities are marked by specific cultural/identity-markers (e.g., ethnicity, biological sex, religious beliefs), and listening is theorized as a variable of communication that is linked to these differences.

In addition to attending to the role cultural difference plays in the practice of listening, research on intercultural listening also indicates and offers suggestions for improving listening effectiveness across communities. Purdy and Manning (2015) contended that listening is always a cultural act, and they advocated the development of self-awareness regarding the role culture plays in shaping listening practices as a strategy for listening interculturally. Timm and Schroeder (2000) analyzed the ways listening training might be used to increase and improve multicultural sensitivity. Bentley (2000) considered the implications of listening across cultural differences in terms of globalization and changing communication technologies, arguing for research regarding effective strategies for listening. Sangster and Anderson (2009) examined the role cultural context, specifically classroom settings, plays in constituting listening practices. Listening, as a factor of communication in intercultural interactions, can be developed, improved, and deployed in the service of a particular kind of intercultural interaction that acknowledges and appreciates cultural differences.

Other approaches to the question of intercultural listening move beyond the questions of listening effectiveness and the role of discrete cultural differences in shaping the practice of listening to consider the broader implications of listening as a cultural act. For example, Arneson's (2010) theory of political listening works to recognize the function of prejudice in shaping interaction and the possibility of listening as an act of developing understandings that reach beyond the limitations of prejudice. Specifically, Arneson suggested that the political rhetoric of women in the United States in the 1800s offers an example of the ways the enactment of listening worked to change existing social structures of democracy and political participation. Advocating for a shift away from a skills-based approach to teaching listening, Baurain (2011) called for a consideration of the moral and relational elements of listening in the context of English language teaching. Both of these examples demonstrate an expanded notion of listening – one that goes beyond the question of effectiveness and skill to that of an act that is constitutive of social and intercultural relationships.

Fung and Miller's (2004) work regarding listening in Taiwanese families similarly moves toward the recognition of the implications of listening as a culturally defined act. In the context of narrative development in Taiwanese families, Fung and Miller articulated listening as an active and privileged part of the narrative process. For example, regarding the significance of the listening role assumed by children in the constitution of family narratives, they contended "that *listening/ learning* would better capture the local meaning of the child's part in this narrative activity" (p. 315). The cultural function and understanding of listening in this context is not a question of skill; instead, the listener is understood as playing an integral role in the development of family narratives. As they explained (p. 316):

> Care givers hold young children to high standards of moral conduct and offer them numerous opportunities to listen carefully and to reflect upon their actions both before and after the fact. Within these didactic interactions, not speaking does not necessarily mean a lack of creativity or critical thinking, nor does listening necessarily imply passive submission or docile obedience. At a very young age, these children already demonstrate a highly reflective form of agency through attentive listening.

In this cultural context, listening is an active process that is culturally privileged and valued as a communicative feature of family development.

Other communication research similarly works to acknowledge the ways listening and silence function, not only in terms of cultural difference, but as specifically cultural acts. For example, Carbaugh (1999) detailed the function of listening as a cultural form of communication amongst the Blackfeet people that constitutes connections between people and physical locations. Muñoz (2014) attended to silence as that which is unsaid or that "leaves something relevant unsaid" (p. 15). Clair (2020) offered a dialectical approach to considering a continuum of figurative and literal uses and understandings of silence that might even occur simultaneously and in opposition. Covarrubias (2007) specified silence as a cultural form that functions communicatively in ways that are not only consumptive, but also generative. She called for a turn away from a Eurocentric evaluation of silence as negative and a move toward an understanding of the cultural function of silence in other communication contexts, such as that of American Indians. Covarrubias pointed to the generative function of silence, explaining: "In generative silence, people are seen as dynamic, affirmed, strengthened, connected, acknowledged, and ontologically empowered" (p. 268).

In a related way, Hao (2011) theorized silence in terms of performance in order to complicate and expand notions of acceptable classroom interaction,

particularly in Western cultural contexts. Hao's work regarding silence in educational practice serves as a corrective to research in critical pedagogy that
maintains a singular cultural perspective regarding the values of speaking and
silence. Rather than treat listening as a variable in intercultural communication
that might impact interactions, these cultural approaches to listening work to
understand the different ways listening and silence are understood. Listening and
silence are not acultural. In other words, the impact of listening on interaction is
always linked to cultural understandings of the functions and values of listening.

The move toward understanding the function and possibility of listening as a
culturally specific act that might impact intercultural communication beyond
questions of skills and efficacy is exemplified in Dutta's (2014) proposal for listening
as a culture-centered approach (CCA) to engaging with communities at the
margins of civil society on questions of inequity and exploitation. Specifically,
Dutta called for listening as a way of engaging with subaltern communities to better
understand and transform the effects of global inequities: "The culture-centered
approach emphasizes listening, defined as opening up dominant discursive spaces to
the voices of the marginalized other, noting that mainstream organizing of spaces
within dominant structures foreclose opportunities for listening" (p. 70). For Dutta,
subaltern voices, in particular, are systemically erased. Listening offers a strategy for
recognizing this erasure and enacting social change. Moreover, from this CCA,
while listening is always constituted and constrained by structures of power, it can
also function as a critical and reflexive act deployed in the service of enacting and
imagining new forms of social change. Dutta explained, "Understanding listening
as imagination is an invitation to co-create understandings of listening through
participation of many different voices, at the same time, working to become
consciously aware of the categories one inhabits and inherits" (p. 79). In this work,
listening is understood not as a discrete skill but as a process of opening up spaces for
the inclusion of a variety of voices and perspectives.

A phenomenology of listening based on participation and dialogue invites
solidarity through the ground-up engagement of community members in creating networks of local and translocal justice, such as in the case of transnational
Black-Dalit solidarity. India and the U.S., the world's largest and oldest (modern)
democracies, respectively, appear to be going through similar struggles with
casteism and racism (Rajgopal, 2021). Systemic practices of Brahminical superi-
ority and White supremacy can be understood as violence against the dignity of
human identity (Wilkerson, 2020). As a mark of translocal solidarity, a public
meeting on Capitol Hill in Washington DC on 13 January 2014, commemo-
rating Martin Luther King, Jr.'s 85th birth anniversary, also called for an end of
oppression of Dalits in India (Paik, 2014). The event was organized by the US
Dalit Freedom Network, the Quander Family, and U.S. Congressperson Eleanor
Holmes Norton, among others (International Solidarity Dalit Networks, 2013).
There are similar translocal solidarity networks such as the World Social Forum
and La Via Campesina (counter-hegemonic network of farmers' organizations)

resisting neoliberal politics and practices (Dutta & Pal, 2020). Performative listening based on shared moral standing and respect can help build solidarity with communities at the margins by creating spaces for translocal networks that work for the margins to come together to address global inequities and injustices.

Listening, ethics, and performative listening

Listening functions as a way of engaging others in a variety of communicative interactions, including intercultural relationships and contexts. Theorizing listening as a communicative act and as a way of engaging others raises questions of ethics and practice (Gehrke, 2009). A central concern of research on listening ethics is the question of how listeners enter into and create relationships with others through the practice of listening (Beard, 2009; Gehrke, 2009; McRae & Nainby, 2015; McRae, 2015b). Scholars interested in developing an ethical approach for creating and maintaining relationships with others through the practice of listening consider the consequences and implications of concepts including empathy, compassion, dialogue, and difference in the context of listening.

Empathic listening, and the use of empathy as a practice for engaging others, is an approach that has raised questions and concerns for communication scholars. Arnett and Nakagawa (1983) provided one of the earliest critiques of empathic listening as a practice that invites the listener to identify the "psychological intentions or internal states of the speaker" (p. 370). Scudder (2016) offered a similar critique of empathy as it pertains to listening in the context and practice of democratic deliberation. As Scudder explained, "Because of the variation in our ability to empathize and our tendencies to project our own views onto others, empathy cannot, in practice, generally be relied upon to play the central role in deliberation that its supporters expect it will" (p. 525).

Stewart (1983) addressed Arnett and Nakagawa's (1983) concerns in his call for "interpretive listening." This approach is informed by hermeneutic phenomenology and emphasizes the act of listening as contextual, constitutive, and emergent. Stewart offered four characteristics of interpretive listening – openness, linguisticality, play, and the fusion of horizons – to clarify the active and constitutive nature of listening in communicative interactions. These characteristics work to define interpretive listening and offer points of contrast between interpretive listening and approaches to listening that foreground empathy. Interpretive listening emphasizes the meanings that emerge and occur in talk between speaker and listener. Ultimately, this approach to listening attends to and is concerned with communicative interaction rather than intentions.

In the special issue of the *International Journal of Listening* on listening ethics, Lipari (2009) directly engaged the critiques of empathy set forth by Arnett and Nakagawa (1983) and Stewart (1983) by calling for a listening grounded in *compassion*. She explained, "the problem with empathy may not reside in the fact that one cannot ever fully know the other, but with the fact that one fails to *feel with* the other" (p. 49). Lipari (2009) called for an ethics of "listening otherwise" that works towards a commitment to compassion that attends to the alterity of the other (p. 49). Lipari explained compassion in the context of suffering to emphasize the ways the other can never be fully known: "The excesses of alterity—of difference, otherness, and strangeness—will always inevitably exceed my knowledge, experience, and understanding" (p. 50). The goal of what Lipari calls "listening otherwise" is to engage the infinite difference of the other in a way that decenters the self but does not assume that the listener can ever understand or fully know the other.

Lipari's emphasis on compassion and alterity is complemented by approaches to listening that center on dialogue as a key characteristic of ethical listening. Shotter (2009) argued for "dialogically responsive listening" as an ethical practice of encountering and engaging others in a way that is an emergent process of creating and sharing understanding within a given location or "set of determining surroundings" (pp. 39–40). Similarly, Cornwell and Orbe (1999) argued for dialogic listening as an ethical position for communicating across difference, and specifically in the context of engaging hate speech. They go on to outline specific elements that constitute dialogic listening. The first element of dialogic listening is listening with an ethic of care. For Cornwell and Orbe, listening with an ethic of care entails engaging with the contextual and emotional experience of others. The second element is a listening to/for culture that emphasizes and centers on the role of culture in shaping communicative interactions. The third element of dialogic listening entails what Cornwell and Orbe referred to as "listening within a power consciousness" (p. 89), that is, listening marked by an attention to and awareness of the ways privilege shapes and informs communication. The final element Cornwell and Orbe outlined is "listening as a both/and process" (p. 90). This quality entails an acknowledgement and recognition of multiple conflicting positions that might emerge in communication. Thus, dialogic listening, as outlined by Cornwell and Orbe, offers a conceptualization of the practice of listening as a dynamic, cultural, and critical act.

Koza (2008) demonstrated an application of listening that similarly emerges from an ethic of critical and cultural awareness of difference. In her analysis and critique of university school of music vocal auditions, Koza demonstrated the various ways these auditions accomplish racial discrimination through the enforcement of particular standards and values. Specifically, Koza argued these auditions listen for affirmations of whiteness. She called for a listening that is critically aware of admission practices and policies that privilege certain people and bodies in exclusion of others, writing, "I invite all music educators, especially those who identify as White, to continue to listen carefully for Whiteness, *not to affirm it*, but to recognize its institutional presence, understand its technologies, and thereby work toward defunding it" (p. 154). Listening, for Koza, functions as a critical act of acknowledging difference and the function of privilege.

Working from Conquergood's (1985) discussion of dialogic performance, McRae (2015a) presented critical compassionate listening as a practice that works towards what Conquergood called "dialogic engagement" (p. 9). Dialogic engagement is a stance that aims "to bring self and other together so that they can question, debate, and challenge one another" (p. 9). He continued by arguing, "Dialogical understanding does not end with empathy" (p. 9). Critical compassionate listening attempts to accomplish dialogic engagement with others through a critical and reflexive consideration of the ways both similarities and differences shape the communicative encounter (McRae, 2015a).

Elsewhere, McRae (2015b) defined a relational ethic of listening that informs the practice of performative listening. Performative listening is "an embodied act of critically and reflexively engaging with and learning from others" (p. 7). This practice of listening is qualified by a relational ethic of listening that entails engagement with others that is centered on a relational stance, critical reflexivity, critical communication pedagogy, and dialogic engagement. The relational ethic of listening is aimed at cultivating an awareness of the ways listening constitutes relationships and the ways the listener is enabled and constrained by larger cultural structures and privileges (p. 59). This ethic of listening is particularly shaped by a commitment to engaging in listening as an act of learning from others. Likewise, what we are calling performative listening works to engage others through critical acknowledgement and consideration of the ways differences mark and constitute relationships. The critical orientation of performative listening is particularly valuable and important for listening in the context of critical intercultural communication.

Performative listening and solidarity in critical intercultural communication

Performative listening is an approach to theorizing and practicing listening that, when extended to the context of critical intercultural communication, offers a way of imagining the act of listening as critical to solidarity and social-justice oriented community engagement. This is an approach that functions within the performative methodological constellation of critical intercultural communication as outlined by Willink et al. (2014). First, performative listening builds on and extends existing scholarship regarding intercultural communication and listening by foregrounding embodiment, reflexivity, and pedagogy. Second, performative listening is a praxis aligned with the goals and aims of critical intercultural communication. Finally, performative listening is a generative approach that can be enacted in the service of forging solidarity and engendering dialogue, especially in relation to marginalized voices.

Approaches to and theories of listening in intercultural communication that focus on listening effectiveness and discrete cultural differences can certainly provide productive ways of enacting listening across difference. Performative

listening, however, foregrounds embodiment, reflexivity, and pedagogy to emphasize the ways listening functions as an act that is always culturally located,
constitutive of relationships, and potentially transformative and instructive
(McRae, 2015b). This approach to listening is characterized by four commitments: A commitment to listening with curiosity, a commitment to listening to
and with the body, a commitment to listening for context and location, and a
commitment to listening with accountability (McRae, 2015b).

Listening with curiosity offers a framework for engaging in the practice of
listening marked by a stance and ethic of openness towards others. This stance
imagines listening as a pedagogical act of learning from others. The second
commitment of listening to and with the body is a commitment that moves
towards a reflexive awareness of the ways our distinct embodied and lived experiences shape the ways we encounter others in our act of listening. In other
words, our performance as listeners is an act that is always marked by our cultural
positions and privileges. McRae's third commitment of performative listening
works to acknowledge and attend to context and location. This commitment
builds on the development of an awareness of our individual position as listeners
by noting the historical, cultural, and social structures that shape our encounters
with others. Finally, performative listening is committed to cultivating accountability for the relations between our individual practices and larger social and
cultural structures (McRae, 2015b). This commitment is informed by Hall's (1985)
notion of double articulation:

> By 'double articulation' I mean that the structure—the given conditions of
> existence, the structure of determinations in any situation—can also be
> understood from another point of view, as simply the result of previous
> practices. We may say that a structure is what previously structured
> practices have produced as a result. (p. 95)

In sum, performative listening is an act that works to recognize the ways the act
of listening is articulated by larger structures, but it is also an act that works to
acknowledge the ways in which listening might be used to transform and
articulate new structures and relationships.

These four commitments of performative listening demonstrate the ways
performative listening works to extend scholarship on intercultural communication and listening, and these commitments also indicate the ways performative
listening functions as a kind of praxis aligned with the transformative goals and
aims of critical intercultural communication. Freire (1970) described revolutionary praxis as "*reflection* and *action* directed at the structures to be transformed"
(p. 126). It is in this sense that performative listening works toward transformation in the context of critical intercultural communication. Performative listening offers a theory of listening as a reflective practice *and* a reflexive action that
is always linked to the production and maintenance of cultural structures,

differences, and relationships. In other words, performative listening is a communicative act that constitutes and is constituted by cultural structures and systems. Enacting performative listening is a matter of accounting for the ways culture produces and is produced by the listener.

In addition to adding to intercultural communication research on listening, and engaging critical intercultural communication, we argue that performative listening offers a strategy and approach that can be enacted in the service of forging solidarity and engendering dialogue, especially in relationships with marginalized voices. To illustrate, we loop back to the four goals of performative listening: A commitment to listening with curiosity, a commitment to listening to and with the body, a commitment to listening for context and location, and a commitment to listening with accountability.

One basic tenet of critical intercultural communication is the recovery of narratives (from the margins of civil society) that have largely been erased/absented or co-opted by intercultural encounters dominated by a Eurocentric knowledge apparatus. Standing in solidarity with the margins (Beverly, 2004/ 1999), performative listening offers a strategy and a framework to performing critical intercultural communication. Dutta and Pal (2010) noted that the act of listening to voices at the margins entails a clear enunciation of intent. Beverly claimed that this intent is not so much about trying to be an objective listener/ partner in the narrativization as it is to put one's (in this case, the critical intercultural communication researcher's) body on the line and attempt to co-script the communication encounter from a stance of solidarity – a stance that is politically motivated to interrogate the silences of marginal narratives in dominant articulations of such communication encounters. Such an act of listening involves putting your body/self at risk of performing against the grain and of being accountable for your performance. As Madison (2005) noted, it involves putting up one's performance for scrutiny and being willing to take the risk of being proved wrong. In other words, the intent of listening is not to excavate/discover exotic and unheard voices from the margins and present them as expert narrations, but to listen with the goal of performing the self out of the narration through a commitment to positioning the researcher self at the center of the narration. Performative listening, in this sense, brings to bear, doubly, the context of the narrative – the context in which the narrative is narrativized and the context that participants in the intercultural communication encounter bring to the narrative. This highlights the omniscient power differential in any intercultural encounter with the margins of civil society and makes explicit the goal to capture, account for, and attempt to interrogate this differential in communicative power. Dutta and Pal (2010) remind us that such a commitment is critical to the act of dialogic solidarity with the margins of civil society.

McRae (2015b) called performative listening, "an embodied practice of critically and reflexively engaging with and learning from others" (p. 31). We argue that this principle lies at the heart of what "Gustavo Gutiérrez calls 'listening to the poor'" (Beverly, 2004/1999, p. 38). This is similar to what Rorty (1998) called the *desire for solidarity*, or in an effort to explore the "possibility of building relationships of solidarity between ourselves and social practices we posit as our objects of study" (Beverly, 2004/1999, p. 39). Embodiment is critical here as a performative and political act of acknowledging that what we do (in intercultural communication) is implicated in some way or another in the social relations of dominance and resistance. The reflexive turn, which calls for a pattern of listening that turns the tables on the researcher engaged in intercultural communication, is critical to this act of solidarity. And this call for solidarity in intercultural communication research and praxis is all the more important as the field expands to position communication acts in the spatial, temporal, historical, and cultural geographies of such acts. This is then a call to recognize that histories formulated at the interstices of marginality/privilege are intercultural communication acts and their products. Indeed, Rigoberta Menchu's (2010) "I, Rigobert Menchu: An Indian Woman in Guatemala" is an intercultural artifact, a testimonio created through an intercultural communication process between the interlocutor and the "author," coming together from privilege and indigeneity, and co-creating a narrative that sustains the political project of changing structures and practices and discourses that create and maintain subaltern/elite relationships (Beverly, 2004/1999). At the heart of this theory and method of writing a testimonio such as "I Rigoberta Menchu" is, what we argue, a way of reflexive listening that causes the listener/interlocutor to make her/himself un-present from the discourse. This act of standing with the margins, of solidarity through performative listening, fulfils one primary political promise of the critical intercultural communication project in the context of globalization, namely re-imagining intercultural communication as a space for social change and participatory justice (Sorrells, 2010).

Conclusion

In this chapter, we theorize a practice of listening in the context of intercultural communication and community engagement that works towards solidarity. Intercultural communication as a field of study has, over the last decade or so, moved toward a critical orientation whereby power differences in an intercultural communication encounter are engaged with to highlight material and discursive inequities. This critical turn can be invigorated through a call for solidarity with cultures at the margins of global civil society. To participate in this call for solidarity, we apply performative listening, or "an embodied practice of critically and reflexively engaging with and learning from others" (McRae, 2015b, p. 31). The four tenets of performative listening are: A commitment to listening with curiosity, a commitment to listening to and with the body, a commitment to listening for context and location, and a commitment to listening with accountability.

Each of these tenets raises questions that could be followed and expanded upon in order to work toward a practice of critical intercultural communication and enacting solidarity. These questions might include: What might be learned by engaging others? How does our embodied and lived experience shape our listening and engagement with others in a given moment? How do cultural, social, and institutional contexts and locations impact and inform our interactions and connections with others? How might we account for the ways our positions, identities, and privileges texture our engagement with others?

In the context of critical intercultural communication, embracing these tenets would mean taking the risk to dialogue with the margins with the aim of deconstructing those theories and methods of intercultural dialogue, of the center, that have historically produced unequal communicative opportunities across the globe. This way, performative listening would serve as a political stance, a theoretical entry point, and a methodological imaginary to practice solidarity in intercultural communication and community engagement.

References

Arasaratnam, L. A. (2015). Research in intercultural communication: Reviewing the past decade. *Journal of International and Intercultural Communication, 8*, 290–310. 10.1080/17513057.2015.1087096

Arneson, P. (2010). Provocation: An ethic of listening in/and social change. *The International Journal of Listening, 24*, 166–169. 10.1080/10904018.2010.513648

Arnett, R. C., & Nakagawa, G. (1983). The assumptive roots of empathic listening: A critique. *Communication Education, 32*, 368–378. 10.1080/03634528309378558

Basu, A. (2022). Afterword: On localocentricity and "Post-AIDS". In A. Basu, A. R. Spieldenner & P. J. Dillon (Eds.), *Post-AIDS discourse in health communication: Sociocultural interpretations* (pp. 245–249). Routledge.

Baurain, B. (2011). Morality, relationality, and listening pedagogy in language education. *The International Journal of Listening, 25*, 161–177. 10.1080/10904018.2011.604604

Beall, M. L. (2010). Perspectives on intercultural listening. In A. D. Wolvin (Ed.), *Listening and human communication in the 21st century* (pp. 225–238). Wiley-Blackwell. 10.1002/9781444314908.ch10

Beard, D. (2009). A broader understanding of the ethics of listening: Philosophy, cultural studies, media studies and the ethical listening subject. *The International Journal of Listening, 23*, 7–20. 10.1080/10904010802591771

Bentley, S. C. (2000). Listening in the 21st century. *The International Journal of Listening, 14*, 129–142. 10.1080/10904018.2000.10499039

Beverly, J. (2004). *Subalternity and representation: Arguments in cultural theory.* Duke University Press. (Original work published 1999).

Broome, B. J., & Collier M. J. (2012). Culture, communication, and peacebuilding: A reflexive multi-dimensional contextual framework. *Journal of International and Intercultural Communication, 5*, 245–269. 10.1080/17513057.2012.716858

Butler, J. (1988). Performative acts and gender constitution: An essay in phenomenology and feminist theory. *Theatre Journal, 40*, 519–531. 10.2307/3207893

Carbaugh, D. (1999). "Just listen": "Listening" and landscape among the Blackfeet. *Western Journal of Communication, 63*, 250–270. 10.1080/10570319909374641

Clair, R. P. (2020). Silence. In D. L. Worthington & G. D. Bodie (eds), *The Handbook of Listening* (pp. 427–438). John Wiley & Sons. 10.1002/9781119554189.ch30

Conquergood, D. (1985). Performing as a moral act: Ethical dimensions of ethnography of performance. *Literature in Performance, 5*, 1–13. 10.1080/10462938509391578

Cornwell, N. C., & Orbe, M. P. (1999). Critical perspectives on hate speech: The centrality of 'dialogic listening'. *The International Journal of Listening, 13*, 75–96. 10. 1080/10904018.1999.10499028

Covarrubias, P. (2007). (Un)biased in Western theory: Generative silence in American Indian communication. *Communication Monographs, 74*, 265–271. 10.1080/0363775 0701393071

Dillon, R. K., & McKenzie, N. J. (1998). The influence of ethnicity on listening, communication competence, approach, and avoidance. *The International Journal of Listening, 12*, 106–121. 10.1080/10904018.1998.10499021

Dutta, M. J. (2014). A culture-centered approach to listening: Voices of social change. *The International Journal of Listening, 28*, 67–81. 10.1080/10904018.2014.876266

Dutta, M. J., & Pal, M. (2010). Dialog theory in marginalized settings: A subaltern studies approach. *Communication Theory, 20*, 363–386. 10.1111/j.1468-2885.2010.01367.x

Dutta, M. J., & Pal, M. (2020). Theorizing from the global south: Dismantling, resisting, and transforming communication theory. *Communication Theory, 30*, 349–369. 10. 1093/ct/qtaa010

de Oliveira, W. F. (2014). For a pedagogy of solidarity. In A. M. A. Freire & W. de Oliveira (Eds.), *Pedagogy of Solidarity* (1st ed., pp. 65–84). Left Coast Press.

Freire, P. (1970). *The pedagogy of the oppressed*. Seabury.

Fung, H. & Miller, P. J. (2004). Listening is active: Lessons from the narrative practices of Taiwanese families. In M. W. Pratt & B. H. Fiese (Eds.), *Family stories and the life course: Across time and generations* (pp. 303–323). Lawrence Erlbaum. 10.4324/9781410610300

Gehrke, P. J. (2009). Introduction to listening, ethics, and dialogue: Between the ear and the eye: A synaesthetic introduction to listening ethics. *The International Journal of Listening, 23*, 1–6. 10.1080/10904010802631023

Hall, S. (1985). Signification, representation, ideology: Althusser and the post-structuralist debates. *Critical Studies in Mass Communication, 2*, 91–114. 10.1080/15295038509360070

Halualani, R. T., & Nakayama, T. K. (2010). Critical intercultural communication studies: At a crossroads. In T. K. Nakayama & R. T. Halualani (Eds.), *The handbook of critical intercultural communication* (pp. 1–16). Wiley-Blackwell. 10.1002/9781444390681.ch1

Hao, R. N. (2011). Rethinking critical pedagogy: Implications on silence and silent bodies. *Text and Performance Quarterly, 31*, 267–284. 10.1080/10462937.2011.573185

Koza, J. E. (2008). Listening for whiteness: Hearing racial politics in undergraduate school music. *Philosophy of Music Education Review, 16*, 145–155. https://www.jstor.org/stable/40327298

International Dalit Solidarity Network. (2013, December 11). *African Americans call for end to oppression of Dalits in India with 'Declaration of Empathy' signing event at U.S. capitol.* http://www.prweb.com/releases/Declare/Empathy/prweb11406890.htm

Lipari, L. (2009). Listening otherwise: The voice of ethics. *The International Journal of Listening, 23*, 44–59. 10.1080/10904010802591888

Madison, D. S. (2005). *Critical ethnography: Methods, ethics, and performance.* Sage.

Madison, D. S. (2006). The dialogic performative in critical ethnography. *Text and performance quarterly*, *26*, 320–324. 10.1080/10462930600828675

McRae, C. (2015a). Compassionate critical listening. In J. T. Warren & D. L. Fassett (Eds.), *Communication: A critical/cultural introduction* (2nd ed., pp. 62–78). Sage.

McRae, C. (2015b). *Performative listening: Hearing others in qualitative research.* Peter Lang.

McRae, C. (2020). Performative listening. In D. L. Worthington & G. D. Bodie (Eds.), *The Handbook of Listening* (pp. 309–407). John Wiley & Sons. 10.1002/9781119554189.ch27

McRae, C., & Nainby, K. (2015). Engagement beyond interruption: A performative perspective on listening and ethics. *Educational Studies*, *51*, 168–184. 10.1080/00131946.2015.1015356

Menchu, R. (2010). *I, Rigoberto Menchú: An Indian woman in Guatemala.* Verso Books.

Moon, D. G. (2010). Critical reflections on culture and critical intercultural communication. In T. K. Nakayama & R. T. Halualani (Eds.), *The handbook of critical intercultural communication* (pp. 34–52). Wiley-Blackwell. 10.1002/9781444390681.ch3

Muñoz, K. L. (2014). *Transcribing silence: Culture, relationships, and communication.* Taylor & Francis.

Paik, S. (2014). Building bridges: Articulating Dalit and African American women's solidarity. *Women's Studies Quarterly*, *42*, 74–96. https://www.jstor.org/stable/24364991

Pence, M. E., & James, T. A. (2015). The role of sex differences in the examination of personality and active-empathic listening: An initial exploration. *The International Journal of Listening*, *29*, 85–94. 10.1080/10904018.2014.965390

Purdy, M. W., & Manning, L. M. (2015). Listening in the multicultural workplace: A dialogue of theory and practice. *International Journal of Listening*, *29*, 1–11. 10.1080/10904018.2014.942492

Rajgopal, S. S. (2021). Dalit/black solidarity: Comrades in the struggle for racial/caste justice. *South Asian Popular Culture*, *19*, 81–86. 10.1080/14746689.2021.1884176

Rorty, R. (1998). *Achieving our country: Leftist thought in twentieth-century America.* Harvard University Press.

Sangster, P., & Anderson, C. (2009). Investigating norms of listening in classrooms. *International Journal of Listening*, *23*, 121–140. 10.1080/10904010903014459

Sargent, S. L., & Weaver, J. B. III. (2003). Listening styles: Sex differences in perceptions of self and others. *International Journal of Listening*, *17*, 5–18. 10.1080/10904018.2003.10499052

Schnapp, D. C. (2008). Listening in context: Religion and spirituality. *International Journal of Listening*, *22*, 133–140. 10.1080/10904010802183074

Scudder, M. F. (2016). Beyond empathy: Strategies and ideals of democratic deliberation. *Polity*, *48*(4), 524–550. 10.1057/s41279-016-0001-9

Shotter, J. (2009). Listening in a *way* that recognizes/realizes the world of 'the other'. *The International Journal of Listening*, *23*, 21–43. 10.1080/10904010802591904

Sorrells, K. (2010). Reimagining intercultural communication in the context of globalization. In T. K. Nakayama & R. T. Halualani (Eds.), *The handbook of critical intercultural communication* (pp. 171–189). Wiley-Blackwell. 10.1002/9781444390681.ch11

Sorrells, K. (2016). *Intercultural Communication: Globalization and social justice.* Sage.

Stewart, J. (1983). Interpretive listening: An alternative to empathy. *Communication Education*, *32*, 379–391. 10.1080/03634528309378559

Thomlison, T. D. (1991). Intercultural listening. In D. Borisoff & M. Purdy (Eds.), *Listening in everyday life: A personal and professional approach* (1st ed., pp. 87–137). University Press of America.

Timm, S., & Schroeder, B. L. (2000). Listening/nonverbal communication training. *International Journal of Listening*, *14*, 109–128. 10.1080/10904018.2000.10499038

Wilkerson, I. (2020). *Caste: The origins of our discontents*. Random House.

Willink, K. G., Gutierez-Perez, R., Shukri, S., & Stein, L. (2014). Navigating with the stars: Critical qualitative methodological constellations for critical intercultural communication research. *Journal of International and Intercultural Communication*, *7*, 289–316. 10.1080/17513057.2014.964150

4

LISTENING AS A TOOL FOR TRANSFORMATIVE CHANGE IN FAMILIES AND NEIGHBORHOODS

The case of SALT

Bobby Zachariah, Joske Bunders-Aelen, and Barbara Regeer

FACULTY OF SCIENCE, ATHENA INSTITUTE, VU, AMSTERDAM

Some of the major contemporary problems of the world, from HIV and AIDS to natural disasters, suicide, and addiction, disproportionately affect vulnerable communities. These communities are, by definition, not in a position of power, and thus their voices are not consistently included in program design. The need and extent of listening to communities in acute and chronic emergency situations should balance and value technical and community solutions. And while there has been greater attention paid to "listening" in recent years, enabling us to better understand how to respond to the needs of the most vulnerable, there is still significant room for improvement.

Indeed, there is no dearth of critiques regarding the low levels of listening in public initiatives (Macnamara, 2020). Scholars have pointed to the fact that citizens' views, while often solicited, are not always fully considered. Most often, these critiques center on the fact that control is not shared, citizen involvement is restricted, and officials are still the primary decision-makers (Hendriks et al., 2019). We see similar dynamics within and between organizations. As Macnamara (2016) observed in his Organisational Listening Project, speaking-related activities far outnumber listening-related activities in public communications. Similarly, Johansson (2017) wrote about international peacebuilders' poor receptiveness to local expertise.

Despite donor organizations' expressed willingness to listen, local partners perceive the lack of interest in taking their experience and knowledge into account as an act of "nonlistening." As a result, participants (or local partners) feel unheard and believe they are not taken seriously. And, Ercan et al. (2019) observed that in contemporary democracies there has been a proliferation of spaces in which citizens can voice their opinions, ideas, and concerns and deliberate and co-design policy programs. While considering this a positive

DOI: 10.4324/9781003214465-4

movement, the authors "take issue with the predominantly expression-centric nature of these spaces" (p. 20). As a result, scholars have argued for redesigning public participation through a more encompassing "architecture of listening" (Macnamara, 2016) that provides sufficient spaces for listening and reflection (Ercan et al., 2019).

Overall, the emphasis in this emerging body of knowledge is on officials and organizations listening better; that is, creating structures to better hear citizens' concerns, and increasing sensitivity to different forms and shapes of citizens' inputs to ensure "citizen knowledge is collected and subsequently incorporated into localised solutions" (Moore & Elliott, 2016, p. 80). Importantly, these architectures of listening address the central question of this book: How can we bring listening to scale? Or, how can listening have outcomes beyond the individual? We concur with Hendriks et al. (2019), who observed that

> those scholars that have taken a specific interest in the role of listening in democracy have focused mainly on the norm of receptivity, whereby decision-makers are considered to be listening to citizens when they are receptive and responsive to messages they receive from them. (p. 139)

While the importance of the receptive side of listening (by organizations and public institutions) is incontrovertible, we see a knowledge gap in the current discourse on listening, the exploration of which may introduce new avenues for bringing listening to scale; avenues that create transformative development in communities. In the following pages, we illustrate this knowledge gap by introducing a framework (Figure 4.1) comprising two dimensions: the first dimension concerns the supposed locality of agency, and the second pertains to the question of bringing listening to scale. We unpack this framework prior to turning our attention to a method we have used for 25 years called SALT – an acronym for Support/Stimulate, Appreciate/Accept, Listen/Learn, and Team/Transfer; the key ways of thinking and behaving that acknowledge and stimulate competence in people. We then draw on our experiences in India, where we have utilized the SALT methodology in three distinct contexts. This chapter concludes by outlining steps practitioners can take to increase the likelihood that community engagement efforts are inclusive and successful.

A framework for bringing listening to scale in community engagement activities

Figure 4.1 provides a graphic illustration of different types of listening-based approaches to community engagement. The left-hand side of the figure illustrates the current pleas for listening at scale. In the bottom-left quadrant, we placed *receptive listening* as a type of listening that puts primacy on the listener – it is about how the listener engages in conversation in order to fully comprehend. In

Large scale

Organisational listening,
Institutional listening

Agency localised
in listener

Agency localised
in listened to

Receptive listening

Other-oriented listening

One-on-one

FIGURE 4.1   Framework to illustrate knowledge gap: focus in literature on bringing listening to scale is on architectures for listening that place emphasis on agency of listener

addition, it is about appropriate responses, like adjusting behavior because of the listening. Agency is localized in the listener. This is the case for one-on-one receptive listening, but equally for receptive listening at a larger scale.

At this larger scale, scholars refer to *organizational listening* (Macnamara, 2018), *strategic listening* (Lewis, 2019), and *institutional listening* (Dobson, 2014; Scudder et al., 2021) as forms of receptive listening beyond one-on-one interactions. As mentioned, architectures of listening are introduced that set requirements for organizations in terms of culture, policies, structure, processes, resources, skills, technologies, and practices (e.g., Macnamara, 2016) and emphasize the need for organizations to examine what was heard, engage with potentially disconfirming and uncomfortable data, consider and understand implications of the acquired understandings, and challenge status quo thinking (Lewis, 2019). More specifically, institutional listening focuses on the relationship between the public sphere and formal institutions and the need to create spaces that ensure that empowered elites pay attention to the voices of marginalized communities (Scudder et al., 2021).

On the right-hand side of the figure, we focus on agency localized in the listened to, which we call *other-oriented listening*, after "other-oriented, feeling-centered listening," which has been labeled in the introduction of this book (Bodie et al., Chapter 1). Others refer to this type of listening as therapeutic (e.g., Watanuki et al., 2018), active-empathic (e.g., Gearhart & Bodie, 2011), or compassionate listening (e.g., Rehling, 2008). This type of listening is healing for the listened to, by acknowledging their realities and the therapeutic effects of feeling heard. Strikingly, we note that this dimension of listening is largely disregarded by those seeking to bring listening to scale. Or, to put it more strongly, therapeutic listening is considered an example of "poor" listening in democracy (Hendriks et al., 2019). In *Listening for Democracy: Recognition, Representation, Reconciliation,* for instance, Dobson (2014) explained why: While acknowledging the value of other-oriented listening for the person who is listened to, with this type of listening, "the only changes that have taken place are in the mind of the person being listened to" (p. 66). Dobson further argued that "there is a problem when this is transferred to the socio-political context [as listening may become] a balm to soothe the anxieties of citizens without changing anything in the circumstances that generate anxieties" (p. 66).

Another argument for largely dismissing other-oriented listening in discussions about bringing listening to scale (i.e., moving from the bottom-right side to the top in Figure 4.1) is that it is allegedly quite difficult, if not impossible. With receptive listening, it is possible to introduce certain tools and technologies that enable listening beyond face-to-face encounters, such as large-scale public consultations, or social research (See Schooler, Chapter 2). This is, however, at least according to the current scholarly discourse, harder to imagine for other-oriented listening. The features of listening involving non-verbal communication (body language, visual stimuli) seem to especially defy the possibility of scaling beyond the face-to-face context (Dobson, 2014).

Even with these critiques, however, there is a recognition that bringing listening to scale might happen through participatory, community-led approaches. For instance, the introduction (Bodie et al., Chapter 1) presents Participatory Action Research (PAR) and Asset-Based Community Development (ABCD) as potential routes to explore. As promising as these approaches are, there is currently a lack of an architecture of listening for these community approaches and an exploration of the role therein of other-oriented listening.

Consequently, we leave the top, right-hand quadrant in Figure 4.1 without a label, and consider this a space to further study. By considering the locality of agency in the listened to, we feel that we can explore a more comprehensive change evoked by other-oriented listening than a change merely taking place in the mind of the person listened to. In this chapter, we explore the possibilities of bringing listening, including other-oriented listening, to scale, especially as we gain more clarity on the outcomes of listening if agency is localized in those being listened to – the members of vulnerable communities.

Before we begin, however, we first need to unpack the notion of upscaling. To do that, we refer to scholars in sustainability transitions research and social innovation and their conceptualization of different types of upscaling of sustainability initiatives. In a recent review of literature on amplifying the impact of sustainability initiatives, Lam et al. (2020) proposed a typology of processes through which to increase impact. The processes are aggregated in three categories: amplifying within, amplifying out, and amplifying beyond. *Amplifying within* refers to processes that seek to increase the impact of one specific initiative, by, for instance, *stabilizing* its existence or *accelerating* the process of impact creation. *Amplifying out* pertains to processes that seek to increase the impact of initiatives by involving more people and places, by, for instance *growing* (when the initial initiative engages a larger number of people or places), or *replicating* (for instance, when the initial initiative is replicated in another context). Finally, *amplifying beyond* comprises *scaling up* the impact of the initiative, by, for instance, changing laws, policies, or institutions; and *scaling deep* to change people's values, norms, and beliefs through the work of the initiative. In the literature on bringing listening to scale, it appears that most of the emphasis is placed on scaling up; organizational and institutional listening are clear examples of this. We imagine that the introduced framework will help us enrich the discussion and provide important clues on the potential role of listening in empowering marginalized communities and tilting power balances on a larger scale, especially given the challenge that "it is much easier to get people to talk than to listen, and this is as true of politics as it is of daily life" (Dobson, 2014, p. 171).

The answer we give in this chapter to the question of how to bring listening to scale and transform communities at the same time is that listening must be embedded in a process that can be structured, learned, and transferred. The approach featured here is the SALT approach. In the following pages, we bring together decades' experience with the SALT approach across a range of persistent challenges in India, in order to establish the key principles and practices that can replicate deep listening across cultures and geographies.

The case of SALT

Initially introduced as the Support to Action Learning Teams approach (Lamboray, 2016), SALT developed as an acronym for Support/Stimulate; Appreciate/Accept; Listen/Learn; Team/Transform/Transfer (Campbell et al., 2021). It stands for a *mindset* that seeks strengths in people, maintains an *attitude* of appreciation for fellow human beings, and encourages *behaviors* that aim to nurture with whom we engage. The approach states that every human being has innate capacities to respond to their concerns (Campbell, 2008). SALT helps to reveal the capacity of communities to build a vision for the future, to assess, to act, to adapt, and to learn in response to a challenge (Nandi et al., 2018). The approach was developed and is employed in the context of the Human Capacity for Response (HCfR) framework, also referred to as the Community Life Competence Process (CLCP; The Constellation, 2022). CLC was first developed as a working model for AIDS competence by Jean-Louis Lamboray and colleagues in the 1990s (Campbell & Rader, 1995; Lamboray & Skevington, 2001).

As communities began to develop local responses to the HIV and AIDS epidemic, other issues in their lives surfaced, and communities recognized their own abilities to respond to them. The Community Competence against AIDS evolved into the CLCP (Lamboray, 2016) and the foundation of the Constellation in 2004 (The Constellation, 2022) – a non-profit organization facilitating local responses to a diverse set of life's challenges, including malaria, polio, maternal health, nutrition, water, sanitation, aging, and post-disaster psycho-social support for communities (Zachariah et al., 2018). Box 4.1 provides further details.

The HCfR framework reflects the belief that people have the capacity to *care, change, hope, lead, and belong as a community*, and that communities can harness these capacities to collectively address challenges (Lamboray, 2016). Communities engage in a process of mutual dialogue about their dreams, taking action together, and evaluating and learning from these experiences (see Box 4.1 for an outline of the adapted process we use in India).

Three contexts

This chapter draws on experiences with the SALT approach in three distinct contexts: A corporate social responsibility (CSR) program in Pune, a suicide-prevention program in Pune, and a drug de-addiction response in Mizoram, Northeast India.

In the first context, the CSR program of a large company offered health, education, and nutrition programs in a low-income neighborhood for a decade, before a group of 18 industry volunteers conducted systematic SALT visits to nearly 500 households. Community volunteers facilitated by the CSR team synthesized the community concerns and hopes into thematic areas of action leading to a series of community-led actions. A suicide-prevention organization that runs a suicide helpline for those in distress implemented SALT home visits to suicide survivors. The third context concerns youth drug de-addiction in Aizawl, the capital of Mizoram, India. A community health organization with active volunteers conducted SALT visits in several neighborhoods to support their response over 25 years. We illustrate various aspects of the SALT approach further.

Data collection and analysis

Documentation is inherent in the SALT approach. The cases concern retrospective analysis of already collected data by or under the guidance of the first author. In all cases, verbal consent was obtained for the home visits, neighborhood conversations, and AER. All participants were notified that they could leave the process at any moment, without giving a reason. Full anonymity is guaranteed in both data storage and reporting. The first author was closely engaged with all programs and facilitated the development of SALT processes therein. The researchers conducted a thematic analysis of the records using the

BOX 4.1 SALT AS PART OF THE COMMUNITY LIFE COMPETENCE PROCESS (CLCP)[1]

SALT is said to be the DNA of the Community Life Competence Approach (Lamboray, 2016). The Community Life Competence Process (CLCP) is a systematic step-by-step methodology used by communities, accompanied by facilitators, of developing a vision, holding honest conversations about the current situation, developing action plans, and learning from action taken (Campbell et al., 2021; The Constellation, n.d.).

Step 1: Who are we? What makes us human?

Facilitators reflect to ground themselves in the common humanity they share with the families they are about to visit. Exploration is done through sharing stories of change and brainstorming about what makes us human.

Step 2: Home visits to affected families

This involves discussion in families regarding their hopes and concerns regarding the issue addressed by the program. During the visit, the program team maintains an attitude of appreciation and seeks to reveal the families' strengths.

Step 3: Neighborhood conversations around concerns, hopes, and strengths

When the concerns, hopes, and strengths have been sufficiently explored in multiple households over a period of time, the team senses the opportunity for a neighborhood discussion to address the previously identified concerns, hopes, and strengths. When the discussion has sufficiently deepened, the community is facilitated to the next step.

Step 4: Where would we like to be? Through which thematic practices?

This involves reflecting and synthesizing dreams of the community members through discussion and drawing exercises. Teams are invited to describe the aspired practices when living the dream and prioritize certain practices.

Step 5: Where are we now?

For each of the practices, participants self-assess where they stand now in comparison to the aspired to, envisioned practice, marking each from 1 (sounds like a good idea) to 5 (the practice is part of our way of life).

Step 6: What are we going to do?

For three selected practices, participants describe the practices, determine at which level (from 1 to 5) they would like the practice to be in three to six months, think of actions that can help move from the current level to the aspired level, check who will be part of their team, how they can see whether they have succeeded (what are indicators, how can we measure this), and when the group will reconvene to check and discuss progress.

Step 7: Let's do it!

Community members take action in their own teams.

Step 8: Where did we get to? What did we learn? How can we share?

After three to six months, the group comes back together and repeats step 5 (Self-assessment) to see if levels of practices have changed and to see if the dream and aspired practices still resonate or need adjustment. A second cycle is then prepared. Step 8 is also used for transfer of lessons learned, through knowledge fairs or learning festivals (Nandi et al., 2018).

After Experience Reflection

After each step in the process, an After Experience Reflection (AER) is done. The reflections are guided by the following questions: (1) What strengths did we see in the families? (2) How did we practice SALT? (3) What are we learning from the experience? (4) How do we adapt our approach based on the learning?

Facilitators

Facilitators of a Community Life Competence Process explicitly do not act as experts. They rather accompany the community as it moves toward ownership of their own challenges, looking for strengths, making contact from human to human, and fully embracing the SALT mindset. Facilitators have been compared to midwives "accompanying the birth of a project that is not theirs" (Lamboray, 2016).

themes listening practices, transformation, and amplifying to understand how to bring listening to scale. We present the results below.

Results

In the following sections, we will elaborate on the elements in the SALT approach that make listening transformative beyond the individual level, i.e., fostering transformation in communities. First, we posit that listening is not just a skill; it is a mindset that can be cultivated. Second, we will show how SALT is embedded in a systematic step-by-step process that instigates spirals of transformation at different levels that are in interaction with each other. Finally, we will see how the empowerment of communities is transferred beyond the boundaries of a particular community through organic sharing between individuals and families across boundaries and through the adaptation of organizational practices. We begin by exploring *deep listening* – the type of listening we view as central to SALT listening practices.

Deep listening

Deep listening in SALT means coming together as human beings and, from that position, being eager to learn from the experiences of others with openness. This openness is particularly pointed toward the conviction that the community has strengths, and it involves a great sense of curiosity to discover these strengths. In deep listening, receptive listening and other-oriented listening are both at play simultaneously, giving rise to transformation by both the listener and the listened to. The listened to is approached with appreciation for their concerns, which may involve deep distress and pain. They are also approached with appreciation for their hopes and their strengths and capacities to respond to their concerns. We will see in this chapter that deep listening cultivates ownership of the issues the community faces and ownership of the response to these issues. At the same time, the listener is receptive to what is shared and develops an in-depth understanding of the communities' concerns, hopes, and capacities, which enables the listener to ask better questions and deepen their mutual understanding. A spiral of mutual, in-depth understanding and strengthening of capacities takes place. Importantly, in SALT, deep listening is always related to learning and action, creating a forward momentum of increased ownership and community response through first localizing agency in the listened to. Below, we further elaborate on the different listening practices that take place in this process, but we will first turn to the listeners and the way a deep listening mindset can be cultivated.

The listeners

In the cases featured, a team of volunteers and program staff took part in the listening practices. At the corporate CSR program, the team included volunteer engineers, mid-level managers, and CSR staff. The suicide-prevention volunteers included stay-at-home parents, students, corporate employees, and retired people. The community health program outreach team included stay-at-home parents, students, and staff members.

A key motivation of this group of listeners was their desire to contribute to social wellbeing. Some felt the need to reciprocate the support they received during their own crisis moments, while others were motivated by the sense of gratitude of a privileged life. In addition, student listeners were eager to ground their academic learning with the lived reality of people, and the organizational staff were motivated to achieve their organizational vision.

How did this diverse group of people align themselves to offer listening as a service? We see the answer to this in the mindsets that grounded the SALT approach. First, the listeners appreciated the common humanity that linked themselves (the listeners) and the families they visited. This meant that the listeners saw the families as equals despite diverse backgrounds. This contrasts with the hierarchical relationships that come from the notion of perceived expertise by virtue of belonging to an organization. This mindset was developed through routinely reflecting on two core questions before community visits: "What makes us human?" and "How did we practice SALT in our personal lives?" The reflection enabled listeners to listen to themselves before listening to others (Sankaranarayan et al., Chapter 9). This led to insights into listening, personal concerns, and efforts at solving them. Thoughts shared include "I realize I need to listen deeper to my wife" and "The challenges in my family need patient handling, but we are making progress," each illustrating the awareness of humanness in listeners.

The debriefing notes from AER revealed the second mindset shift in listeners – increased confidence in the community's capacity to be resilient and solve their own challenges. For instance, one listener said, "I am moved to witness how content the family is, though they earn a fraction of what I do." Another reflected that, "The experience of losing their only child to suicide has made the parents become activists for suicide prevention in their neighborhood." During this process, volunteers learned that their role was to listen and stand alongside the families as they worked out their own solution.

The role of home visits

Much of the work listeners accomplished was located in personal spaces of the listened to. In particular, home visits emerged as a key SALT practice that allowed the listeners to enter the intimate lived reality of families and experience life as they do. The security of the home environment enabled families to feel comfortable in expressing conflicts, fears, and hopes. The listeners received insights into the relational strengths, intensity of family challenges, and the yearning for hope – a context in which change could be facilitated.

How did the listeners enter the homes? A factor that increased acceptance of the listening visits is the organizations' provision of institutional services. The community health program provided counseling, wound dressings, and treatment for drug users; the CSR program offered adolescent tuition classes, health services, and a nutrition program; and the suicide prevention NGO ran a suicide helpline, a school suicide prevention program, and counseling to suicide survivors. Thus, there seemed to be goodwill toward the organizations in these communities.

The second factor was the listeners' skill in recognizing and responding to opportunities for home visits. Such invitations were sometimes explicit; others were implied during counseling conversations. The listeners visited families who were new to the program and were transparent about their identity and the purpose of the visits when they introduced themselves. For instance, the community health team introduced themselves using this template:

> We are from the [name] program. Your son has been availing our dressing services and expressed his anguish about the distance he feels in your love. He requested a home visit. May we have an hour of your time to discuss your concerns regarding this situation?

Although the families could choose to deny permission for the visits, humble, congenial, and caring conversations often resulted in an invitation. On occasions when the invitation was not accepted, the team left a pamphlet about organizational services and contact numbers. Some families conducted background checks of the organization, observed outcomes of similar home visits in their neighborhood, and invited the team.

In the next section, we show how deep listening during home visits is embedded in specific listening practices that are geared toward cultivating community ownership of concerns and responses. We also explore the nature of the listening that makes it transformative both to the families and the listener.

Spiraling in: deep listening

The first set of listening practices pertain to what facilitators listen *for*, as this is very specific in SALT. Indeed, SALT listeners do not just "lend an ear"; rather, they specifically listen for family concerns and hopes that open the way to listen for existing human capacities and strengths. In the beginning, sample questions include "What are your concerns as parents?" and "As a school Headmaster, what are your concerns about the mental health of students?" This differs from inquiring about their "wants," which often results in a "shopping list" that the listeners are expected to provide. While there are genuine material necessities, reflections on their concerns led families to reflect on the deeper challenges that jeopardize the realization of their hopes. For instance, one individual from the suicide prevention project said, "I am worried about the impact of drug use on my son," while another commented, "After the suicide of my daughter, my husband is hallucinating that my daughter is inviting him to join her by killing himself." We also note that skilled listeners explore the concerns in depth, allowing for deeper reflections of the cause and impact of the concerns. For instance, a father in the CSR program said, "I now realize that the root cause of my son's academic failure rests also in our lack of parenting and not just neighborhood influences as I had originally thought."

While listening to concerns, the listeners rephrased the emotions and the underlying needs, similar to the traditions of Non-Violent Communication (Rosenberg, 2012). For instance, a listener in the suicide prevention program reflected to a group of girls, "I hear you are quite upset at having to marry early against your consent. Your need is to explore your full educational potential before you commit to a married life." To a group of school students, the suicide prevention volunteers said, "You feel frustrated your parents fight in front of you and you desire peace in family life." When people felt understood and acknowledged, the resulting respect and mutual trust facilitated further sharing. In the earlier instance, the girls responded by saying, "Nobody cares what we feel … we had accepted it as our fate. But you seem to have understood us." The listening and respectful dialogues around concerns peeled back layers of conflicts, hurt, anger, and potential for new engagements and reconciliation in the home and neighborhood.

A second theme explored by listeners is hopes, which helped people articulate their desires, including reconciliation, a life of full potential, fulfillment, and competent citizenship. As part of the CSR program, parents of young people in the community reflected that "Many school drop-out children now attend school because of your programs. Now we want 100% enrolment." Discussions about people's hopes provided a balance to the hard feelings evoked during the discussions regarding their concerns.

The third theme that supports fruition of hopes is people's strengths. The listening team skillfully interwove questions and observations about the strengths of the families, in particular loving care, changes among people, strength derived from relationships, and the actions people took. For example, a mother in the CSR program commented "I am not used to thinking of my strengths, but I now realize I am resilient," while a leader stressed "We are a caring neighborhood and support one another in need."

A fourth key concept that listeners explored in SALT-based listening is the notion of response, which signifies people's agency represented as the will and actions to address concerns and achieve their hopes by drawing on their strengths. They include individual, family, and collective actions undertaken; as well as conversations, desires, and emotions regarding the impact of concerns in their lives. The individuals in these situations made use of their strengths, mobilized support, included affected individuals, and accessed resources. Responses of the affected people in the case studies signified ownership and leadership for change.

The listeners asked and listened to stories of people responding to their concerns. An interesting point to note is the vast amount of community responses abandoned midway. Several reasons contributed to this, including lack of support from other family or community members, opposition from those who are part of the problem, lack of skills in raising the challenges appropriately, and lack of energy to pursue solutions. For instance, a woman in the suicide prevention program said, "When I confronted my husband about his undisciplined lifestyle, he was furious and became abusive. I withdrew and accepted it as my fate." A community leader in the suicide prevention program mentioned that "We banned child marriages. However, parents ignore this." The past responses thus provided insights into ways in which the families have responded to their concerns, their emotions, and their level of enthusiasm to explore further solutions.

By staying neutral in conflicts, acknowledging emotions of people, expressing appreciation for positive intent behind actions, and provoking reflections, SALT listeners facilitated deeper insights for future actions. For instance, the wife from the aforementioned instance, who had withdrawn after the pushback from her husband, shared, "I should have spoken to him in a non-confrontational manner when he was in a good mood and listened to his side of the story." A community leader in the suicide prevention program stated, "We did not take time to understand the challenges faced by parents while banning child marriages. We need to include the parents in future decision making." The families in question wanted listeners capable of understanding of their deep concerns, supporting them in processes of reconciliation, providing advice on ways to address their challenges, and assisting access to technical support and resources.

Spiraling out: mutual listening and listening across differences

While the first set of listening practices involved "spiraling in" to deeper layers of understanding through listening for concerns, hopes, and capacities in the home context, the second set of listening practices expands the conversations to the neighborhood context with a focus on stimulating discussions that cultivate community response to concerns shared across households. In particular, the listeners proposed a neighborhood discussion to facilitate a shared understanding of concerns and joint exploration of solutions when they recognized similar concerns shared across families (step 3, Box 4.1). Joint discussions seemed to support open discussions about the impact of stigmatizing issues, identifying resources for solutions, and increasing understanding about potential for a solution. A listener from the suicide prevention NGO asked, "We listened to your neighbours who were undergoing domestic violence like you. Do you think it will be useful for all to meet at your home for a time of listening to collective perspectives and deciding next steps?"

Listening to separate groups of people who are involved in a conflict revealed different aspects that need to be addressed to resolve the problem. For instance, in the case of suicide prevention, listeners listened to young girls' distress about early marriage, parents regarding their fears for the safety of their daughters, and community leaders regarding their frustration with parents not adhering to their decision to ban child marriage. Consequently, the neighborhood-based listening provided a forum for respectful mutual understanding, considering the needs of all members, and acknowledging their feelings. This listening practice, learned from the listeners, provided neighborhood families with different perspectives and potential for inclusive approaches. Families apparently derived solidarity and mutual strength in knowing that they can respond together as a group, providing and receiving support from one another. We also note that the practice of confidentiality, that inadvertently creates stigma and hinders people from seeking and receiving help in families, changed to one of *shared confidentiality*. With shared confidentiality, the families shared their secrets in the neighborhood context with whom they chose and as much as they wanted to share.

Listening to feelings and felt needs of all parties promoted understanding and mutual appreciation. For instance, during the community discussion at the Pune CSR program, the women shared their distress about domestic violence due to excessive alcohol consumption of men, whereas men said that alcohol eased their aches and pains from hard labor. For the men, there was no intent to abuse their wives. The husbands acknowledged that they consumed excessive amounts of alcohol while drinking with friends. This shared understanding created appreciation and allowed decisions for change. The men resolved to drink alcohol at home in limited quantities and avoid losing sense of right and wrong. The listening team stayed alert to preventing mutual accusations, addressing overwhelming emotions about the scale of the problem, and facilitated sharing regarding notions of hope and change.

As communities implemented their agreements (step 7), the listeners continued their home visits (step 2) to listen to challenges, offer encouragement, and understand emerging perspectives. A crucial aspect of listening in neighborhood change involved reflections regarding the impact of actions following implementation. These reflections allowed learning, adaptation of actions, and building confidence in the neighborhood. The following story, narrated by a listener, illustrates learning.

> There was deep anger and frustration against addiction felt by the community leaders. They resolved to take strong action against drug peddlers despite us trying to facilitate inquiry into the reasons why drug peddlers choose this career. One drug peddler was caught red-handed, tied at the city square, assaulted and humiliated. A follow-up visit by the listening team to the peddler's home revealed the humiliation he felt and how he has now resolved to sell more drugs. During the reflection session, the leaders realized the

negative impact of their decision and decided to reach out to drug peddlers and help them find an alternative source of income.

Listening to self

A final observation about the practice of deep listening concerns listening to oneself, one's inner voices, similar to the practice of mindful self-care (Posluns & Gall, 2020). Listeners have experienced that being aware of strengths, feelings, and thoughts helps them notice and control their responses to the person to whom they are listening. For instance, a listener in the drug de-addiction program reflected,

> I think it is stupid that the community cremated the young man and his belongings who died of HIV due to their irrational fear of spreading HIV. However, I will stand alongside the community and seek opportunities for a discussion.

Listening can also result in self-work in diagnosing and working out solutions for individual challenges. As a listener said at an AER,

> Listening to the abuse faced by the young woman from her mother-in-law brought up bouts of anger in me due to what I have experienced in the past. I realize I need help to resolve this, before I am of help to the young woman.

The AER notes from the case studies revealed a pattern of discernment regarding listeners' own strengths and vulnerabilities and adaptation in behavior and practices to the emerging needs and strengths in the program, localizing agency in the listener. For instance, as the communities opened wound dressing clinics in the neighborhood, the program team reduced their own clinical operations. The listening approach thus resulted in change in the communities, the listeners, as well as their associated institutions.

Bringing listening to scale

Now that we have covered the primary components of SALT, we turn our attention to two factors that expanded the scale of the program – the changing role of the institutions to which the listeners belonged and the spread of a listening culture to connected communities. First, the change in listeners produced change in institutional practices as the organizations formed deep connections with the communities and adapted their services based on community needs. We saw this happening in two ways. Primarily, the listeners recognized emerging confidence in the community to take ownership to listen and implement services in their neighborhoods. For instance, the community health team supported the start of a community clinic, with fundraising, identifying former drug users as counselors and affirming emerging initiatives. We observed that the community health organization transferred a working culture of listening to some organizations in Mizoram; the suicide prevention NGO cultivated listening-oriented peer education, helpline, and survivor support programs in the city in partnership with other institutions; and the CSR experience has now produced a city-wide collective action model based on the agency building of youth for transformation resulting in changing laws, policies, or institutions. These institutional changes have supported an increasing scale of listening practices through transfer between institutions.

The second approach was that several neighborhoods have embraced the listening culture and transferred it to neighborhoods connected to them. In one case, we have witnessed a vast lateral community-to-community transfer as illustrated in Figure 4.2, affecting hundreds of neighborhoods. Note that the figure just shows the reported transfer of one of the original communities (Dinthar) and one of the secondary communities (Dawrpuii), but one can imagine the extent of transfer if all 22 original communities were traced.

What does transfer of listening mean in this context? There are both visible and intangible changes. The culture of listening and caring, acceptance of individuals and support was felt by individuals and families. The opening of clinics that offer counseling and rehabilitation services was the visible emblem of change. A counselor from Dawrpuii, one of the communities which adopted the approach from the Dinthar community, said:

> I applied for a post of Counsellor after being prodded by a friend, though I did not have the necessary qualification of Masters in Social Work. However, when the committee heard my story of change from being a former drug user and the impact of the Dinthar community program (first community) in my life, they recruited me. Now, I find that the drug users in Dawrpuii community and their parents prefer to speak to me since they feel I understand their experience better.

Thus, the second community has adopted the caring culture and listening practice to meet their needs.

In case of Mizoram, a visible change is that SALT-based listening is now part of the policy of several social institutions. For instance, the staff at a residential childcare program conducted home visits to understand parents' concerns and hopes regarding raising children at home and why they felt the need to leave their children at the residential center. Deep-rooted concerns that emerged included alcoholism, HIV in families, and broken family relationships. As families worked their way through these challenges and listened to each other, reconciliation in relationships surfaced. As family ties stabilized, they expressed their desire to take the children back from the residential care institution to their own families. The number of children under residential care decreased, which initially worried the Centre Heads. At the same time, however, this decrease facilitated admission for more children from broken homes, thus expanding the listening services to more neighborhoods. Though listening to drug users was the entry point, deep listening is now standard practice across social care centers run by the organization. Caring relationships expressed in homes and neighborhoods are thus implicit in large-scale change.

Discussion

In this chapter, we have explored how to bring listening to scale through an analysis of listening practices in three cases that employed the SALT approach – an approach to community engagement that features listening. We have seen two distinct sets of listening practices. First, *spiraling in*, which is characterized by deep listening for concerns, hopes, strengths (or capacities), and responses; and, second, *spiraling out*, which takes the deep listening practice from individuals and homes into communities, organizations, and beyond. The listening practices in SALT can be described as simultaneous spirals of deep listening, mutual listening, and transformative listening, when, taken together, bring about changes in the listened to and the listener; in individuals, communities, and organizations. Moreover, the profound nature of these changes sparked the transfer of the listening practices, and associated impacts, to many other communities. Let us look at these processes in more detail.

The *deep listening* that takes place when *spiraling in* is characterized by listening *for* very specific things, in a specific order. Similar to approaches such as ABCD, it builds on the assumption that local people have the capacity to build strong communities (Bodie et al., Chapter 1, referring to, among others; Mathie & Cunningham, 2003). From SALT, we can learn that before attending to the strengths and capacities of communities, deep listening for concerns and hopes is essential. Only then does the listening practice reveal deeper, underlying concerns that, when recognized and addressed, can have a lasting impact. Listening for concerns and hopes involves "listening from a deep, receptive, and caring place in oneself, to deeper and often subtler levels of meaning and intention in the other person. It is listening that is generous, empathic, supportive, accurate, and trusting" (Rome & Martin, 2010, p. 58, cited in Laryea, 2018). The initial stages of the deep listening practice – listening for concerns and hopes – are empowering and lead to feelings of being validated, being heard, and sparking healing (Geller & Greenberg, 2012). In contrast, listening in SALT moves beyond healing by listening for strengths and capacities. In the systematic SALT process, listening for innate human capacities is an essential step and includes listening for the capacity to care, form a community, change, hope, and embody leadership. Irrespective of where you find them (communities, institutions, policymakers,

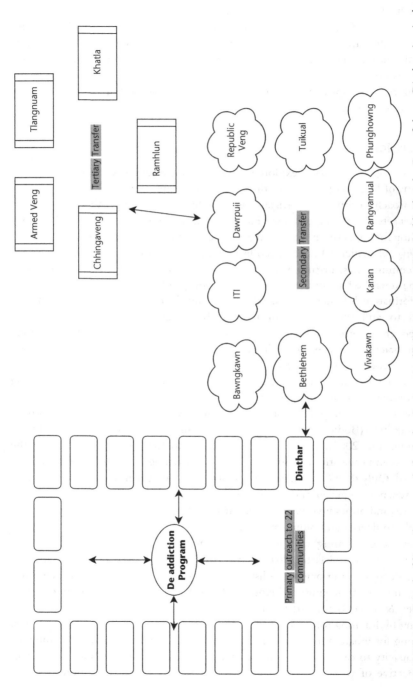

FIGURE 4.2 Spread of listening approach from the community health program to 22 neighborhoods. One of these, Dinthar, inspired ten neighborhoods. Dawrpuii, one of these neighborhoods, transferred it to five new neighborhoods

researchers, academics), listening to and acknowledging people's human capacities makes them feel truly valued and appreciated, thus stimulating further thoughts and actions. Because "Communities are usually only too well aware of their weaknesses ... but are frequently unaware of their strengths" (De Rouw et al., 2020, p. 133), SALT facilitators ask questions that encourage community members to start recognizing their own capacities and earlier achievements to enable them to mobilize these assets in response to common concerns.

The listening that takes place in the *spiraling out* movement entails taking the deep listening practices into the community (and beyond). This *mutual deep listening* practice involves dealing with differences and even conflict, or, as it has been named elsewhere, "listening across differences" (Bodie & Godwin, 2022; Hendriks et al., 2019) and builds on the deep listening practices described above. People who feel they have been heard are more willing to open themselves to another's perspective (Bruneau & Saxe, 2012), and sharing personal information creates connections between community members (De Rouw et al., 2020). In addition, deep listening for concerns and hopes, like the practice of listening to feelings and underlying needs in non-violent communication (Rosenberg, 2012), helps not only to heal old wounds, but also to resolve inner and interpersonal conflicts. Listeners may disagree with what is being said and cut themselves off, especially when it concerns deeply rooted, conflicting values. The ability to learn how to listen for underlying concerns, hopes, feelings, and unmet needs helps to accept conflict and dissent, to remain open and with the other person. In SALT, facilitators enable the inclusion of divergent people and views in the community, by creating a space in which isolated and conflicting voices are listened to and considered by all participants in considering their next steps. These spaces for listening seem to allow for community members to deeply listen to each other's viewpoints and create a sense of mutual understanding and solidarity for change.

The *spiraling out* movement can then further move into *transformative listening* as it encourages a community-level response to shared concerns. While communities use their capacities and strengthened connections to act, the organizations involved need to adapt to the community transformation and organizational listening that occurs (Macnamara, 2018). Importantly, organizational adaptation takes place only in response to and in pace with community transformation. As the Mizoram case shows, organizations must be sensitive to increasing confidence within the community to take up the program and be ready to pare down institutional services in response, while also taking on new roles like facilitating neighborhood conversations and cultivating community responses. This is markedly different from forms of institutional listening that are structured by the organization (e.g., through providing channels for people to voice their views), which often delineate the scope, time, and timing that listening occurs. Hence, we see that deep listening, mutual listening, and transformative listening can bring about changes in the listened to and the listener, in individuals, communities, and organizations in multiple, simultaneous, and iterative spirals.

Let us now turn back to Figure 4.1, where we brought in the dimension of locality of agency. We saw a tension in the literature between other-oriented, feeling-centered listening while also bringing listening to scale. First, important elements of other-oriented, feeling-centered listening are hard to imagine in large-scale, non-face-to-face contexts (Bodie et al., Chapter 1). In addition, "the exercise of [compassionate] listening implies nothing regarding taking action as a consequence of what is heard" (Dobson, 2014, p. 65). In other words, other-oriented, feeling-centered listening may change something in the mind or heart of those who are listened to, but it is of little (or no) consequence in terms of having a larger social impact. We do not concur. Based on the study presented in this chapter, we would argue that other-oriented, feeling-centered listening (which we would say is an essential part of our understanding of deep listening) can be of consequence. Broader impact and transformation can result from this type of listening as long as (1) listening is geared toward community response; (2) listening is embedded in a systematic process; and (3) listening has certain characteristics (i.e., deep listening for concerns, hopes and capacities, stimulating mutual listening across differences). As illustrated in Figure 4.3, creating impact and bringing listening to scale through vertical receptivity (left side) is, in our study, replaced by a spiraling movement, connecting one-on-one listening with larger-scale listening (vertical axis), and connecting community transformation with organizational or institutional transformation (horizontal axis).

In *Listening for Democracy* (2014), Andrew Dobson asked whether listening in the socio-political context is a matter of changing individuals or changing structures. Do we need a growing number of individuals to embody the virtues of listening, or do we need to change institutional structures so that dialogic listening would be central to democracy? The experiences with SALT, as presented in this chapter, show that we may be able to go beyond an either/or question in addressing the upscaling problem. If upscaling is understood as generating lasting impacts, we argue that this process already starts with deep, other-oriented, feeling-centered listening to individuals. We have seen that deep listening practices do not merely serve as instruments to generate input for programs or policies. Such listening changes people – both the listener and "listened to" – and can be seen as a process of stabilizing the new practice, one of the amplifying impact pathways as identified by Lam et al. (2020). Moreover, they would naturally bring their changed mindsets along with them into other situations (see also Zachariah et al., 2018), which accelerates the process of creating impact. In the cases presented, we see further spreading, and hence increased impact, through the growing number of people connected through and affected by the listening intervention as well as replication of the approach in neighboring communities. We see scaling up through adaptations of program design in the organizations involved and their adoption of new roles: From providing services to facilitating community responses. Finally, we see scaling deep in the changed mindsets of all involved. Let us focus on one important change in the mindset of the listeners, namely listeners from institutions that are used to providing services and bringing in expertise: The change from being an expert to being a listener.

In the SALT approach, taking a non-expert position is the assumed starting point, and listeners are trained as such. As is evident from the case studies, this is harder for those who need to unlearn being an expert than it is for those new to the work. In his book *What Makes Us Human*, in which Jean-Louis Lamboray reflected on decades of experience with SALT, he wrote about one of the facilitators in the Democratic Republic of Congo, Antoine:

> Antoine likes to remind us that old habits die hard, and it is easy to resume the role of an expert. 'The old man is asleep in us. He can wake up at any moment!' But when we have tasted the joy of sharing, and when we choose to appreciate the strengths of each person, of each family, of each community, then we progressively lose the desire to resume that role. (Lamboray, 2016, chapter 4)

In addition to repeated and consistent engagement with the practice of listening, the focus on common humanity seems to be conducive to strengthening the non-expert role in the SALT approach. Deep listening is grounded in the idea that listening, and opening one's mind and heart to others, involves

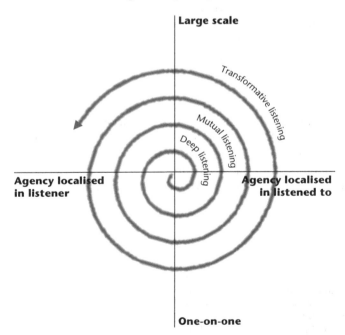

FIGURE 4.3 Adapted framework illustrating the listening practices and transformation at play when listening is embedded in SALT process

connecting deeply with oneself too. In these listening practices, people meet beyond roles and functions; they meet as human beings. While the importance of grounding listening in common humanity is widely recognized in listening literature (e.g., Hamelink, 2020 Wilmer, 2018), SALT offers a concrete method to operationalize this. In SALT, home visits and community conversations are preceded by a structured team reflection on people's common humanity, which helps to make a deeper connection with oneself. These discussions allow project staff to recognize points of connection with the community and tune their minds for deep listening. The question "What makes us human?" can also be the start of the community conversations, where communities come together to establish a common identity grounded in mutual humanity (e.g., De Rouw et al., 2020).

We end this chapter by recognizing that the insights shared here have been developed in interaction with communities over decades. Our understanding of different listening practices (deep, mutual, and transformative listening) that are conducive to community engagement, ownership, and response, as well as the listening architecture (SALT) that forms the scaffolding around these listening practices, reflect communities' experiential knowledge. SALT practitioners have recognized this and learned from communities. The scientific community can learn from this, in turn, by, for instance, recognizing that while it is possible to make analytical distinctions between different types of listening (e.g., receptive listening, other-oriented listening), in practice they are highly interwoven. SALT practitioners have shown all of us that becoming a listener involves learning and unlearning. They have shown the generative and transformative power of listening. And they have shown what it is to be human.

Acknowledgments

The experiences that form the base of the analysis for this chapter emerged from three decades of labor of love by a team of practitioners consisting of program staff, volunteers, and community champions. We particularly acknowledge Dr. Ian D. Campbell, Alison Rader Campbell from Affirm Facilitators, and The Constellation for Community Life Competence Team for their mentorship to SALT initiatives in India.

Note

1 Note that SALT and CLC approach are sometimes used interchangeably (see e.g., Nandi et al., 2018) or referred to as SALT-CLCP (Community Life Competence Approach, n.d.). In this chapter, we will use the approach as practiced by the author and facilitators in India – which is a slightly adapted form of the Community Life Competence Process, and includes principles of non-violent communication (NVC) and active listening, and refer to it as the SALT approach.

References

Bodie, G. D., & Godwin, P. (2022). On the limits of listening for bridging divides and cross-cultural understanding. In L. Chao & C. Wang (Eds.), *Communication across differences: Negotiating identity, privilege, and marginalization in the 21st century* (pp. 225–243). Cognella.

Bruneau, E. G., & Saxe, R. (2012). The power of being heard: The benefits of 'perspective-giving' in the context of intergroup conflict. *Journal of Experimental Social Psychology*, *48*(4), 855–866. doi:10.1016/j.jesp.2012.02.017

Campbell, I. D. (2008, June). *Human capacity development for response to HIV.* [Paper Presentation]. The HIV Implementers Meeting, Kampala, Uganda. https://www.affirmfacilitators.org/docs/Ian_Campbell_Speaker_Notes_with_Slides_4June2008_HCD.pdf

Campbell, I. D., Campbell, A. R., & Chela, C. (2021). A community development approach to HIV care, prevention and control. In T. Lankester & N. J. Grills (Eds.), *Setting up community health programmes in low and middle income settings* (4th ed., pp. 350–367). Oxford University Press. doi:10.1093/med/9780198806653.001.0001

Campbell, I. D., & Rader, A. D. (1995). HIV counselling in developing countries: The link from individual to community counselling for support and change. *British Journal of Guidance & Counselling*, *23*(1), 33–43. doi:10.1080/03069889508258058

De Rouw, M., Kuan, A., Forth, P., Nanda, R. B., & Constantin, L. B. (2020). Four principles of community-based primary health care. In M. Schleiff & D. Bishai (Eds.), *Achieving health for all: Primary health care in action* (pp. 127–152). Johns Hopkins University Press. doi:10.1353/book.77991

Dobson, A. (2014). *Listening for democracy: Recognition, representation, reconciliation.* Oxford University Press. doi:10.1093/acprof:oso/9780199682447.001.0001

Ercan, S. A., Hendriks, C. M., & Drysek, J. S. (2019) Public deliberation in an era of communicative plenty. *Policy & Politics*, *47*(1), 19–35. doi:10.1332/030557318X15200093925405

Gearhart, C. C., & Bodie, G. D. (2011). Active-empathic listening as a general social skill: Evidence from bivariate and canonical correlations. *Communication Reports*, *24*(2), 86–98. doi:10.1080/08934215.2011.610731

Geller, S. M., & Greenberg, L. S. (2012). *Therapeutic presence: A mindful approach to effective therapy.* American Psychological Association. doi:10.1037/13485-000

Hamelink, C. J. (2020). *Communication and peace: Celebrating moments of sheer human togetherness.* Springer. doi:10.1057/978-1-137-50354-1

Hendriks, C. M., Ercan, S. A., & Duus, S. (2019). Listening in polarised controversies: A study of listening practices in the public sphere. *Policy Sciences*, *52*(1), 137–151. doi:10.1007/s11077-018-9343-3

Johansson, P. (2017). Feeling for the game: How emotions shape listening in peacebuilding partnerships. *E-International Relations.* https://www.e-ir.info/2017/05/17/feeling-for-the-game-how-emotions-shape-listening-in-peacebuilding-partnerships/

Lam, D. P., Martín-López, B., Wiek, A., Bennett, E. M., Frantzeskaki, N., Horcea-Milcu, A. I., & Lang, D. J. (2020). Scaling the impact of sustainability initiatives: A typology of amplification processes. *Urban Transformations*, *2*, 1–24. doi:10.1186/s42854-020-00007-9

Lamboray, J. L. (2016). *What makes us human?: The story of a shared dream.* Balboa Press.

Lamboray, J.-L., & Skevington, S. M. (2001). Defining AIDS competence: A working model for practical purposes. *Journal of International Development*, *13*, 513–521. doi:10.1002/jid.800

Laryea, K. (2018). A pedagogy of deep listening in E-Learning. *Journal of Conscious Evolution*, *11*(11), Article 2. https://digitalcommons.ciis.edu/cejournal/vol11/iss11/2

Lewis, L. (2019). *The power of strategic listening*. Rowman & Littlefield.

Macnamara, J. (2018). Toward a theory and practice of organizational listening. *International Journal of Listening*, *32*(1), 1–23. doi:10.1080/10904018.2017.1375076

Macnamara, J. (2020). Listening for healthy democracy. In D. L. Worthington & G. D. Bodie (Eds.), *The handbook of listening* (pp. 385–395). Wiley.

Macnamara, J. R. (2016). *Organizational listening: The missing essential in public communication*. Peter Lang.

Mathie, A., & Cunningham, G. (2003). From clients to citizens: Asset-based community development as a strategy for community-driven development. *Development in Practice*, *13*(5), 474–486. doi:10.1080/0961452032000125857

Moore, K. R., & Elliott, T. J. (2016). From participatory design to a listening infrastructure: A case of urban planning and participation. *Journal of Business and Technical Communication*, *30*(1), 59–84. doi:10.1177/1050651915602294

Nandi, R., Nanda, R. B., & Saha, S. (2018). Sense of ownership as capacity building: Experience of using SALT among domestic workers for systematic self-assessment. In A. Brahmachari & S. Ghosh (Eds.), *New directions for evaluations: Visibility, voice and value* (pp. 115–126). Daya Publishing.

Posluns, K., & Gall, T. L. (2020). Dear mental health practitioners, take care of yourselves: A literature review on self-care. *International Journal of Advanced Counselling*, *42*, 1–20. doi:10.1007/s10447-019-09382-w

Rehling, D. L. (2008). Compassionate listening: A framework for listening to the seriously ill. *International Journal of Listening*, *22*(2), 83–89. doi:10.1080/10904010701808516

Rosenberg, M. (2012). *Living nonviolent communication: Practical tools to connect and communicate skillfully in every situation*. Sounds True.

Scudder, M. F., Ercan, S. A., & McCallum, K. (2021). Institutional listening in deliberative democracy: Towards a deliberative logic of transmission. *Politics*. [First Online]. doi:10.1177/02633957211060691

The Constellation. (2022). *About us. Our approach*. https://www.communitylifecompetence.org/our-approach.html

Watanuki, S., Tracy, M. F., & Lindquist, R. (2018). Therapeutic listening. In R. Lindquist, M. Snyder, & M. F. Tracy (Eds.), *Complementary alternative therapies in nursing* (8th ed., pp. 29–46). Springer. doi:10.1891/9780826144348.0003

Wilmer, F. (2018). Empathy as political action can empathic engagement disrupt narratives of conflict in Israeli-Palestinian relations. *Journal of Social Science Research*, *13*, 2860–2870. doi:10.24297/jssr.v13i0.7934

Zachariah, B., de Wit, E. E., Bahirat, J. D., Bunders-Aelen, J. F., & Regeer, B. J. (2018). What is in it for them? Understanding the impact of a 'Support, Appreciate, Listen Team' (SALT)-based suicide prevention peer education program on peer educators. *School Mental Health*, *10*, 462–476. doi:10.1007/s12310-018-9264-5

5

LIGHT ON SYRIA

Performance, listening, and community engagement

Andrew Cessna Jones[1] *and Aubrey Helene Neumann*[2]

[1]CONTEMPORARY COMMUNICATION DEPARTMENT, LCC INTERNATIONAL UNIVERSITY; MORRISON-NOVAKOVIC CENTER FOR FAITH AND PUBLIC POLICY, DAVIS & ELKINS COLLEGE
[2]DEPARTMENT OF THEATRE AND FILM, DAVIS & ELKINS COLLEGE

One of the first Lithuanian folk tales Andrew Jones – communication scholar and co-author of this chapter – heard when he moved to the port city of Klaipeda on Lithuania's Baltic coast was the tale of Eglė the Queen of Serpents. The tale warns the hearer about the dangers of foreigners from across the sea by recounting how Eglė is tricked into marrying the king of the grass snakes and taken away to live in his palace under the lagoon. There she has four children, whose names translate into English as Oak, Ash, Birch, and Aspen. Eglė slowly forgets her homeland until her oldest son inquires about where she is from, and she decides to take her children home to meet their relatives. After a series of trials, Eglė and her children are allowed to return home, but warned not to summon the king of serpents except in dire need. Eglė's brothers, however, never forgave the serpents for stealing away their sister and secretly threaten each of the children unless they give away the secret of calling forth their father. The older children resist their uncles' threats, but the youngest child, Aspen, reveals the secret. Eglė's brothers summon the king of serpents and slay the king with their scythes. In mourning, Eglė turns her children into trees – oak, ash, birch, and quaking aspen. Finally, she turns herself into a spruce tree, which in Lithuanian is called Eglė to this day.

While there are many morals to any folk tale, one overriding lesson Eglė the Queen of Serpents is a wariness towards strangers from across the sea. Jones was reminded of this story in 2019 when he was asked to consult on a collaborative project that would bring together students in the Middle East Scholars program at LCC International University, representatives and resources from the United Nations High Commission on Refugees, and the City of Klaipeda, for the city's annual festival of lights. Eglė's story formed the cultural backdrop for the project.

Kenneth Burke (1969) called such stories "representative anecdotes," because they summarize a repetitive set of circumstances and provide language users with

DOI: 10.4324/9781003214465-5

the ability to respond symbolically to those circumstances. As such, they transcend the moment and allow for motivated action rather than mere motion in response to external stimuli. In the example of Eglė the Queen of Serpents, incursions into Lithuanian territories from neighboring tribes demanded a cultural shorthand to explain the complex nature of the threat, and promise, of accepting strangers into the familial bond. Eglė is initially tricked into marrying a foreign dignitary, and the resistance of her ken is insufficient to keep her home, much as a raiding party might capture the youth of a coastal village and take them away to foreign lands. Likewise, Eglė's return brings both the promise of an expanded alliance with neighboring powers and the threat that those powers might diminish the autonomy of the culture allied with them. As Burke (1973) explained, the usefulness of the vocabulary provided by any representative anecdote is its power for providing "*strategies* for dealing with *situations*" where "another name for strategies might be *attitudes*" (pp. 296–297, emphasis in original). Thus, a story like Eglė the Queen of Serpents is not only useful for ancient Baltic tribes facing foreign invaders, but also for the pagan state of Lithuania targeted for conversion by Teutonic Knights; the remnants of the Grand Duchy of Lithuania, partitioned between the Russian, Prussian, and Austrian empires; the republic of Lithuanian, occupied by the Soviet Union; and the restored republic of Lithuania, contemplating the European Union's call to settle migrants and refugees.

While Jones has written previously on political rhetoric in Lithuania (Jones, 2021) and on listening to viewpoints in intercultural communication pedagogy (Jones & Kungienė, 2022), this chapter follows a more performative model, recounting the incorporation of listening in and through the process of devising an artistic work aimed at facilitating the integration of externally displaced persons. And that is the purpose of this chapter, to explore the role of listening in the process of devising and performing community-engaged theatre. Toward this aim, we detail the contributing circumstances and development of Al Kallas's art installation. We then analyze the role of listening in the piece through the lens of existing performance scholarship, paying particular attention to critiques of existing practices with externally displaced persons. While acknowledging the contextually specific nature of the installation, the conclusion underscores elements of Light on Syria that could be adapted for use in future peacebuilding efforts.

The annual Klaipeda festival of lights

On 14 February 2020, the Lithuanian port city of Klaipeda held their annual festival of lights, a small tourist attraction that breaks up the monotony of long winter nights in the only ice-free seaport on the Baltics. This year, however, with the support of the United Nations High Commissioner for Refugees (UNHCR), and the Middle East Scholars program of LCC International University, Syrian scenic designer and installation artist Souhel Milad Al Kallas created a multi-media installation designed to help residents of the Klaipeda region listen to the stories of displaced persons who have settled in the Baltics over the past several years. A major goal of the event was to transform Klaipeda into a "welcoming intercultural port," as the title of a series of talks associated with the event proclaimed.

Al Kallas's installation is significant for discussions of listening in the context of community engagement and peacebuilding in two ways. First, the development of the piece reveals the vital role of listening in cross-cultural devised art. The project, intended to bridge differences between Syrians and natural-born Lithuanians, at times became a microcosm of existing cultural divides, necessitating greater listening from all parties involved. Second, the multi-media nature of the installation presents an alternative to existing depictions of externally displaced persons. The opportunity for dialogue between Syrian docents and audience-participants paints the former as agential beings capable of contributing to their new communities rather than mere victims of their circumstances. In this section, we identify the collaborators, outline their process for working together, and describe the installation.

The collaborators

LCC International University is an English medium institution founded at the collapse of the Soviet Union to serve students from the former Soviet states. Over the past 30 years, the reach of LCC has expanded as students from around the world have found the small, private, liberal arts university paradigm appealing as an alternative to larger state schools. While most students still come from former Soviet republics, the student population now represents over 50 countries (LCC International University, 2021). Furthermore, as more internally and externally displaced students have arrived from Ukraine, Georgia, and other war-effected regions, the University has worked to expand its support for war-affected students by providing specific programming and scholarships for these populations.

In 2016, LCC International University started their "Middle East Scholars" program, which was designed to welcome students from Syria, Iraq, and Afghanistan to their satellite campus in Georgia (Sakertvella). While the original goal of the program was to prepare students for acceptance to English medium education in Europe and North America, the growing humanitarian crises associated with forced migration required a restricting of the program, bringing the faculty, staff, and students back to the main campus in Klaipeda, Lithuania. This complex move at the height of the refugee crises in Europe has ultimately proven successful. The program began with four Syrian students in 2016 and has since grown to over 50 students from all three countries (LCC International University, 2018).

In February 2020, on the cusp of the global pandemic, organizers of the Light Festival in Klaipeda city welcomed Syrian artist Al Kallas to design an installation shining a light on Syria. However, the unique context of the event sheds light not only on Syria, but also on listening as an embodied practice to promote peace-building in the midst of several ongoing humanitarian crises. In the Middle East alone, the U.S.'s assassination of Iranian commander Qasem Soleimani prompted increased violence in Iraq, the Saudi Arabian-led intervention in Yemen had escalated yet again on the northern border, and Turkish forces together with Syrian rebels prepared to push back against the Russian-backed regime. While focused on Syria, Al Kallas's country of origin, Renata Kuleš, UNHCR representative in Lithuania, emphasized the broader implications of the project: "It's important for people in Lithuania to understand why so many flee their country … it becomes more clear that refugees run for their lives" (Steinke, 2020). Jones was asked to consult on this project by Aistė Motekaitienė, then Vice President of Communications at the LCC International University. Motekaitienė was aware of Jones's work as both a consultant in the community and as an assistant professor at the University, who regularly incorporated aspects of performance studies into his teaching. With collaborators from the Middle East, North America, and Europe, learning to listen across cultures was a constant challenge throughout the process.

The process

The first problem was to decide the contribution the event would make. When developing this project, Al Kallas's vision was to show the audience that what had happened to him could also happen to them. To communicate this, his original vision was to create sculptures of light to emulate the work of an installation in Copenhagen, which used figures of wire-framed lights. The initial meetings were largely brainstorming sessions designed to decide what we should do. It was generally agreed that there should be an opening night event with city leaders to be hosted on the campus. The following program would then be coordinated with the festival of lights and make use of the resources available through UNHCR, but the specifics of the event were left open.

Early on, the idea of projection became a central theme of the discussions. Al Kallas and his collaborators had access to the film *Sea of Sorrows, Sea of Hope* through our connection with UNHCR, so the plan was to project the film on the exterior of the Klaipėda Kultūros fabrikas (Culture Factory). However, the Cultural Factory was at a distance from the center of old town, and potentially too far from the epicenter of the lights festival for audiences. Subsequently, a plan was proposed to create a tunnel of light leading from the site of the destroyed Anglican church, which was closer to old town, to the rear of the Culture Factory, where the projection would be set up. John's Hill, and the fortifications that surround an old moat, has a tunnel leading from one site to the other, and would have provided an interesting canvas for Al Kallas's light sculptures. However, the issue of looping a projection until late into the evening in a mixed-residential area posed a problem, as did the unknown expense of projection and audio equipment.

Rather than abandon this initial idea, Jones raised the question of moving the projection to non-residential parts of the old town closer to the center of the light festival. Part of Al Kallas's initial vision was to highlight the similarities between Klaipėda and Syria, and one way to do this was through altered reality enabled by projection. For example, the team brainstormed creating renderings of landmark buildings destroyed by bombings, and then projecting those renderings onto the buildings themselves, thus highlighting the potential for Klaipėda to experience what Syria was experiencing. Unfortunately, this ran into the same budgetary concerns as projecting onto the Culture Factory, not only for the projection equipment, but also commissioning an artist to create the renderings and animations. One potential solution, which became important to the final design of the installation, was Jones's discovery of an exhibition at the Klaipėda castle featuring actual images from the Second World War showing the destruction of the city. Several existing buildings, including the Viktorija Hotel, were almost destroyed as the city was captured and recaptured by Soviet and Nazi troops. Though the final installation did not include these images, they become an important touchstone for the project as they served to highlight how recently Lithuanians had experienced what Syrians were currently experiencing.

As it became clear that projections were not a viable option, we began to explore virtual reality (VR) options. Al Kallas worked with friends to acquire VR headsets and a video of a drone flight through major landmarks in Syria. The idea was to place the VR headsets on pedestals around a space so that audiences could "tour" the spaces in the photographs from the UNHCR collection. Jones recommended that, instead of a passive experience where participants picked up and put on headsets that were just lying around, the artist could station individuals around the space to engage audience members in conversation. Having lived near New Orleans in the aftermath of Katrina, Jones was wary of dark tourism and associated critiques of voyeurism. Ultimately, it was decided that the VR headsets would emphasize the technology and detract from the goal of the installation. However, Al Kallas kept the idea of recruiting Syrian-born friends to act as docents – a casting that, as discussed in later sections, deviated from the more passive role often relegated to externally displaced persons (Figure 5.1).

The installation

Al Kallas and his crew worked frantically, preparing and installing until the moment the doors opened. The space of the Viktorija Hotel was ideal for the installation. The hotel had been a landmark building for the city, but years of neglect marred the interior. From the grand entrance, visitors had to walk up to a cage, part of an old video rental store that had once been located in the space.

FIGURE 5.1 Al Kallas focusing a lighting instrument on a photograph for the exhibition

Source: Image credit Vira Kravchuk.

Through the barred doors, visitors then walked up a half flight of steps and turned into the grand ballroom. The polish and lacquer of the herringbone patterned wooden floors had worn off long ago, and the raw wood creaked underfoot. Plaster walls had spots of peeling yellow paint. Panels had been erected around the room showcasing a selection of photographs from the UNHCR's collection, a mixture of persons and buildings, some mirroring the very building we stood in with obvious signs of distress. This echoed Al Kallas's desire to show the proximity of Syria and Lithuania, highlighting the possibility of the things he witnessed at home happening in this new home. The center of the space was dedicated to rows of chairs facing a shallow proscenium stage against the back wall. The UNHCR-sponsored film *Sea of Sorrow, Sea of Hope* played on a loop as audiences crisscrossed the space (Figure 5.2).

FIGURE 5.2   Audience viewing *Sea of Sorrows, Sea of Hope*

Source: Image credit Vira Kravchuk.

The 30-minute documentary film tells the story of Manal, a mother who is forced to leave her children behind in Syria while she seeks a safe place for her family in Denmark. The film filled the space with the sound of crashing waves as Manal told her story in Arabic with subtitles in English and Lithuanian. Manal had worked for the Syrian Ministry of Justice and was therefore at great risk if she remained in Syria, but she could not afford to bring her children with her on her trip. Planning to reunite with them shortly after her arrival, she left her children and sought asylum in Denmark. Once she arrived, however, she learned that it could take up to three years for her family to have permission to join her. Out of desperation, she turned to smugglers to bring her three children from Syria through Turkey and into Greece. It took over a year of searching, but in October 2015 her children boarded a dinghy bound for Lesvos. At this time, a boat making the same crossing sank, an event that made international news when the image of two-year-old Alan Kurdi's body was widely circulated. Manal had no way of knowing whether or not her children were in the same boat. As the promotional website for the film explains, "By the fourth day, Manal found a photo of a drowned boy who looked just like her 8-year-old son Karam. He has the same curly brown hair, the same eyes, the same innocent face. The photo was blurred but it could easily have been him" (Bach, 2018). Manal had to wait ten more days to learn that her children were safe. They had been aboard a different boat, which had broken down and been forced to return to Turkey. It took another month for Manal's children to make the crossing and for Manal to finally be reunited with them in the resettlement center in Copenhagen. As Manal concluded, "no one should have to cross an ocean and risk their lives to reunite with their family" (Bach, 2018, para. 13).

Rather than sit and watch the film from beginning to end, most audience members wandered the space. A photo exhibit from the UNHCR archives displayed images of Syria from before and after the war. The photographs were displayed against cracked plaster walls, surrounded by peeling paint and bare concrete where time had worn down the once grand interior of the Viktorija Hotel. Pieces of architectural salvage were also propped against the wall. Wrought iron window fans, relics of Soviet architecture, were placed beside scraped metal bedframes. The photos were mounted on black metal stands that also leaned against the walls. Standing lights were connected to cords that crisscrossed the space, powered by a generator, as the abandoned building had neither heat nor electricity on a frosty February day.

Al Kallas is an accomplished scenic artist. His installation (Figure 5.3) incorporated elements of his background in scenic design, which are immediately obvious when you enter the space as the dramatic staging of his installation implies action within and against elements of the space. Four translucent figures stand against the wall immediately across from the entrance to the grand ballroom. Behind them is the outline of a bricked-in door – closed permanently behind them. To their left is a floor-to-ceiling arched window, the beginning stages of renovation for the space. Through the window, the port city of Klaipėda glowed with festive lights shining back against the long cold winter nights from approximately 4 pm until late in the morning. The four figures are two adults and two children. Al Kallas explained that the adults started as part of the scenic design for the University's Christmas pageant – Mary and Joseph. The repurposing feels appropriate as the contemporary story of externally displaced persons harkens back to the ancient story of externally displaced persons. The male figure wears a plaid shirt, untucked, beneath a dark blue cardigan with matching toboggan and faded jeans. His eyes are closed beneath dark brows, and his mouth is turned slightly down at the edges beneath a full beard. He holds a large red bag in his right hand, while his left hand holds the hand of a child. The child wears a duffle coat, like the one Paddington Bear wears in the children's books. His face has a blurred appearance, like the images from the news coverage of children drowned

FIGURE 5.3   Al Kallas's installation

Source: Image credit Vira Kravchuk.

while fleeing war. The flaps of his hat are tied securely under his chin, holding it warmly in place. His right hand clutches his father's hand, and his left hand clutches his mother's.

The mother figure is the centerpiece of Milad's installation. She wears jeans and a white blouse with a white head covering and a black vest. However, the center of the vest is cut out in the shape of Syria. The incision reveals the figure's ribs, and a red light fills the cavity. Her right hand holds the hand of an older child, and her left rests on the head of a small child clutching her knee. In an interview with the campus newspaper, Milad, describing the installation, noted, "the installation is a summarization of what the refugees are going through. The mother's heart will always be the lighthouse for her children and represents both

Syria and motherhood" (Steinke, 2020). The smallest figure, a child, wears a grey-striped toboggan and a small jacket. The child clutches their mother's leg, and like the older child, has no distinguishing features on their face – allowing the face to appear blurred.

Summary

In the sections above, we identified the organizations and individuals who collaborated on this project, outlined the process of bringing the installation together, and described the installation itself. With a team of collaborators from the Middle East, across Europe, and North America working together to bring this project together, there were several opportunities for everything to fall apart – either in the process of bringing the installation together, or during the performance itself. Thus, our analysis first considers how listening across cultures facilitated the process of devising the installation, and then explores how the installation foregrounded listening as an agential act.

Analysis

In this section, we examine the process of devising *Light on Syria* and the subsequent performance. In this process analysis, we use theatre artist and theorist Augusto Boal's (1985) concept of the Joker to explain Jones's role in guiding the organizers and artists to listen across cultures. In the next section, we argue for listening as an agential act through an analysis of the performance.

Process analysis: listening across cultures

Throughout the process, interactions between artist and organizers revealed cultural differences indicative of the larger division the project aimed to overcome. Motekaitienė's approach to the project reflected several cultural traits of Northern Europe, including a detached business-like approach to the project and low-context communication.[1] For example, Motekaitienė would bluntly state that an idea wouldn't work or was unfeasible. Al Kallas took more of a Middle Eastern approach through high-context communication that saw the project as an extension of the interpersonal relationships between members of the project. For example, Al Kallas interpreted a comment on the feasibility of an idea as an intimate betrayal and suggested scrapping the entire project. Jones's role became that of facilitator, listening to both parties and providing meta-communication. His comments encouraged all to return to the shared goal of the work by highlighting how different approaches to communication were disrupting the process.

In many ways, this facilitation resembled the work of the Joker in Boal's forum theatre. An extension of Boal's initial work on theatre of the oppressed, which blends elements of Paulo Freire's pedagogy of the oppressed and Jerzy Grotowski's aesthetic of poor theatre, forum theatre aims to be a *"rehearsal of revolution"* (Boal, 1985, p. 141, emphasis in original). Performances depict instances of social injustice and play out possible solutions to existing oppression. Rather than the more passive role of spectators, the work engages audience members as "spect-actors" – a joining of the roles of spectator and actor – capable of entering or altering the performances, with the help of a playful "Joker."

Carrying forward the promise of drama in classical Greece, which Crick (2015, p. 140) identified as "always striving to be something greater than what we are," Boal personifies the comic corrective in the role of a Joker. As Boal (2002, p. 244) explained forum theatre:

> One of the actors, or someone else, must also exercise the auxiliary function of Joker, the wild card, leader of the game. It is up to him or her to explain the rules of the game, to correct errors made and to encourage both parties not to stop playing. Indeed, the effect of the forum is all the more powerful if it is made entirely clear to the audience that if they don't change the world, no one will change it for them and everything will inevitably turn out exactly the same – which is the last thing we would want to happen.

In forum theatre, the Joker stands outside of the drama, while the other actors – including the spect-actors – are inside of the drama. That is, the Joker can perceive the implications of minor alterations to the performance as spect-actors replace the protagonist and role-play alternatives while the actors remain focused on maintaining their presence.

In fulfilling the role of the Joker, Jones emphasized three tasks of the Joker: (1) explaining the rules of the game, (2) correcting errors, and (3) encouraging participants to keep playing. Here, the rules of the game are the parameters of the project. By explaining the rules of the game, the Joker keeps everyone focused on the goal of the collaboration. For example, when Al Kallas wanted to set up a projection system in a mixed-use residential area, Jones encouraged the artist to listen to the organizer's concerns about how residents of the neighboring buildings might react and about the prohibitive cost of outdoor projection. Here, the rules of the game required Al Kallas and the organizers to recognize not only the practical impossibility of setting up the projection system, but also the artistic vision that would require projecting onto residential buildings. By returning to the overall purpose of the project, to shine a light on Syria, Al Kallas and the organizers devised a solution together.

Error correction is not about pointing out things that were done wrong, but about instilling doubt when a magical solution is being proposed. Magical solutions, for Boal, are the Deus ex machina – theatrical illusions that cannot be implemented in everyday life: such as suddenly obtaining a large grant to cover all production expenses, or an artist agreeing to compromise their vision because it would be easier for the organizers. Rather than bluntly intervening and calling out an error, Jones as Joker questioned whether artist's and organizers' proposed solutions were instances of magical thinking. For example, when organizers wanted to create a passive installation and sequester interactive elements of the installation at the university campus 30 minutes from the actual venue, Jones encouraged Al Kallas to emphasize the importance of listening for – and making space to listen for – the difficult and different experiences of others. As Boal (2002) clarified, the Joker is not in charge of the game, but simply responsible for ensuring that "those who know a little more get the chance to explain it, and that those who dare a little, dare a little more and show what they are capable of" (p. 245). Jones's Joker was not meant to preside over the collaboration, but to facilitate listening amongst the collaborators, instilling doubts about solutions that appear to fix every problem while maintaining a focus on the goal – shining a light on Syria.

Finally, the Joker role is about encouraging participants to keep playing the game, that is, to continue with the collaboration. Boal described this as being a midwife, assisting in the birth of all ideas and of all actions (Boal, 2002, p. 262). Al Kallas's installation went through several iterations during the collaborative process, few of which were under his direct control. Finding ways to bring artist and organizers back into the game again required frequent return to the goal of performance. For example, when Al Kallas wanted to use VR headsets so that audiences could take a drone tour of archeological sites in Syria, Jones asked if this would put light on Syria or if it would instead put light on the VR headsets. Al Kallas eventually decided that the technology would steal the focus away from the goal of the installation. Likewise, there were points where it would have been easier to simply have a film showing, followed by scholarly discussion of migration trends in Northern Europe. However, when prompted to explain how this fit with the purpose of the event, the organizers could hear that their description of a film screening and scholarly discussion left out both the displaced Syrians and natural-born Lithuanians. The Joker is also responsible for ensuring that actors are listening to each other – an ethical action "undertaken with a spirit of mutual respect void of goals to marginalize or otherwise suppress competing voices" to borrow from the definition in the introduction of this volume (Bodie et al., Chapter 1).

The Joker role facilitated the process by encouraging artist and organizers to listen for how others were attempting to contribute to the goals of the installation. When actual or potential miscommunication arose, the Joker encouraged collaborators to listen for the contributions that others were making. For example, when potential conflict arose because of differences between low- and high-context communication, Jones, in the role of the Joker, was able to question whether blunt, low-context assertions were personal attacks and whether polite high-context equivocations were acceptance. Boal's Joker played an important role in the cross-cultural communication necessary to bring this project into existence. In the following section, we transition from the process to the performance, exploring how the installation focused on the shared precarity of displaced Syrians and natural-born Lithuanians.

Performance analysis: listening as an agential act

Collectively, the many elements of *Light on Syria* combine to form what Jan Cohen-Cruz (2010) would deem an "engaged performance." The term surpasses mere description to delineate a group of performative practices aimed at facilitating dialogue between artist and participants. As Cohen-Cruz (2010) elucidated, "The term 'engaged' foregrounds relationships at the heart of making art with such aspirations, and dependence on a genuine exchange between artist and community such that the one is changed by the other" (p. 3). The emphasis here lies with mutual transformation on the part of both artist and participants for the purpose of broadly defined communal growth. At first glance, Al Kallas's intended aim – namely to reveal the shared precarity of displaced Syrians and natural-born Lithuania's – requires greater transformation on the part of the audience-participants. Yet scholars in the parallel field of applied theatre practice have long hypothesized and critiqued the impact of testimony on refugee-artists.

Applied theatre scholar-practitioner James Thompson (2009) contended that trauma studies extolling the virtue of testimony as well as a slippage as to what constitutes trauma have created an "imperative to tell" (p. 56; See also Chapter 12). Most evident in the trauma studies of psychiatrist Dori Laub (1995) is the imperative to tell details of a belief that survivors:

> ... need to *tell* and thus to come to *know* one's story, unimpeded by the ghosts from the past against which one has to protect oneself. One has to know one's buried truth in order to be able to live one's life. (p. 63, italics original)

While narrative therapy and testimony have proven useful for many, Thompson questions the universality of this statement. What works for one individual in one cultural context may prove wholly unproductive for another.

To counter this imperative, Thompson proposed not a shift away from storytelling altogether but a greater respect for culturally specific responses. The multi-media nature of *Light on Syria* offers another alternative. *Sea of Sorrow, Sea of Hope* relies heavily on storytelling. Organizers even invited the documentary's protagonist to the performance, with the intention of giving Manal the opportunity to retell her story in person and observe the reception of the film. In contrast, the photographic display and four figures eschewed the spoken word in favor of nonverbal communication. Although Al Kallas still shared a story, this visual take on the refugee experience leaves greater space for interpretation. The photographs of destroyed buildings set against the hotel's crumbling walls encouraged viewers to draw connections to their current location. Meanwhile, the quotidian clothing and blurred expressions, illustrated in Figure 5.3, invited the audience to superimpose their own stories on the figures. Some viewed the figures and recall Manal's struggles; others the story of Alan Kurdi as told and retold on news and social media.

Still others began to draw connections to their own experiences and that of family members and loved ones as quickly became apparent in conversations between the docents – Al Kallas's Syrian friends – and the many Lithuanian-born audience members. After viewing the destruction in Syria through the photographs, audience members would often speak to the docents of the Second World War and the subsequent Soviet occupation: the destruction of the war, the forced collectivization, the deportation of relatives. In listening to audience members, the docents assumed a very different role than that normally reserved for externally displaced persons: not victim/testifier, but helper/witness.

Externally displaced persons are often required to re-enact victimhood to obtain and maintain residency in a new country. In her analysis of bureaucratic performance, applied theatre scholar-practitioner Alison Jeffers (2008) asserted, "all asylum seekers are assumed to be lying unless they can prove otherwise. In the absence of material evidence, one of the few ways to do this is through a convincing and compelling narrative of persecution, meaning that asylum seekers are often forced to perform the role of victim in order to expedite their case for asylum" (p. 218). Though Jeffers's focus lies in the UK, other scholars have noted similar trends globally (e.g., Balfour et al., 2015; Thompson, 2009). Such bureaucratic performances, together with the theatrical penchant for drama, contribute to "an aesthetic of injury" (Salverson, 1999). While the performance of victimhood may at present prove necessary in judicial and legal settings, replications of such narratives in art perpetuate the othering and objectification of externally displaced persons.

"If, however," Salverson (1999) argued, "participants learn to use the medium of theatre deliberately, to create their own images and play with them consciously and willingly, then artists, participants, and audience members might remain present, seeing and being seen, hearing and being heard" (para. 17). The interaction between Syrian docents and Lithuanian-born audience did exactly this. Al Kallas cast his Syrian friends in a position of power – the docent – capable of guiding enquiry but not an object of direct scrutiny. Docents could choose to share parts of their story with audience-participants or keep the conversation focused on the photographs. Audience-participants encouraged to see Syrian docents as more than mere victims, in turn, became more comfortable sharing their own stories – or those of the previous generation.

While difficult to ascertain a change in either party, the relationship shows a marked difference from that between refugee-testifier-victim and audience-witness-helper. Through dialogue, both parties had opportunities to listen and be heard, creating a relationship of mutual exchange rather than one-way assistance.

As Beard (2009) contended in his call for an ethic of listening, a model for ethical listening must explore choices beyond the simple dichotomy of listening or not listening. Beard summarized the five choices we make in our listening practices: (1) to listen individually, (2) to listen selectively, (3) not to listen, (4) to listen together, and (5) to listen to each other.

Audience members listened individually to the story of Manal through the film screening, however, as Beard (2009) noted "no one can read the cultural studies literature without some suspicion that listening alone is anti-communal" (p. 18). Through the multi-media nature of the installation, audience members could choose to listen selectively. The choice to focus selectively on aspects of the installation even when they wailed against "the soundscape, the ideologies, that we find safe" encouraged "a kind of parasocial openness to those different from us and our communities" (Beard, 2009, p. 19). The choice not to listen, Beard noted, is ethically unclear – Beard compared this to the choice of listening or not listening to a Holocaust denier. Applied to the context of *Light on Syria*, the choice may be framed as listening or not listening to stereotypes of migrants, refugees, and externally displaced persons. With the looped screening of *Sea of Sorrow, Sea of Hope*, audience members and docents were positioned to listen together to the story of Manal, which allowed both audience members and docents to listen to each other. Beard framed this as the final choice, which can only happen after the cultivation of a listening self through the prior choices to listen individually, selectively, not to listen, and to listen together. On a microlevel, the choice to listen to each other underscores the potential for externally displaced persons to contribute to their new communities. That is, the choice to listen to each other moves from clearly defined dyadically dependent roles such as refugee-testifier-victim and audience-witness-helper and instead allows for a constantly changing relationship in which roles are donned, shared, and resisted.

This relationship of mutual exchange again recalls Cohen-Cruz's (2010) engaged performance, which she connects to the practice of call-and-response. Building on the work of African and African American studies scholar Geneva Smitherman, Cohen-Cruz (2010, p. 2) highlighted both the political and social nature of such work:

> The 'call-and-response' dynamic of engaged art brings a community together for both political and spiritual reasons. Political because it provides a way for a group of any status to participate in a public discourse about issues that affect their lives; spiritual because a purpose is embedded in the process and goal of such work that goes beyond material results an out day-to-day existence. Both the political and the spiritual provide a model of how we live together, suggesting something bigger than our individual selves.

With *Light on Syria*, the model of "how we live together" became grounded in shared listening. We conclude the chapter, considering the efficacy and ethics of such listening to better support future arts-based peacebuilding efforts.

Listening for alternative narratives

Returning to the folk tale Jones heard when first moving to Lithuania, the story of Eglė the Queen of Serpents serves as a cultural backdrop for Lithuania's broader relationship with externally displaced persons. As a representative anecdote, the folk story warns against the easy acceptance of foreigners who come from across the sea. Yet the story holds out a promise alongside its warning – the promise of strengthening relationships with one's neighbors, both near and far. The story does not memorialize Eglė's brothers for killing her husband. Rather, Eglė and her descendants, the fruits of foreign influence, are the heroes of the story. Oak, ash, birch, quaking aspen, and spruce are held in high esteem. While the story does warn of recklessly embracing all others, it also speaks to the potential benefits of performance, listening, and community engagement.

With this in mind, we offer two things that practitioners could carry forward from this project. The first is the efficacy of the Joker role from Boals' work in facilitating listening during potentially fraught collaborations. The second is that listening may pose an antidote to the aesthetic of injury by allowing both performers and audiences alike to exist beyond the dichotomous tripartite roles of refugee-testifier-victim and audience-witness-helper. We have argued that Boal's Joker fulfills the promise of drama in classical Greece by bringing to light new possibilities in otherwise intractable situations. Practitioners could bring the role of Joker into future collaborations by listening for alternative narratives through the three tasks of the Joker: explaining the rules of the game, correcting errors, and prompting participants to keep playing. From the Joker's task of explaining the rules of the game, practitioners may encourage listening for alternative narratives by focusing not only on what collaborators say, but also on how and why they said it. There is also wisdom in attending what is left unsaid. From the Joker's task of error correction, practitioners may encourage listening for alternative narratives by making space for collaborators to listen for the words of those who might know a little more than themselves. Finally, from the Joker's task of prompting everyone to keep playing the game, practitioners may encourage listening for alternative narratives by reminding them of their shared goal.

The installation itself also offers alternative narratives. The multi-media event allowed audience members and performers alike to navigate between the five listening choices outlined by Beard: (1) to listen individually, (2) to listen selectively, (3) not to listen, (4) to listen together, and (5) to listen to each other. The last choice carries ethical value in community-engaged and peacebuilding practices. In contrast to existing narratives, which often oversimplify the relationship between performer and audience, testifier and witness, victim and helper, the act of listening to each other provides alternate, arguably more complex narratives. As Al Kallas intended, natural-born Lithuanians come to see some of their own story in that of externally displaced Syrians. Through listening, the Syrian docents assist in this process and assume a more agential role than refugees and asylum seekers are often allowed. Future practitioners may consider how incorporating similar listening together could help create more complex stories and, in doing so, rehearse more desirable relationships between externally displaced individuals and others of their communities.

While it would be pleasant to think that this installation provided the groundwork for a new era of cooperation in Lithuania, 2021 saw Lithuania building detention centers and refugee camps along the Belarusian border. Lithuanian officials claim that Belarusian Dictator Lukashenko encouraged people to fly to Minsk and then travel to neighboring EU states. However, as Thompson (2009) argued, perhaps what this piece offers is the affect of those involved – particularly the affect of beauty that can arguably be seen in the coming together of two perspectives. Thus, the installation foregrounded the significant role of listening as an ethical activity (Beard, 2009).

Note

1 Low- and high-context communication are connected to low- and high-context culture, from the work of Anthropologist E. T. Hall. Low-context cultures engage in communication that explicitly conveys information through verbal messages without relying on assumed contextual knowledge shared by communication partners, while high-context cultures engage in communication that implicitly conveys information by relying on content from either the physical surroundings or internal to the relationship between individuals (McKay-Semmler, 2017).

References

Bach, C. (2018). *No one should have to risk their life to reunite with their family.* UNHCR: The UN Refugee Agency. Nordic and Baltic Countries. https://www.unhcr.org/neu/16784-no-one-risk-life-reunite-family.html

Balfour, M., Bundy, P., Burton, B., Dunn, J., & Woodrow, N. (2015). *Applied theatre: Resettlement - Drama, refugees and resilience.* Bloomsbury Methuen Drama.

Beard, D. (2009). A broader understanding of the ethics of listening: Philosophy, cultural studies, media studies and the ethical listening subject. *International Journal of Listening, 23,* 7–20. 10.1080/10904010802591771

Boal, A. (1985). *Theatre of the oppressed* (C. A. McBride & M. L. McBride, Trans.) Theatre Communications Group.

Boal, A. (2002). *Games for actors and non-actors* (2nd ed; A. Jackson, Trans.). Routledge.

Burke, K. (1969). *A grammar of motives* (1st ed.). The University of California Press.

Burke, K. (1973). *The philosophy of literary form: Studies in symbolic action* (3rd ed.). The University of California Press.

Cohen-Cruz, J. (2010). *Engaging performance: Theatre as call and response.* Routledge.

Crick, N. (2015). *Rhetoric & power: The drama of classical Greece*. The University of South Carolina Press.

Jeffers, A. (2008). Dirty truth: Personal narrative, victimhood and participatory theatre work with people seeking asylum. *Research in Drama Education, 13*, 217–221. 10.1080/13569780802054919

Jones, A. C. (2021). Juozas Urbsšys and the case for Lithuanian Independence. *Southern Communication Journal, 86*(1), 46–57. 10.1080/1041794x.2020.1854335

Jones, A. C., & Kungienė, E. (2022). Intercultural communication pedagogy in Lithuania: Listening to viewpoints. In M. C. Minielli, M. N. Lukacovic, S. A. Samoilenko, M. R. Finch, & D. Buecker (Eds.), *Communication theory and application in post-socialist contexts*. Rowman & Littlefield.

Laub, D. (1995). Truth and testimony: The process and the struggle. In C. Caruth (Ed.), *Trauma: Explorations in memory* (pp. 61–75). John Hopkins University Press.

LCC International University. (2018). *Middle East scholars*. https://lcc.lt/about-lcc/middle-east-scholars

LCC International University. (2021). *30 years together*. https://lcc.lt/assets/lcc-facts (en).pdf

McKay-Semmler, K. L. (2017). High- and low-context cultures. In Y. Y. Kim (Ed.), *The international encyclopedia of intercultural communication*. Wiley. https://onlinelibrary.wiley.com/doi/full/10.1002/9781118783665.ieicc0106

Salverson, J. (1999). Transgressive storytelling or an aesthetic of injury: Performance, pedagogy and ethics. *Theatre Research in Canada/Recherches théâtrales Au Canada, 20*(1). https://journals.lib.unb.ca/index.php/TRIC/article/view/7096

Steinke, C. (2020, February 15). Shadowing the light on Syria. *International University Chronicle*. https://iuc.news/2020/02/15/shadowing-the-light-on-syria/

Thompson, J. (2009). *Performance affects: Applied theatre and the end of effect*. Palgrave Macmillan.

6

PATTERNS OF ENGAGEMENT

Identifying associations between listening styles and community-news consumption

Eike Mark Rinke[1], Patricia Moy[2], and María E. Len-Ríos[3]

[1]SCHOOL OF POLITICS AND INTERNATIONAL STUDIES, UNIVERSITY OF LEEDS
[2]DEPARTMENT OF COMMUNICATION, UNIVERSITY OF WASHINGTON
[3]HUBBARD SCHOOL OF JOURNALISM AND MASS COMMUNICATION, UNIVERSITY OF MINNESOTA

It is a simple truth that the world around us is complex, and the increasing intricacies of media ecosystems have only posed obstacles to better understanding how individuals navigate their sociopolitical environments (Bail, 2021). Whereas half a century ago, the media landscape was dominated by organized mass media, today's landscape is interactive and evolving, featuring a plethora of outlets with endless news streams and partisan media. From a normative standpoint, one can argue that greater access to information should increase democratic engagement (Dahl, 1989; Delli Carpini, 2004). After all, such access should afford individuals more opportunities to harness specific media channels that would allow them to engage with community issues and public affairs in general. Unfortunately, greater media access does not necessarily translate into such normatively desirable outcomes. Indeed, society today bears witness to heightened political polarization (Már, 2020; Pew Research Center, 2014), with problems attributed to individuals' unwillingness to talk or listen to those who hold dissonant views. Indeed, social media and technology have created echo chambers and tribes, ultimately eroding vital elements of the public sphere (Arora et al., 2022; North et al., 2021).

At a basic level, in today's hyper-mediated social world, "listening" to one's community involves attending to, interpreting, evaluating, and responding to messages from both mediated and non-mediated sources. Thus, our model of community engagement suggests an important distinction between *interpersonal engagement*, which involves "traditional" forms of listening to others, and *mediated engagement*, which captures the extent to which individuals turn to news media and attend to news about their community. This distinction is critical given longstanding discussions about the effects of mass versus interpersonal communication (e.g., Chaffee, 1982; Katz & Lazarsfeld, 1955) and more recent research illustrating the "differential gains" to be had by individuals who engage in both

DOI: 10.4324/9781003214465-6

interpersonal and mediated communication (Hardy & Scheufele, 2005). In short, to fully understand how people engage with media, research should attend also to how people engage with each other, and vice versa.

In the study presented in this chapter, we examine an array of news media consumption behaviors to determine whether a distinct pattern of community-oriented engagement with news exists. We then ask about the extent to which people's proclivity to use and pay attention to community news is related to their listening preferences. Put another way, we ask: Do people who report distinct "habits" of listening also report differential inclinations to engage with their community through the media?

Scholars have long noted the potential of listening to ameliorate problems arising at the interpersonal (e.g., Bodie & Denham, 2017), small-group (e.g., Bodie & Godwin, 2022), organizational (e.g., Macnamara, 2016), and societal levels (e.g., Bickford, 1996; Dobson, 2014). Regardless of the number or type of individuals impacted by a problem, engagement with that community of stakeholders requires listening, and listening is central to community formation (Purdy, 1991). And, yet, even with the consensus that listening is important, questions of exactly *how* listening relates to community engagement have, to our knowledge, largely escaped scholarly scrutiny. This chapter focuses on how tendencies to listen in particular ways relate to patterns of community news engagement in the context of the 2016 U.S. presidential election. Elections provide much grist for the scholarly mill as campaigns generate heightened levels of media coverage and increase the likelihood of interactions with others around particularly salient or contentious issues. We use a data set collected from a panel of U.S. adults who identify as Hispanic or Latino/a and who voted in the 2016 U.S. presidential election.

Our investigation is situated in the U.S. Latino/a community because, among those issues registered voters in the U.S. reported as "very important" in 2016 (Pew Research Center, 2016), immigration "emerged as the leading substantive issue of the campaign" (Jones, 2015). In addition, immigration became a salient issue given news media coverage of then presidential-candidate Trump's statements and position on the U.S. southern border with Mexico (e.g., Faris et al., 2017; Joshi, 2017). From the larger data set, we explore the association between interpersonal engagement (in this case: interpersonal listening) and mediated engagement (in this case: news-media consumption). We examine the extent to which individuals' specific listening styles, as defined in Bodie et al. (2013), relate to their use of community-news media and their attention to news content about their community.

Listening styles and mediated community engagement

Stemming from the Latin root *commūnitās,* the word community is often equated with kinship, sharing, fellowship, and social relationships. Whether geographically bound or diasporic in nature, or whether bound by profession, avocational interest, or identity, communities offer structures, frameworks, and guidelines through which individuals make sense of their world. As Bellah et al. (1985, p. 153) noted, communities offer "a context of meaning" that allows people to connect their aspirations and interests with the aspirations and interests of those closest to them, as well as the goals of a larger whole. Identifying these connections allows people to understand how their efforts contribute to a common good. Crucial to this process is communication, which creates and sustains community (Purdy, 1991). As some view it, only after individuals have learned to communicate with and accept one another do they become a community (Peck, 1987). This process of learning to communicate with one another includes speaking, by which individuals' ideas are shared, and listening, by which these ideas are interpreted. Put another way (Purdy, 1991, p. 60):

> what is attended to, how information is perceived, the interpretations that are created, the ideas that are remembered, and the response that is given, are all determined to a large degree by the community of which the listener is a member.

Communication and community are thus inextricably linked, as interactions beginning at the interpersonal level shape the community that emerges, and the very rules of this community, in turn, shape the interactions that ensue.

To make sense of the communities and the world around them, individuals attend to information with goals in mind. These goals are in place whether the information comes through media or via conversations with friends and family. In the context of mediated information, individuals process content through their level of attention to news and/or through their depth of processing (Eveland, 2002). Such cognitive elaboration links this mediated information with other pieces of information (gleaned from media or elsewhere) (Lin et al., 2022) and often reflects a strategy designed to cope with information the receiver deems incomplete, inaccurate, or confusing (Kosicki & McLeod, 1990).

Notably, today's media ecosystem, with its prevalence of social media and partisan media outlets, has complicated matters. With the proliferation and balkanization of media outlets, audiences have become increasingly fragmented. No longer faced with a limited array of outlets to which they can turn, they can actively avail themselves of content that resonates with their political beliefs and attitudes (Stroud, 2011; Van Aelst et al., 2017). In addition, search engines and algorithms create filter bubbles – or information ecosystems that have been personalized (Pariser, 2011) – that insulate individuals from potentially dissonant material and ultimately restrict the breadth of information to which individuals are exposed. In today's high-choice media ecosystem, messages are amplified and reverberate among like-minded individuals in echo chambers (Jamieson & Cappella, 2008) that fuel group polarization.

Regardless of how simple or complex the media ecosystem is, individuals may turn to and process mediated information with particular goals in mind. Decades of research in uses and gratifications scholarship have illustrated that media audiences do not merely passively receive messages. Rather, individuals' selection of media is often "goal-directed, purposive, and motivated" (Rubin, 2002, p. 527). Indeed, scholars have long identified individuals as motivated to engage with news media content, whether to learn about the latest political events (Blumler & McQuail, 1969) or to obtain nuggets of information for social interaction (Palmgreen & Rayburn, 1979). Research in the past half-century has confirmed this model of an active audience member whose motivations vary in contexts ranging from traditional media to social media (Whiting & Williams, 2013).

Of course, such motivations are only part of a larger array of factors – "prereception orientations" – that determine not only which individuals are more likely to be exposed to a message, but also how that message might impact them (McLeod et al., 2009). These motivations, which include the need for information, can involve cognitive, structural, and/or cultural orientations. For instance, cognitive orientations that relate to individuals' level of democratic engagement can shape news consumption patterns. Individuals who are more interested in politics or those who feel they are more capable of effecting change are more likely to turn to news content (see Delli Carpini, 2004). In addition, demographic characteristics that are either innate (e.g., race and ethnicity) or structural in nature (based on, for example, education or neighborhood of residence) can shape people's life experiences and the type of media content to which they turn. Similarly, worldviews and values can influence media consumption. Namely, compared to those who hold strong material values, individuals who express strong postmaterial values (e.g., political freedom and participation, helping others) are more likely to turn to news content (McLeod et al., 1998). In the political realm, values are inherently intertwined with partisanship, which in today's highly partisan media ecosystem, serves as a heuristic for news use.

Instrumental goals might similarly be in play when individuals engage in interpersonal discussions and listen to their interlocutors (Watson et al., 1995). In fact, listening styles and mediated engagement with one's community can both represent habitual responses to how communication gets processed and how meaning gets ascribed. In other words, individual-level listening dispositions may well be based on a set of core orientations that also underlie community engagement.

Research has traditionally conceptualized listening styles as "attitudes, beliefs, and predispositions about the how, where, when, who, and what of the information reception and encoding process" (Watson et al., 1995, p. 2). This early work identified four different dimensions, each involving a specific orientation. Listening might be *people-oriented*, which means that individuals' listening is driven by their concern for others. Put another way, people-oriented listening foregrounds care and concern, with individuals attempting to build rapport and establish common interests. Listening can also be *action-oriented*, often reflected in individuals' preferences for concise, well-organized presentations that are devoid of errors. When people engage in *content-oriented* listening, they pay attention to details presented and evaluate the information provided before passing judgment; these listeners are not averse to receiving complex information. Finally, *time-oriented* listeners are prone to engaging in efficient communications, partaking in brief or hasty interactions. To be clear, while these four listening styles represent different tendencies, they are not mutually exclusive, individuals rely on multiple styles depending on the situation (Imhof, 2004).

After finding evidence that the LSP-16, the original scale developed to measure listening styles, failed to produce robustly valid data (Bodie & Worthington, 2010; Williams et al., 2012), more recent scholarship (e.g., Bodie et al., 2013; Gearhart et al., 2014) has relabeled these four narrative listening styles as: *relational* (in which listeners build rapport and work to understand others' feelings); *analytical* (in which listeners withhold judgment and consider multiple sides of an issue); *task-oriented* (whereby the listeners work to ensure that their time is not being wasted); and *critical* (when listeners work to identify errors and inconsistencies).

How do these listening styles relate to engagement in one's community? Relational listening, which is motivated by an individual's desire to build relationships and connections, might be characterized as listening to or hearing out one's interlocutor to remain in a particular social system or to create connections among otherwise disconnected elements of the community. Individuals who engage in analytical listening might be most strongly motivated by their need to obtain information, engage in surveillance of the information environment, and attain a good epistemic (i.e., not necessarily social) understanding of one's community. Task-oriented listeners might be most strongly motivated to "get things done" and be pragmatic in their communication styles, striving to solve problems. This particular listening style may imply that the individual possesses an ego-centered orientation at odds with a general concern for one's community. In other words, task-oriented listeners may focus their attention on community information relevant to addressing and solving their own problems, perhaps at the expense of learning about or dealing with issues that impact the community at large. Finally, motivated to find errors and inconsistencies in information they receive, critical listeners may be agnostic as to whether the information is oriented toward the community, and thus it is unclear whether they are any more or less inclined to engage with their community via news media.

With these orientations toward information that is communicated via media and interpersonal discussions, our study empirically examined three research questions related to interpersonal engagement with one's community (via listening) and mediated community engagement:

RQ1: To what extent can we identify patterns of engagement with community news?

RQ2: Does community news media use relate to interpersonal listening styles?

RQ3: Does community news attention relate to interpersonal listening styles?

Methods

To examine how patterns of community-news use and attention related to preferences for specific listening styles, we drew on data from a single wave of an online Qualtrics consumer panel survey fielded December 7 to 17, 2016. The panel comprised adults self-identifying as Hispanic or Latino/a[1] who lived in the United States or its territories and had voted in the 2016 U.S. presidential election. Quotas were set to recruit an equal number of male and female participants as well as a variety of ethnicities (N = 720). The mean age of participants was 33.8 years (SD = 12.8), and just over half (50.3%) identified as female. Participants averaged just over three decades' of residence in the U.S. (M = 31.0, SD = 13.0) and were diverse in educational background (median education level = some college or an associate degree). Of the sample, 66.5% identified as Mexican American, 11% as Puerto Rican, 7% as Cuban American, 3% as multiethnic Hispanic, and 2.1% as Dominican; the rest were divided among other Central, South American, and Spanish ethnicities.

As shown in Table 6.1, our sample reflected the Hispanic population in terms of gender breakdown. It also generally resembled the Hispanic population in terms of Latino identification, though it included a slightly larger proportion of Mexican Americans and Cuban Americans. However, our sample was more educated than the Hispanic population at large, where more than three in five had earned at most a high-school education or equivalent.

Interpersonal listening styles

We measured listening styles using an eight-item short form of the Listening Styles Profile-Revised, the LSP-R8 (Rinke, 2016; see also Bodie & Worthington, 2017). This short form allows for the self-report measurement of listening styles in general-population surveys. To the best of our knowledge, the survey we draw on in this chapter was the first general-population survey ever that implemented a validated measure of interpersonal listening styles.

The LSP-R8 consists of eight items, each using a seven-point Likert scale ("strongly disagree" to "strongly agree") to operationalize four dimensions of individuals' listening styles. A confirmatory factor analysis showed that the theoretical four-factor model with correlated factors fit the data well, $\chi^2(14)$ = 30.023,

TABLE 6.1 Sample demographics and Latino population

	Sample of Hispanic voters (%)	Census data of Hispanic voters in 2016 (%)	Census data of Hispanic population (%)
Education			
Less than high school	2.8	N/A	31.5
High-school graduate/GED	19.3		30.6
Some college or associate degree	45.4		21.5
Four-year degree	23.3		11.1
Advanced degree	9.2		5.3
Latino identification			
Mexican	66.5	N/A	60.0
Puerto Rican	11.0		10.8
Cuban	7.0		3.8
Other Latino	15.5		24.0
Gender			
Male	49.8	45.0	50.2
Female	50.3	50.0	49.8

Note: Census data of Hispanic voters in 2016 come from the Current Population Survey (U.S. Census Bureau, 2016a). Census data of Hispanic population come from the Current Population Survey, Annual Social and Economic Supplement (U.S. Census Bureau, 2016b, 2016c).

$p = .008$, CFI = .989, RMSEA = .040, 90% CI [.020, .060], SRMR = .023. Estimated correlations among latent variables were as follows: RL–AL, .57; RL–TOL, .00; RL–CL, .41; AL–TOL, .02; AL–CL, .33; CL–TOL, .28. For all analyses reported below, item responses for each factor (two items each) were averaged. Table 6.2 reports descriptive statistics for the four resulting two-item listening style scales.

The items that measure *relational listening* emphasize empathy and concern for others' feelings, emotions, and moods ("When listening to others, I am mainly concerned with how they are feeling" and "I listen to understand the emotions

TABLE 6.2 Descriptive statistics for listening styles (LSP-R8)

	Mean	SD	Reliability
Relational listening (RL)	5.02	1.23	.65
Analytical listening (AL)	5.52	1.20	.77
Task-oriented listening (TOL)	4.84	1.44	.72
Critical listening (CL)	5.22	1.20	.77

Note: Cell entries are the arithmetic mean (Mean), the standard deviation (SD), and the internal consistency reliability as measured by the Spearman-Brown Coefficient (Reliability). All scales ranged from 1 ("strongly disagree") to 7 ("strongly agree").

and mood of the speaker"). *Analytical listening*, reflected in one's hearing others out to secure additional information before reaching a conclusion, was tapped by the following items: "I wait until all the facts are presented before forming judgments and opinions" and "I fully listen to what a person has to say before forming any opinions." *Task-oriented listening*, a general desire to have efficient and effective interactions when listening to others, was measured by asking respondents about their level of agreement or disagreement with the following items: "I am impatient with people who ramble on during conversations" and "I find it difficult to listen to people who take too long to get their ideas across." The final two items gauged *critical listening*, the general tendency to assess and evaluate the accuracy and consistency of messages received in conversation: "I often catch errors in other speakers' logic" and "I tend to naturally notice errors in what other speakers say."

News use and attention

To identify types of news users within the U.S. Latino population (RQ1), respondents were asked, "In general, how often do you … : Watch local TV news; Watch national network TV news (CBS, ABC, or NBC); Watch cable TV (e.g., CNN, FOX News, MSNBC); Read information and news from social media; Watch local Spanish-language news; Watch national Spanish-language TV news (e.g., Noticiero Univisión); Read a local English-language newspaper; Read a local Spanish-language newspaper; Read a national newspaper (e.g., *USA Today, New York Times, The Washington Post*); and read magazines (online or in print)?" Responses to each item were measured on a 10-point scale (1 = "never"; 10 = "all the time"). A separate item captured participants' *attention to community news* by asking them, "In general, how much attention do you pay to: News about your community?" This item also utilized a 10-point response scale (1 = "no attention at all"; 10 = "a great deal of attention").

Analytic procedures

We first explored whether U.S. Latino news users form distinct groups that vary in their patterns of news engagement across different news media, including community-news channels (RQ1). This was done following a two-step approach to cluster analysis that combines hierarchical and non-hierarchical (*K*-means) clustering for refined identification of groups from the data (see Hair et al., 2019, Ch. 7). In a first step, we used hierarchical cluster methods to identify the number of clearly distinct groups of Latino news users that could be recovered from the data. This number informed the second step of the analysis, in which we improved the clustering solution and classified each participant into one of the clusters (media user groups or "types") in a *K*-means partitioning of the data into the number of clusters, *K*, that was previously identified in the completely inductive first step. We then compared the news media use profiles of the identified types of Latino news-media users to see if they involved distinct patterns of engagement with community news.

We then examined how community news use (RQ2) and attention (RQ3) are associated with interpersonal listening styles. Corresponding with earlier findings (e.g., Bodie et al., 2013, p. 76), the four listening styles are correlated with each other to varying degrees. Because our analytical goal in this chapter is to identify the unique associations of each listening style with mediated community engagement, we first estimated the partial correlations of each individual listening style with the three community news engagement measures in our data; these estimates reflect the correlation that would be observed between the three forms of engagement and each listening style if the other listening styles did not vary. We then followed up on this analysis with a canonical linear discriminant analysis. This descriptive analysis goes back to the news-engagement clusters identified earlier to explore how well the identified Latino news-engagement clusters could be separated from each other based on the four listening styles. The survey questionnaire and analytical code used in this study are available on the Open Science Framework (https://dx.doi.org/10.17605/OSF.IO/XKBC4).

Results

To answer RQ1, whether distinct patterns of community news use exist in the U.S. Latino community, we followed the cluster-analysis approach previously described and generated a taxonomy of Latino news media users.[2] The results are shown in Figure 6.1.

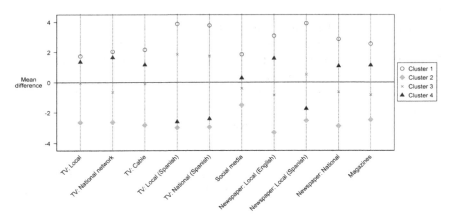

FIGURE 6.1   News-Use Profile Plot for Four Types of Latino Media Users (Based on K-means Cluster Analysis)

Note: Cluster 1 ("Universally engaged," *n* = 177), Cluster 2 ("Universally disengaged," *n* = 197), Cluster 3 ("Community-engaged," *n* = 178), Cluster 4 ("Mainstream-engaged," *n* = 164).

Despite some ambiguity, the first, fully inductive step of this analysis suggested that four clusters best represent the news-media use-patterns of U.S. Latinos in our sample. In the second step, we specified four clusters for non-hierarchical *K*-means clustering, classifying each survey participant into one of the four identified clusters. Following that, we computed for each participant how much they differed from the grand mean of each of our ten news-use variables, as an indicator of how much they differed from the average participant in the sample. Figure 6.1 plots how much each of the four identified clusters differed, on average, from the sample-wide grand mean on each of the ten news-use variables.

Based on the profiles represented by four different markers in Figure 6.1, we can identify four types of Latino news users. *Universally engaged users* (Cluster 1, circle) is the group of Latino individuals who most consistently expose themselves to news through each of the ten media channels included in the analysis. They are "news buffs," and their media diet includes much use of Spanish-language newspapers and TV news, which they use more than any of the three other clusters of news users. Their inverse consists of *universally disengaged users* (Cluster 2, diamond), who consistently tune out the news and consequently record the lowest average exposure to news use for each of the ten media channels included in the analysis. A more nuanced picture emerged for the final two types. *Community-engaged users* (Cluster 3, X) are characterized by slightly below-average exposure to news across channels, with an important exception: While not particularly engaged with general news media, they consume an above-average amount of community-news media (i.e., local Spanish-language news-papers and TV news) as well as national Spanish-language TV news. Of particular note is that their consumption of (English-language) local TV news is virtually indistinguishable from that of the entire sample. Finally, *mainstream-engaged users* (Cluster 4, triangle) are characterized by the inverse pattern of community-engaged news users: They show somewhat above-average use of non-community "mainstream" news media, but largely tune out community-news media. They follow the general-population discourse, but not so much the community-specific discourse provided by these latter media offerings.

In sum, this analysis shows that community-news use indeed *is* a distinct pattern of news use within the U.S. Latino community. Roughly a quarter of U.S. Latino individuals surveyed engaged with community news as part of a wider pattern of "news omnivorism," while about half of those surveyed hardly engaged with news from and about their community. Mainstream-engaged Latino news users seemed to act in a targeted manner, side-stepping Spanish-language community news, while universally disengaged Latino users generally avoided news of any kind. But community-engaged news users, which consti-tuted about a quarter of surveyed participants, could be characterized as engaging with community media in a targeted, specific manner, just like the mainstream-news user group – in particular, they exposed themselves to Spanish-language local TV news and Spanish-language local newspapers. Given the results of this cluster

TABLE 6.3 Partial correlations of listening styles with mediated community engagement

	Listening styles			
	Relational	Analytical	Task-oriented	Critical
Use of community news media				
Local Spanish-language TV news	.11 (.004)	.06 (.124)	−.13 (.001)	−.07 (.078)
Local Spanish-language newspapers	.09 (.017)	.02 (.596)	−.11 (.004)	−.03 (.463)
Attention to community news content	.09 (.024)	.16 (.000)	−.03 (.497)	.03 (.511)

Note: Cell entries are partial correlation coefficients controlling for the three respective other listening style dimensions, with *p*-values in parentheses.

analysis, we next focused on individuals' use of Spanish-language local TV news and Spanish-language local newspapers in a first step towards understanding the link between listening styles and use of "community media."

To answer RQ2 and RQ3, we first estimated partial correlations of the four listening styles with the use of community-news media (RQ2) and attention to community news (RQ3), while controlling for the other three listening styles.

As seen in Table 6.3, relational listening consistently exhibited a small, positive association with all three measures of mediated engagement. Specifically, Latino individuals who report being generally more inclined to listen to others with empathy and concern for others' feelings, emotions, and moods also tend to make greater use of various media to engage with their community. These media included Spanish-language TV news (*r* = .11) and newspapers (*r* = .09). The data also reveal a similar relational component to people's attention to community news (*r* = .09).

Analytical listening manifested slightly different relations with mediated engagement. It was positively related to paying attention to community news, but not to use of either reading Spanish-language newspapers or watching Spanish-language local TV news. In other words, as individuals who report a tendency to hear others out to get as much information as possible before forming a judgment, analytical Latino listeners do not differ statistically from those less inclined to engage in analytical listening in their use of specific community-oriented news media. However, they are more likely to engage with their community by paying greater attention to news about their community when they hear it.

Task-oriented listening, which is characterized by a tendency to listen "transactionally" and a preference for interactions to be efficient, was associated with less engagement with community-news media (Spanish-language newspapers and Spanish-language local TV news), but not with the degree of attention paid to news about the community. Notably, the partial correlation coefficients for task-oriented listening are in direct contrast to those for relational listening.

From this analysis, it would appear that the instrumental nature of task-oriented listening expresses itself in a tendency to avoid using Spanish-language local news media, but without translating into less attention to community news when one encounters it.. This pattern suggests that task-oriented listeners are just as interested as non-task-oriented listeners in attending to relevant community information, but they are less likely to use specifically community-oriented news media like Spanish-language local newspapers and TV news.

Finally, in contrast to the other three listening styles, critical listening was not statistically associated with mediated community engagement. The extent to which individuals report listening to others with the goal of evaluating the accuracy and consistency of what has been said does not appear to make a difference for the degree to which they engage with their community – either through their use of Spanish-language local media or through attention paid to news about their community.

While these broad correlational findings are instructive, we next examined more closely how people's engagement with community news was associated with their interpersonal listening orientations. To do so, we performed a descriptive canonical linear discriminant analysis, in which we treated the four clusters of news engagement found in our initial cluster analysis as a group variable and the four listening styles as variables discriminating the four clusters (i.e., "news-user types" or "news-engagement groups"). This analysis allowed us to assess the separability of the different patterns of Latino's news engagement based on how people tend to listen to others, giving more detailed insight into whether regular engagement with community news is associated with different listening styles. In other words, our goal in this analysis was to identify the relative contribution of the four listening-style variables to the separation of the four Latino news-engagement groups.

The four listening styles (relational, analytical, task-oriented, and critical) were entered concurrently in the discriminant function analysis. The linear equations performed well, with the first two linear discriminant functions accounting for almost all the variance between news engagement clusters (the first function for about 71%, the second for about 29%). According to Table 6.4, which shows the

TABLE 6.4 Standardized canonical discriminant function coefficients

	Function 1	Function 2
Relational	.68	−.48
Analytical	.19	.03
Task-oriented	−.61	−.72
Critical	.10	−.32

Note: Cell entries are standardized canonical discriminant function coefficients from canonical linear discriminant analysis separating four news use clusters as a function of listening styles. Function 3 was omitted as it accounted for a minimal proportion of the total variance in the discriminant scores, Wilk's $\lambda = 1$, $F(2, 710) = 0.08$, $p = .925$.

TABLE 6.5 Discriminant function values for each news engagement cluster

	Function 1	Function 2
Universally engaged (Cluster 1)	.29	.03
Universally disengaged (Cluster 2)	−.31	.04
Community-engaged (Cluster 3)	.05	.15
Mainstream-engaged (Cluster 4)	.01	−.24

Note: Cell entries are group means on canonical variables from canonical linear discriminant analysis separating four news use clusters as a function of listening styles. Function 3 again was omitted as it accounted for a minimal proportion of the total variance in the discriminant scores, Wilk's $\lambda = 1$, $F(2, 710) = 0.08$, $p = .925$.

standardized discriminant function coefficients (loadings) for these two functions, the dominant first discriminant function contrasts relational listening (.68) to task-oriented listening (−.61) in line with a zero-order analysis. The subordinate second function adds nuance to by further separating those with lower and higher scores across relational (−.48), task-oriented (−.72), and critical listening (−.32) from each other, but not analytical listening (.03). In all, two of the four listening styles, analytical listening and critical listening, have little discriminating ability for the four news-engagement groups.

Table 6.5 shows the group means on the canonical variables, giving some indication of how the four news-engagement clusters are separated by listening styles. The means on the first function show that the universally engaged and universally disengaged groups are separated farthest from each other by this function (.29 and −.31, respectively), which separates relational from task-oriented listeners. Thus, the relational–task-oriented contrast seen in the first function (Table 6.4) appears to be driven mostly by what we have labeled "universal engagement" with news, not by engagement with specifically community or mainstream news. The means on the second function indicate that the community-engaged and mainstream-engaged groups (.15 and −.24, respectively) separated farthest from each other on this function, though the contrast is not overly strong.

Finally, Table 6.6 displays the discriminating variable summaries for each of the four news-engagement groups. These data provide a direct look at the differences in average listening styles across the four news-engagement clusters. Specifically, where relational listening is concerned, community-engaged news consumers do not report engaging in relational listening as much as the universally and mainstream-engaged news consumers. They were, however, more likely than the universally disengaged to score highly on relational listening. This particular set of findings adds important nuance to the partial correlations presented in Table 6.3, whereby relational listening was positively related to all three measures of mediated engagement. It appears that these positive relationships are driven mostly by the universally engaged news consumers, not those who are focused on community news.

TABLE 6.6 News engagement cluster means for each listening style (LSP-R8)

	Mean (SD)	Universally Engaged (Cluster 1)	Universally Disengaged (Cluster 2)	Community-engaged (Cluster 3)	Mainstream-engaged (Cluster 4)
Relational	5.04 (0.23)	5.28	4.70	4.96	5.20
Analytical	5.52 (0.13)	5.69	5.33	5.48	5.59
Task-oriented	4.83 (0.24)	4.56	5.06	4.62	5.09
Critical	5.23 (0.11)	5.26	5.11	5.14	5.39
N		176	197	178	164

Note: Cell entries are the grand and group means on listening styles variables for four news engagement clusters, based on estimation sample from canonical linear discriminant analysis, with standard deviation for grand means in parentheses. All listening scales ranged from 1 ("strongly disagree") to 7 ("strongly agree").

In contrast, community-news consumers were somewhat less analytical than the universally and mainstream-engaged in their listening style. In other words, analytical motives play a stronger role in general news engagement than in engagement with community news specifically.

The greatest differences between news-engagement clusters emerged in the case of task-oriented listening. A comparison of the community- and mainstream-engaged news clusters indicates the greatest contrast, with the former much less likely to be predisposed to task-oriented listening. However, the relatively low mean levels of task-oriented listening were similar for community-engaged news consumers and the universally engaged. At the same time, mainstream news consumers were almost as task-oriented as the universally disengaged in their listening. Further illuminating Table 6.3, which revealed community-news engagement to be positively associated with relational listening and negatively with task-oriented listening, the findings shown in Table 6.6 indicate that a less transactional/goal-oriented approach to others predicts a pattern of engagement with primarily community news as well as universal engagement with news.

Finally, the group means for critical listening indicate great levels of similarity across the four news-engagement clusters, although use of community-news media is associated with a somewhat less critical approach in listening to others.

Discussion

Against a backdrop of media balkanization, increased access to information, and deepening societal cleavages, talking "across the aisle" has become fraught as individuals attend to information that resonates with their own viewpoints. We examined how individuals' listening styles are associated with their use of specific types of media and how they might attend to news about their community. Analyzing survey data collected from a national sample of Latino voters shortly after the 2016 U.S. presidential election, we showed how examinations of individuals' community engagement can be enriched by the simultaneous study of mediated and interpersonal engagement (in this case, listening to others). A multidimensional view of engagement highlights myriad ways in which interest in community life can be piqued, acted upon, and potentially sustained by individual motivations, interpersonal relationships, language and culture, and media messages, as well as the interactions among them.

We found, first, that news media use among Latino respondents clustered into distinct patterns. At the extreme ends were the universally disengaged and the universally engaged users, individuals who, respectively formed the groups with the least and the most use of all media types for news consumption. Between these extremes, the mainstream engaged showed an above-average use of English-language news media, while the community engaged were above-average consumers of Spanish-language local and national news media. Our cluster analysis indicated great variance in the degree to which Latino individuals engage with news about their own community, following a pattern of either community-specific or more general news attention. We thus showed that selective community-news use is a distinct pattern of news use among U.S. Latinos. Future research should replicate this in a more nationally representative sample as well as in other communities.

Second, we examined how interpersonal listening styles relate to community-news use. Our data illustrate how different listening styles are indeed associated with specific patterns in how people use community-news media. Specifically, Latino/a individuals who report higher tendencies toward relational listening also used (Spanish-language) community-news media more. Conversely, more transactional, task-oriented listeners were consistently less likely to use media that would present news specific to their community, perhaps because of the extra effort that may be required, lack of Spanish-language proficiency, and/or lack of felt community connection to Spanish-language news media. These and other mechanisms should be tested in future empirical work and theory building.

Interpersonal listening styles also relate to community-news attention, but these patterns of association differ slightly from how the same styles are related to the use of Spanish-language news media. Namely, relational and analytical listening both predicted greater attention to community news, whereas task-oriented and critical listening tendencies did not appear to be related to attention.

Why would analytical listening be related to how much *attention* individuals pay to community news, but not their *use* of community-news media? This differential finding might stem from the primarily cognitive approach to their community taken by analytical listeners, who tend to engage with as much information as possible before forming judgments. While the requirements of this approach may be satisfied by paying extra attention to mainstream media, relational listeners may be driven by more social-moral motivations and a desire to connect, which may push them to also turn more often to community-news media. The extra effort needed to follow community-news media compared to just generally paying attention to community news (regardless of medium) might also explain why task-oriented listeners are less likely to use community-news media but are *not* any less likely to follow community news in general. In a transactional approach to one's community, it might just be "cost-effective" to pay attention to news about the community when incidentally exposed to it, but it might seem prohibitively costly to adapt, and perhaps extend, one's news media repertoire just to follow the community.

With these general relationships emerging between listening styles (here, a reflection of interpersonal engagement) and community-news use and attention, it is important to provide some caveats. First, although our survey items on listening styles and news use and attention were framed broadly to elicit general tendencies, it is very possible that the timing of the survey itself – on the heels of a highly contentious election that was still quite salient – may have elicited responses grounded in more recent, contextual behaviors (Tourangeau et al., 2000). In other words, respondents' reported levels of using community-news media may more closely resemble campaign-related patterns of mediated engagement than such levels of use during a politically routine period.

Second, while the survey overall measured the thoughts, attitudes, and behaviors of Latino voters, and while many measures can be adopted wholesale into surveys of other groups, others might not be so easily transferable. In particular, because use of Spanish-language television and newspapers were part of the items analyzed in the fully inductive cluster analyses, it is unclear what specific community-oriented media news consumers who speak only English would use. Regardless, while community engagement, mediated or not, can take many forms and involve multiple tongues, in our view, language can serve as a useful, conservative proxy to indicate actual engagement with a community centered around that language.

Overall, this study uncovered clear differences in the patterns of mediated community engagement within the U.S. Latino community. It also uncovered links between interpersonal listening styles and the amount of mediated community engagement that warrant further investigation. Specifically, the link between relational listening styles and community-news engagement suggests a systematic affinity between the two. This highlights the social-moral and social-belonging dimension of (mediated) community engagement: Engaging specifically and systematically with one's community, even in mediated forms, has a specifically relational aspect to it. In this sense, community engagement emerges as a "labor of love" that stands in opposition to engagement that is more transactional and instrumental in nature. Two key findings underscore this relationship. First, mediated community engagement, captured empirically in this study by the tendency to consume local Spanish-language newspapers and TV news, *generally* is lower for task-oriented listeners in the Latino community. Second, *selective* mediated community engagement (i.e., consuming community news and not mainstream news) appears to be less attractive to task-oriented, transactional listeners, too. In other words, people who take a non-transactional approach to connecting with others around them will be more likely to tune into their community, *even if they otherwise avoid the news.*

In all, this study shows that different patterns of mediated community engagement appear related to different approaches to interpersonal relationships as expressed by different general listening styles. That mediated community engagement *overall* appears to be relationally and socially oriented illustrates that community media may not only be serving an informational function (one they normatively are expected to serve), but also a social one. Such a finding reminds us that, contrary to the traditional view that political engagement is grounded only in issues of substance, information that serves to build connections and foster cohesion may be equally compelling.

Notes

1 As an inclusion criterion, the survey asked respondents whether they identified as "Hispanic or Latino/a." To simplify our references to group membership, we will use "Hispanic" or a version of "Latino/a."
2 We first performed two types of fully inductive agglomerative hierarchical cluster analysis, one using the average-linkage and the other using the Ward agglomeration method (using Euclidian distance and squared Euclidian distance as the distance measure, respectively), to identify the number of news media user clusters (or "user types") in the U.S. Latino sample. Following these analyses, we inspected the respective dendrogram and used the Caliński–Harabasz pseudo-F and Duda–Hart Je(2)/Je(1) indices, two stopping rules that have been shown to allow for valid cluster recovery (Milligan & Cooper, 1985), for solutions of up to 15 clusters to find the "best" number of clusters (i.e., Latino-news media user types). The general practice for deciding the number of groups based on the Duda–Hart stopping-rule table is to find one of the largest Je(2)/Je(1) values that corresponds to a low pseudo-T-squared value with much larger T-squared for adjacent cluster solutions. This strategy, combined with the results from the Caliński–Harabasz and dendrogram results, especially for the Ward cluster analysis, indicated that a four-group solution is optimal for the data analyzed here.

References

Arora, S. D., Singh, G. P., Chakraborty, A., & Maity, M. (2022). Polarization and social media: A systematic review and research agenda. *Technological Forecasting and Social Change, 183,* Article 121942. 10.1016/j.techfore.2022.121942

Bail, C. (2021). *Breaking the social media prism: How to make our platforms less polarizing.* Princeton University Press.

Bellah, R. N., Madsen, R., Sullivan, W. M., Swidler, A., & Tipton, S. M. (1985). *Habits of the heart: Individualism and commitment in American life.* University of California Press.

Bickford, S. (1996). *The dissonance of democracy: Listening, conflict, and citizenship.* Cornell University Press.

Blumler, J. G., & McQuail, D. L. (1969). *Television in politics: Its uses and influence.* University of Chicago Press.

Bodie, G. D., & Denham, J. P. (2017). Listening in(to) close relationships. In M. M. Stoltz, K. P. Sodowsky & C. M. Cates (Eds.), *Listening across lives* (pp. 41–61). Kendall Hunt.

Bodie, G. D., & Godwin, P. (2022). On the limits of listening for bridging divides and cross-cultural understanding. In L. M. Chao & C. Wang (Eds.), *Communication across differences: Negotiating identity, privilege, and marginalization in the 21st century* (pp. 225–243). Cognella.

Bodie, G. D., & Worthington, D. (2010). Revisiting the Listening Styles Profile (LSP-16): A confirmatory factor analytic approach to scale validation and reliability estimation. *International Journal of Listening, 24,* 69–88. 10.1080/10904011003744516

Bodie, G. D., & Worthington, D. L. (2017). Listening Styles Profile-Revised (LSP-R). In D. L. Worthington & G. D. Bodie (Eds.), *The sourcebook of listening research* (pp. 402–409). Wiley. 10.1002/9781119102991.ch42

Bodie, G. D., Worthington, D. L., & Gearhart, C. C. (2013). The Listening Styles Profile-Revised (LSP-R): A scale revision and evidence for validity. *Communication Quarterly, 61*(1), 72–90. 10.1080/01463373.2012.720343

Chaffee, S. H. (1982). Mass media and interpersonal channels: Competitive, convergent, or complementary? In G. Gumpert & R. Cathcart (Eds.), *Inter/media: Interpersonal communication in a media world* 2 nd ed., (pp. 57–77). Oxford University Press.

Dahl, R. A. (1989). *Democracy and its critics.* Yale University Press.

Delli Carpini, M. X. (2004). Mediating democratic engagement: The impact of communications on citizens' involvement in political and civic life. In L. L. Kaid (Ed.), *Handbook of political communication research* (pp. 395–434). Lawrence Erlbaum Associates.

Dobson, A. (2014). *Listening for democracy: Recognition, representation, reconciliation.* Oxford University Press.

Eveland, W. P., Jr. (2002). News information processing as mediator of the relationship between motivations and political knowledge. *Journalism & Mass Communication Quarterly, 79*(1), 26–40. 10.1177/107769900207900103

Faris, R., Roberts, H., Etling, B., Bourassa, N., Zuckerman E., & Benkler, Y. (2017). *Partisanship, propaganda, and disinformation: Online media and the 2016 U.S. presidential election.* Berkman Klein Center. https://cyber.harvard.edu/publications/2017/08/mediacloud

Gearhart, C. C., Denham, J. P., & Bodie, G. D. (2014). Listening as a goal-directed activity. *Western Journal of Communication, 78*(5), 668–684. 10.1080/10570314.2014.910888

Hair, J. F., Black, W. C., Babin, B. J., & Anderson, R. E. (2019). *Multivariate data analysis* (8th ed.). Cengage.

Hardy, B. W., & Scheufele, D. A. (2005). Examining differential gains from internet use: Comparing the moderating role of talk and online interactions. *Journal of Communication, 55*(1), 71–84. 10.1111/j.1460-2466.2005.tb02659.x

Imhof, M. (2004). Who are we as we listen? Individual listening profiles in varying contexts. *International Journal of Listening, 18*(1), 36–45. 10.1080/10904018.2004.10499061

Jamieson, K. H., & Cappella, J. N. (2008). *Echo chamber: Rush Limbaugh and the conservative media establishment.* Oxford University Press.

Jones, J. M. (2015). *One in five voters say immigration stance critical to vote.* https://news.gallup.com/poll/185381/one-five-voters-say-immigration-stance-critical-to-vote.aspx

Joshi, A. (2017, February 28). Donald Trump's border wall – An annotated timeline. *HuffPost*. https://www.huffpost.com/entry/donald-trumps-border-wall-an-annotated-timeline_b_58b5f363e4b02f3f81e44d7b

Katz, E., & Lazarsfeld, P. F. (1955). *Personal influence: The part played by people in the flow of mass communications*. Free Press.

Kosicki, G. M., & McLeod, J. M. (1990). Learning from political news: Effects of media images and information-processing strategies. In S. Kraus (Ed.), *Mass communication and political information processing* (pp. 69–83). Lawrence Erlbaum Associates.

Lin, X., Lachlan, K. A., & Spence, P. R. (2022). "I thought about it and I may follow what you said": Three studies examining the effects of elaboration and source credibility on risk behavior intentions. *Journal of International Crisis and Risk Communication Research, 5*(1), 9–28. 10.30658/jicrcr.5.1.2

Macnamara, J. (2016). *Organizational listening: The missing essential in public communication*. Peter Lang.

Már, K. (2020). Partisan affective polarization: Sorting, entrenchment, and fortification. *Public Opinion Quarterly, 84*(4), 915–935. 10.1093/poq/nfaa060

McLeod, D. M., Kosicki, G. M., & McLeod, J. M. (2009). Political communication effects. In J. Bryant & M. B. Oliver (Eds.), *Media effects: Advances in theory and research* (3rd ed., pp. 228–251). Routledge.

McLeod, J. M., Sotirovic, M., & Holbert, R. L. (1998). Values as sociotropic judgments influencing communication patterns. *Communication Research, 25*(5), 453–485. 10.1177/009365098025005001

Milligan, G. W., & Cooper, M. C. (1985). An examination of procedures for determining the number of clusters in a data set. *Psychometrika, 50*(2), 159–179. 10.1007/BF02294245

North, S., Piwek, L., & Joinson, A. (2021). Battle for Britain: Analyzing events as drivers of political tribalism in Twitter discussions of Brexit. *Policy & Internet, 13*(2), 185–208. 10.1002/poi3.247

Palmgreen, P., & Rayburn, J. D., II. (1979). Uses and gratifications and exposure to public television: A discrepancy approach. *Communication Research, 6*(2), 155–180. 10.1177/009365027900600203

Pariser, E. (2011). *The filter bubble: What the internet is hiding from you*. Viking.

Peck, M. S. (1987). *The different drum: Community-making and peace*. Simon & Schuster.

Pew Research Center. (2014, June 12). *Political polarization in the general American public*. https://www.pewresearch.org/politics/2014/06/12/political-polarization-in-the-american-public/

Pew Research Center. (2016, July 7). *Top voting issues in 2016 election*. https://www.pewresearch.org/politics/2016/07/07/4-top-voting-issues-in-2016-election/

Purdy, M. (1991). Listening and community: The role of listening in community formation. *The Journal of the International Listening Association, 5*(1), 51–67. 10.1207/s1932586xijl0501_4

Rinke, E. M. (2016, May 14). *A general survey measure of individual listening styles: Short form of the Listening Styles Profile-Revised (LSP-R8)*. 71st Annual Conference of the American Association for Public Opinion Research, Austin, TX. https://www.mzes.uni-mannheim.de/d7/en/publications/presentation/a-general-survey-measure-of-individual-listening-styles-short-form-of-the-listening-styles-profile-revised-lsp-r8

Rubin, A. M. (2002). The uses-and-gratifications perspective of media effects. In J. Bryant & D. Zillman (Eds.), *Media effects: Advances in theory and research* (pp. 525–548). Lawrence Erlbaum Associates.

Stroud, N. J. (2011). *Niche news: The politics of news choice.* Oxford University Press.

Tourangeau, R., Rips, L. J., & Rasinski, K. (2000). *The psychology of survey response.* Cambridge University Press.

Umphrey, L. R., & Sherblom, J. C. (2018). The constitutive relationship of listening to hope, emotional intelligence, stress, and life satisfaction. *International Journal of Listening, 32*(1), 24–48. 10.1080/10904018.2017.1297237

U.S. Census Bureau. (2016a). *Voting and registration in the election of November 2016. (Table 6.2: Reported voting and registration, by race, Hispanic origin, sex, and age, for the United States: November 2016).* https://www.census.gov/data/tables/time-series/demo/voting-and-registration/p20-580.html

U.S. Census Bureau. (2016b). *The Hispanic population in the United States: 2016. (Table 6.2. Population by sex, age, and Hispanic origin type: 2016).* https://www.census.gov/data/tables/2016/demo/hispanic-origin/2016-cps.html

U.S. Census Bureau. (2016c). *The Hispanic population in the United States: 2016. (Table 6.6. Educational attainment of the population 25 years and over by sex and Hispanic origin type: 2016).* https://www.census.gov/data/tables/2016/demo/hispanic-origin/2016-cps.html

Van Aelst, P., Strömbäck, J., Aalberg, T., Esser, F., De Vreese, C., Matthes, J., ... & Papathanassopoulos, S. (2017). Political communication in a high-choice media environment: A challenge for democracy? *Annals of the International Communication Association, 41*(1), 3–27. 10.1080/23808985.2017.1288551

Watson, K. W., Barker, L. L., & Weaver, J. B., III. (1995). The Listening Styles Profile (LSP-16): Development and validation of an instrument to assess four listening styles. *International Journal of Listening, 9*(1), 1–13. 10.1080/10904018.1995.10499138

Whiting, A., & Williams, D. (2013). Why people use social media: A uses and gratifications approach. *Qualitative Market Research, 16*(4), 362–369. 10.1108/QMR-06-2013-0041

Williams, B., Brown, T., & Boyle, M. (2012). Psychometric properties of the Listening Styles Profile (LSP-16): A replication study. *Evaluation & the Health Professions, 35*(4), 440–446. 10.1177/0163278712448772

7

ACTIVE LISTENING AND "SERIAL CALLING"

Negotiating public space in interactive radio

Iginio Gagliardone

DEPARTMENT OF MEDIA STUDIES, WITS UNIVERSITY

The study of interactive media in Africa has been characterized by contradictions and paradoxes. In the early stages of the diffusion of the Internet and the mobile phone, these innovations were welcomed as multipliers of economic and social development, levelers, and "liberation technologies" (Diamond, 2010), which could help ordinary citizens fight corruption, abuse, and challenge dictators. Heavily normative frameworks were projected onto the continent, imagining unfettered citizens using media to root for their leaders or demand accountability. Interactive media were pitched as channels for erecting a new "architecture of participation" to "reconceptualise participation as a radicalized notion of citizenship involving a multi-scaled agency, or involvement" (Thompson, 2008, p. 826). In the case of interactive radio, which is the focus of this chapter, the projection of salvific and progressive qualities onto technical objects displayed possibly its most contradictory quality. As Brisset-Foucault (2016, p. 260) remarked,

> whereas in Western culture, talk radio has often been characterised as a threat to democracy, a paragon of cheap talk, it has acquired letter of nobility in Africa. Interactive radio shows have continuously been one of the favoured targets of support by international NGOs and institutions, and particularly used with the vision of transforming individual citizens' commitment to the community and as vehicles of civic spirit.

Notably, this celebration of the potential effects of interactive media on civil culture occurred in the same period the continent was either emerging from or still engulfed in many violent conflicts – from the Rwandan genocide (see Mugume et al., chapter 12) to the open war between Ethiopia and Eritrea (see Beyne & Mengistu, chapter 11), the collapse of Somalia, and civil wars in Sierra Leone, Northern

DOI: 10.4324/9781003214465-7

Uganda, and Darfur. These were the years when Binyavanga Wainaina wrote "How to write about Africa" (2005), where he provocatively juxtaposed "AK-47," "guerrillas," and "naked warriors" with "celebrity activists" or "qualified Westerners who care about Africa" to account for the distortions in the representation of the continent and its perception as a canvas on which different actors could project their hopes and fears, often simultaneously.

A decade later, in an arguably less violent conjuncture, research on the relations between communication and power in Africa seems to have experienced a dramatic – and apparently bizarre – turn, almost ditching explorations of empowering and leveling uses of digital media, becoming increasingly focused on studying phenomena such as hate speech and information disorder (Gagliardone et al., 2021; Wasserman & Madrid-Morales, 2022). Digital media have shifted from being sites where differences and conflicts are solved to spaces where they are exacerbated; invisible forces within or beyond a country's border maliciously spread false, inaccurate, or misleading information, seeking to score political or economic gains. Optimistic expectations that digital media could give rise to a new public sphere have given way to the skepticism that behind vocal citizens taking to the airways or using digital walls to denounce wrongdoings and abuses could lie malicious intent to cunningly tarnish the image of an opponent or a group. And yet, Africa is rising. Tech giants – from Google and Facebook to a coalition of Chinese companies operating under the umbrella of China's Digital Silk Road – are docking undersea cables of unprecedented capacity on African shores.

This chapter seeks to account for some of these contradictions, highlighting the disconnections between actual uses of communication technologies and the frameworks adopted – or in some cases imposed – to study them. It looks retrospectively – through the lenses of the changes in narratives and paradigms adopted to approach digital media – at fieldwork conducted in radio stations in Kenya and in Somalia between 2011 and 2013, and published in two separate articles (Gagliardone, 2016; Stremlau et al., 2015), to achieve a set of interrelated goals.[1]

First, by relying on empirical insights gained from ethnographic engagements with radio stations and journalists as well as their callers, audiences, and communities, this chapter seeks to provide a picture of the complex forms of interactions co-existing in interactive media, eschewing unidirectional hypotheses aiming to prove either their empowering potential or to denounce manipulative or conflict-provoking uses. It does so in conversation with a recent wave of interactive media studies that have challenged stereotypes and supposedly clear boundaries between "passive mass media audiences and hyperactive digital media users" and have accounted for how audiences in different locales have "distinctive, conventional modes and styles of making meaning" (Willems & Mano, 2016, p. 22); or have offered a more granular and detailed understanding of the factors determining who listens to and participates in interactive shows (Srinivasan & Lopes, 2020).

Second, building on these findings, this chapter exposes some of the dangers carried by frameworks that are too rigid and normative, elaborated in centers of knowledge that are both conceptually and geographically distant from the spaces in which they are applied. The evidence presented in it, as well as in some closely related works cited throughout the chapter (see, for example, Bob-Milliar, 2012; Brisset-Foucault, 2013; Selormey, 2013), emerged from fieldwork that predates the turn from conceptualizing interactive spaces as civil and emancipatory to uncivil and contentious, which can be located in the mid-2010s, following scandals such as Cambridge Analytica. And yet, this fieldwork already offered examples of ambiguous and manipulative practices occurring in interactive spaces, even if these defied idealized conceptions of the public sphere that were still dominant at the time the research took place. In a way, this was an instance when sensitivities and grounded approaches in the Global South predated conceptual innovations in academia in the Global North, by challenging and resisting the imposition of conceptual and methodological straightjackets.

Finally, it suggests a pragmatic, rather than normative, approach to comprehending participatory practices, which suppresses the impulse to categorize them as authentic or in-authentic, and recognizes instead how many forms of interaction tend to be self-interested, often related to expected gains in visibility, popularity, or financial incentives. This does not mean embracing a cynical view of interactions in digital and hybrid media. As the next sections illustrate, and other ethnographic studies on interactive radio in Africa have stressed (Brisset-Foucault, 2016; Cante, 2018, 2020), individuals and groups creating or occupying interactive spaces at the intersection of different media and modes of communication often make use of them to educate themselves and others. They may still experiment with various forms of participation, but they often do so away from institutional politics, in ways that are radically distinct from bureaucratic rationality and idealized citizens-state relations.

Rethinking participation and governance

International organizations, NGOs, and academics have developed an approach toward using and analyzing media in conflict and post-conflict scenarios that is more reliant on broad assumptions regarding their role in supporting processes of state and nation building than on actual evidence of whether and how this actually happens (Schoemaker & Stremlau, 2014). As a popular and adaptable medium', radio has been at the center of these debates. With the growth of mobile phones and social media platforms, call-in radio programs have become increasingly accessible and have gained popularity not only among audiences (Gunner et al., 2012; Willems, 2013), but also among researchers and practitioners.

Call-in programs allow the convergence of different media, as calls, text messages, and social media are aggregated and returned to audiences for further elaboration. They have progressively merged performance, entertainment, information, and ideological messages; and because they have facilitated public participation and interaction between journalists, audiences, and public figures, they have also been seen as instruments for accountability from below. As described by Thornborrow and Fitzgerald (2013), "radio phone-in provides a rare context for direct interaction between members of the public and their political representatives, where voters can hold politicians to account for their policies by asking questions" (p. 3). It is this latter dimension that has attracted particular attention in debates on development and post-conflict reconstruction, especially in sub-Saharan Africa. Call-in programs dealing with local news, especially those that feature elected representatives or political leaders responding to people's questions and complaints, have been regarded as excellent ways to spread political news widely and help build local accountability (Devas & Grant, 2003).

Indeed, NGOs and international organizations have progressively incorporated call-in programs into their efforts to promote "good governance." The United Nations sponsored call-in radio programming to raise awareness about initiatives it supported, such as Somalia's constitution making process (Williams, 2018). Similarly, the World Bank experimented with interactive radio to expand opportunities for citizens to speak to public officials (Governance Partnership Facility, 2016). At its core, this approach emphasizes the role of call-in programs in facilitating "voice," typically citizens or civil society groups that are expected to encourage the "accountability" of a particular actor, most often the government. It assumes that a challenge of governance is the asymmetry of information, whereby the media, and those who call-in, are able to provide information that will encourage action. This approach is rooted in transparency initiatives that are intended to open up government and develop spaces for broader participation, thereby improving the accountability of institutions and their leaders.

The emphasis on media, and on call-in programs in particular, as tools for accountability downplays how radio programs are constructed, or how they follow a particular logic to structure interaction between audiences, journalists, and public authorities to ultimately be "staged events," where "the seeming spontaneity and authenticity of audience participation are constructed through the media's programming practice and the actor's discursive practice" (Lee & Lin, 2011, p. 1). By taking a less normative approach, the research presented here illustrates how radio stations promote debate by developing formal and informal rules to govern the conversations that often run against the idealized conception of a public sphere (Fraser, 2007; Habermas, 1991). In resonance with studies on gatekeeping and public participation (Dori-Hacohen, 2012; Ytreberg, 2004), the next sections offer clear examples of how call-in programs, despite their apparent open nature, reproduce power imbalances both at the macro level, reflecting who has access to resources in a particular community, and at the micro level, facilitating the presence of specific figures and favoring forms of interaction that implicitly exclude others. These imbalances are arguably more significant in conflict and post-conflict scenarios. This does not mean that individuals cannot make use of call-in programs as platforms to denounce abuses and encourage accountability of public authorities; however, these efforts must be considered in their broader structural context.

Interactivity in local radio stations

The research presented here was conducted on three radio stations, all head-quartered in Kenya, but reaching significantly different constituencies. Pamoja FM in Nairobi and Radio Nam Lolwe in Kisumu are local radio stations (Fardon & Furniss, 2000) catering to a limited audience and geographic area. Pamoja FM was launched in 2007 as a community radio station for the people living in Nairobi's largest informal settlement, which, at the time the fieldwork took place, was commonly known (and is still often addressed) as Kibera. In the late 2010s, Kibera went through a bottom-up process of renaming, promoted by its own residents, and reappropriating the original name Kibra, which in Nubian means forest or jungle (Wanjiru-Mwita, 2021). As a result, Pamoja FM went from being "the voice of Kibera" to being "the voice of Kibra." In Kibra, almost all Kenyan ethnic groups are represented, but they occupy different layers in its complex socio-economic structure. While Luo are the majority, most landlords are Nubian and Kikuyu, creating problematic fault lines between economic survival and ethnic divisions. Pamoja means 'together' in Kiswahili and, according to its funders, was established with the goal of promoting unity in this complex landscape.

In contrast, Nam Lolwe, which means Lake Victoria in Luo, was started as a political radio station by Jakoyo Midiwo, a member of parliament (MP) for the Orange Democratic Movement (ODM) and caters to the Nyanza province, where Luo represent the dominant ethnic group. It initially served as a platform for the ODM to support its political campaign in an area recognized as an ODM stronghold, but after the 2007 elections it gained greater independence, adopting a fresher approach and trying to take a more active stance toward local political actors.

Star FM occupies an original and somehow unique position. Like the other two radio stations, it focuses on a specific community, but it does so on a much wider scale. It broadcasts from Nairobi, but it reaches Somali audiences well beyond its location in Eastleigh neighborhood, including many other Somali communities in Northern Kenya and in Somalia through relay stations in Wajir, Madogo in the Tana River Valley, and Mandera in the northeast province of Kenya. In addition, Star FM has FM stations in Mogadishu and Guriceel. The expansion of Star FM in south-central Somalia has been partially supported by the international NGO Internews, with funding from USAID. By virtue of this expansion and the audience it reaches, Star FM is regarded as an important Somali-language radio station in the region, with growing influence.

In each radio station, I conducted ethnographic work both in the studios and in the communities reached by the stations, with the support of research assistants. For Pamoja FM and Radio Nam Lolwe, fieldwork took place between July and September 2011; fieldwork for Star FM took place from December 2012 to January 2013. In all sites, we relied on a combination of data collection methods to understand interactions from the perspective of different actors. Participant observation in the radio stations' studios and newsrooms revealed the practices used by journalists and presenters to collect and make use of information coming from people who are calling and texting. This also included people who were contacting journalists directly on their personal mobile phones and visiting the radio station to make sure their demands were given full attention. In all cases, the focus of the study progressively narrowed toward breakfast shows, as they displayed the richest forms of interaction and regularly connected journalists, audiences, and public authorities to debate issues of both local and national relevance.

Ethnographic work involved sitting with presenters during their breakfast shows, taking notes, asking questions while songs were playing, and observing the interactions with callers. At the end of each show, we often spent time with the show hosts, asking them to reflect on specific interactions they had with callers and public authorities. In some occurrences, we also accompanied journalists outside of the studio while they were collecting information and interacting with residents.

The observations we collected in the radio stations were then compared with audiences' perceptions of the exchanges they were taking part in and their possible repercussions on governance processes. The most active and engaged users were identified based on their frequent interactions with the station and then interviewed either in person or through the phone.

Finally, in the three sites, individuals working at different levels of the local administration were interviewed (district officers, chiefs, assistant chiefs, MPs), as well as individuals working in formal and informal institutions involved in in the provision of services identified as particularly relevant for the surveyed community. These public authorities were contacted and interviewed to better understand how they perceived the interactions and debates taking place on the radio.

In total, we interviewed more than 80 people. The interaction with different interviewees, however, varied significantly: from repeated interactions with radio presenters spanning across weeks, to sustained engagement with some regular callers and public authorities who were interviewed on multiple occasions, to single, brief interviews (between 10 and 45 minutes) with members of the communities reached by the three radio stations.

Presence and performance

The breakfast programs broadcast by all three radio stations follow a similar structure: They "wake up" their communities and offer them a space to exchange greetings and discuss issues of the day. There is a balance between local, national, and sometimes international news, mostly picked up from national newspapers and the Internet – and occasionally the opportunity to talk with leaders. The presenters act as brokers among various constituencies in their communities. In line with the rhetoric highlighting how the convergence between radio and digital technologies is supporting "participatory development processes" (Gilberds & Myers, 2012), presenters often remark that they are offering a platform for people to raise their concerns. As one of the hosts of Pamoja's morning program noted:

> At the beginning, when we started our morning show, we could go on for three hours without receiving any call. And when people were calling they were afraid, they did not feel comfortable talking on the radio. Now they are much more confident; they know what they want and how to say it. Before, people were talking about just a few issues, but now they can talk about politics, about corruption; they can accuse and say what they do not like in the community.

Assertions like this may seem to reinforce the image of the radio empowering ordinary citizens, as advanced by donor agencies and NGOs concerned about transparency and accountability. As it became increasingly clear during fieldwork, however, while these interactive spaces are open to all listeners with access to a phone, they are, in practice, inhabited by a much smaller cohort of recurrent characters. Presenters recognize their voices, and some callers are addressed by their nicknames, such as "the bull fighter," "senior citizen," and "the governor." One of the hosts of Ye Lolwe, Nam Lolwe's show, acknowledged that, on a normal day, two-thirds of callers are recurrent. Outside of the radio, the prevalence of some voices over others has led people to think calls are arranged in advance. As one listener in Kibra alleged, "the presenters know before who is calling, because they recognize the number." But the view from the studio revealed this was not the case, simply because the technology used to manage calls was too rudimentary to show a caller's number. Rather, in resonance with other research on radio talk shows (Chignell, 2011; Dori-Hacohen, 2012; Willems, 2013; Ytreberg, 2004), this phenomenon is rooted in the constructed and managed nature of audience participation.

Over time, the radio stations have created new public figures, people who know what language to use on air, respect the format, and are able to adopt a "participant role" (Ytreberg, 2004). Their emergence challenges the simplistic rhetoric of democratic engagement at various levels. In Ghana, recurrent callers have been labeled "serial callers" (Bob-Milliar, 2012; Selormey, 2013), users activated and paid by political parties to call radio stations and advance a particular view. Selormey (2013, p. 158) has advanced a definition of the "serial caller" as:

> An individual, who is a frequent and persistent caller to radio programmes, particularly primetime programmes and political talk shows, with the intention of swaying public opinion about all manner of issues, including politics. This individual may be a foot soldier of a political party or an individual who receives rewards in cash or in kind from a political party, or influential persons in society.

This definition was formulated in 2013, when attention and research on information manipulation was still limited. Reading it in hindsight of the numerous scandals and studies on electoral interference, mis/disinformation, and the myriad conspiracy theories that have emerged since, it immediately evokes now familiar imagery of troll armies, sock puppets, or paid influencers. Brisset-Foucault (2016, p. 256) warned, however, of accepting normative dichotomies and flagging serial callers as people:

> keeping genuine citizens from participating [or] encouraging a process of commercialization of electoral politics. [This characterization] prevents from paying attention to the sideway, unexpected uses of these spheres of discussion [and] from reinserting them within their historicity and from understanding their significance within particular political contexts.

Many callers may embark on their careers as active participants in call-in shows to build their reputational network. Several examples of this emerged during my previous ethnographic analysis, published in Gagliardone (2016, p. 8). For example, as a recurrent caller of Nam Lolwe's program commented, "I feel that my role in my community has increased. People around can tell me that they heard me on the radio, and I said something that was important, that they agreed with." Similarly, another caller stated, "Now I can be heard. Before people did not know me. But now my presence is felt in the community. If I go to a funeral now my presence is acknowledged." As I explained in the article, which focused specifically on Radio Pamoja and Radio Nam Lolwe,

> in rural Kenya, funerals are not only moments of mourning; they are also a political back to their constituency, allowing people to reach them and express their claims. They can also become spaces where other individuals test their political weight and where the popularity they acquired through the media can be assessed among peers. For the funeral of a respected member of the community, an MP is likely to come.

In the case of Star FM, some recurrent callers were able to reap even larger benefits from their active participation. For instance, Star FM journalists reported that one of their frequent callers was subsequently elected to a political position in Garissa, a development that was credited to the popularity he gained by regularly contributing to Star FM's morning call-in program. A second example cited was the similar case of a businessman, another very active caller to Star FM's morning program, who was subsequently elected as an MP and continued to remain actively engaged with the program, particularly about issues related to his constituency.

Across different cases, relationships between recurrent callers and radio stations are often mutually beneficial, as they help sustain a format that is both engaging and supports the idea of radio as a forum for public participation (see also, e.g., Gaynor & O'Brien, 2017). Callers are given, and seize, the opportunity to challenge public authorities, but they must follow certain norms; inappropriate and irrelevant calls are screened out. While the radio-mobile convergence has been touted as powerful and democratizing in Africa because it also extends opportunities to raise voice to individuals with low literacy levels (Gilberds & Myers, 2012), in reality, callers are implicitly required to display a type of competence that is far from being widespread among communities in the margins.

In numerous interviews, serial callers asserted how their presence in call-in programs and ability to be more impactful than ordinary callers were opportunities to represent their own communities, act as their spokespersons, and encourage public authorities to act. Or, as Brisset-Foucault (2016) vividly illustrated in her research on Radio Buddu and Better FM in Uganda, participation may not be interpreted as an opportunity to enhance good governance or democratization, but to "take responsibility for one's own fate [...] a remedy against inaction and moral decay" (p. 265).

The same individuals who are moved by strong ambitions to represent their communities and be heard may also be the ones who, because of their popularity, are approached by more powerful actors and co-opted into promoting messages that benefit a specific party or group, in exchange for cash, airtime, or future compensation. Flagging them as saboteurs of genuine forms of interaction because of these practices, however, would amount to refusing to appreciate not only the complexity of real – rather than imagined – practices of participation, but also the role these individuals play in creating the very spaces to which listeners choose to return, and the power they can mobilize in supporting different causes.

Active listening and the complex networks connecting voice and action

This section shifts the attention from active participants to different categories of listeners, with a particular focus on those who have the power to do something with the information collected on air. Innovations may increase the ability of citizens to participate in public debates and take an active role in the provision of public goods and services, but whether this increased participation has the power to eventually affect decision making and processes at scale depends on how other actors interpret and incorporate it into their agendas.

Also, in this case, the faith of international organizations and NGOs in the power of new technologies to promote change in Africa has seemed disconnected from – or unaware of – how these mechanisms operate in societies with arguably more accountable and responsive institutions. As Macnamara (2016) illustrated through the study of government, non-government, and corporate organizations in Australia, the United Kingdom, and the United States, only a tiny fraction of resources in these institutions have been devoted to listening to stakeholders. Instead, the vast majority has been allocated to speaking to them, often with the aim of influencing their views. So, one may ask, if public authorities in countries with supposedly more efficient bureaucratic systems – often the same countries funding projects to improve governance in Africa – have made very limited efforts to listen to their stakeholders, why should more responsiveness be expected from public authorities in an African context? In my experience, first in international development, and later in academia, I came across numerous projects aimed at promoting good governance or mitigating conflict in Africa. While I am fully aware my knowledge in this regard is anecdotal, rather than based on a systematic survey, I never came across a project that could answer – or even pose – this question.

Despite this mismatch between expectations and the concrete ability of specific tools and processes to promote change, the research conducted in the communities reached by the three radio stations offered indications that public authorities recognized new spaces created by mobile-radio interactions as significant and useful for collecting information to perform their activities. Substantial differences, however, emerged in how these powerful listeners indicated they were making use of this information. Some of these differences can be traced back to the nature of the relationships connecting different nodes in local networks. In numerous cases, it was not just a demand for greater accountability or a sense of civic duty to encourage authorities to act. Other types of – often informal rather than formal/bureaucratic – connections, appeared as more relevant to trigger a response.

In the case of Kibra, district officers, chiefs, and other public authorities were less likely to follow up on claims made by citizen callers. They argued that citizens should place their demands and complaints to the state (see Gagliardone, 2016, p. 11). As one assistant chief explained:

> If someone calls the radio and denounces someone else for having done this and that, it is not an official communication. People now tend to forget this. They think that they can just call the radio, denounce something, and that is it. But in many cases, it is not enough, you need to come to an office of the administration and denounce what has happened, provide evidence, so that we can follow up. The residents may think that the media have the power to act, but they do not.

Interviews collected among the Kibra residents offered a very different take on a claim like this. One of the reasons to call the radio, rather than approaching the police or an assistant chief, was the lack of faith in these formal, government-affiliated institutions; they remained unconvinced that anything would be done with the information provided to public authorities. The radio, in their view, would at least make a claim public, putting pressure on authorities, or, given the unwillingness or inability of authorities to act, encourage other groups or individuals to self-organize. Within the period covered by fieldwork, claims made on the radio seemed to have the most impact on relatively limited spheres of action, such as small emergencies (e.g., fire outbreaks or children getting lost), rather than being able to affect deeper and more structural issues, such as service delivery or corruption. As one listener of Radio Pamoja put it, "It is much better to go to a place and help when you hear from a radio there is a fire because if you wait for the police, they will never come."

In contrast, Kisumu public authorities had a less adversarial view of the relationship between information and communication technologies and the state. As a result, they were more willing to collect and act on information through the radio. As a chief I interviewed toward the end of my fieldwork in Kisumu (see Gagliardone, 2016, p. 11), described:

> We can act through the radio. When I hear something on the radio, I do act. I may decide to send my people there. [...] I can learn for example that an area in Kisumu was raided by people who are known in the community. So why would I wait before acting on that? Even if what I hear in the radio is just an allegation, I have to act on what I hear. Then I can decide to have a baraza, so that people can talk to us. A baraza can allow us to get the facts from the ground.[2]

The diverging approaches of Kibra and Kisumu public authorities were confirmed in interviews with journalists and audiences from each area who pointed to ethnicity as a main reason for that divergence. As I have reported elsewhere (Gagliardone, 2016), Kibra's complex ethnic diversity "made it harder for chiefs and their assistants to react to some of the claims collected by radio stations, for fear that more deep-rooted grievances might be behind these cases" (p. 11). In contrast, Kisumu's more homogeneous networks linking citizens to public authorities increased the likelihood that the latter would act. For Kibra, ethnicity became an obstacle preventing public authorities from acting on some claims (and thus producing tangible results), while Kisumu's ethnicity allowed them to act in cases where Kibra authorities could not. As a journalist in Kisumu explained to me (Gagliardone, 2016, p. 12):

> Here in Kisumu, we mostly belong all to one tribe, so when something happens the authorities feel that they have to follow up, they are expected to, they may know who is involved, and that there is less risk that this event is simply made up. But if you are in Kibera, where there are a lot of different tribes, you don't really know if what is said may be the result of an ethnic tension, a tension between different groups, so you have to be more careful.

The comparison between the two radio stations, and their communities, highlights the importance, also in this case, of adopting open frameworks that can deepen the understanding of what connects voice and listening in practice, even if these mechanisms eschew mainstream conceptions of state-society relations. The tendency of most is to consider ethnicity a destructive, rather than a productive force in studies on communication and power, or communication and conflict in Africa (Ismail & Deane, 2008; Kellow & Steeves, 1998). Fewer attempts have been made to understand how ethnicity can also represent a productive force in connecting demands and actions. From a normative standpoint, one may interpret the inclusion of a variable like ethnicity problematic in practical attempts to more closely connect voice and listening, as it raises difficult questions about inclusion and exclusion in complex societies. This, however, should not prevent researchers from studying its relevance in everyday interactions, rather than holding too tightly onto idealized conceptions or unrealistic hypotheses.

Moving on to the case of Star FM, the relation between information and opinions shared on air and their ability to produce or encourage action, displayed features that at the same time resembled those encountered in the case of the two other radio stations, but was also further complicated by the protracted conflict in South-Central Somalia. As both journalists and callers emphasized, the radio represented a unique source of information from areas that are often inaccessible, but there were little expectations that the government could act on them, given its limited reach and the constant threat posed by Al-Shabaab. As a journalist explained during fieldwork originally reported in Stremlau et al. (2015, p. 1521):

> When the public calls, they were reporting new ... cases that the government was not even aware of. The caller may report that in his/her district [there was] a robbery, or a woman was raped, or a person was robbed of his personal phone.

As the journalist elaborated, the government has little to no capacity to act on such information, and callers may expect that other authorities – such as clan elders – may intervene once this information has become available.

In other cases, understanding the harsh conditions that journalists, but also callers, may face in conflict areas, is used to interpret the meaning of what is being shared on air. As a caller explained (and previously reported in Stremlau et al., 2015, p. 1521):

> Star FM gives information about my area, but I know that the local reporters are not free to tell all what happens. *I know the brother of one of them* and can trust the information they give, but I'm aware that the government does not control that area, and they have to be always careful with their reports.

In contrast to Kibra, where public authorities and citizens offered often opposing interpretations on the standing of local institutions – the former purporting their ability and willingness to act, the latter displaying utmost distrust – in the case of the communities reached by Star FM, callers and public authorities seemed to share the awareness that the state was often incapacitated to act in areas where it had limited or no control.

Conclusion

The research presented in this chapter sought to offer a grounded perspective on the complex forms of interactions emerging at the intersection of old and new media. It eschewed simple dichotomies presenting interactive media as tools that can either deepen or solve conflicts, and users as either authentic agents of change or self-interested individuals seeking to manipulate information in their favor or in ways that can favor groups to which they are connected. In particular, through the analysis of the motivations and forms of participation of "serial callers," the chapter sought to account for the serial callers' complex and often contradictory role, as highly competent participants who make use of their skills and visibility to serve multiple agendas. While some of their actions and strategies, such as paid contributions seeking to favor specific political actors or to support/contest a specific issue, resemble those pursued by agents of disinformation on social media, their visibility and reputation in their communities make them relatively unique characters in the increasingly diverse media ecologies that have emerged in Africa and globally.

With specific reference to listening, the chapter highlighted three important phenomena, which are relevant not only to studying interactive media in Africa, but also to developing a more realistic understanding of the relationship between speaking and listening in fostering democracy (Macnamara, 2020). The first is the radical situatedness of processes connecting citizens' claims and the actions – or lack of actions – of public authorities. The comparison between Radio Nam Lolwe and Radio Pamoja suggests how in more homogeneous communities, authorities tend to be less suspicious of and more responsive toward demands publicly articulated on interactive media. On the contrary, in more diverse communities, public authorities are more likely to downplay the role of inter- active spaces as legitimate venues to advance requests or articulate criticism. The arguments chiefs and assistant chiefs in Kibra advance – that complaints and ac- cusations should be made formally in their offices – has little to do with their ability to follow up on those requests – as lamented by Kibra's residents – but rather seeks to reclaim or expand spheres of power, in spaces where state authorities compete with multiple other forms of authority – from ethnic groups, to religious organizations, NGOs, and criminal networks.

The second phenomenon, highlighted by the presence and role of serial callers, relates to the supposed ability of interactive spaces to reduce the distance between citizens and those in power. As argued in the introduction of this chapter, the "romantic" view of interactive media as power levelers, after having reached its apex in the late 1990s and early 2000s, has since faded. The case of serial callers offers nonetheless unique contributions toward explaining why that view contained several fallacies. Aside from the resonance with now more familiar cases of information manipulation discussed above, the recurrent presence of these characters on air highlights the relevance of skills and understandings of the medium/format for influencing public debates, which are not equally shared among the population, as some initially posited. Even if serial callers are unlikely to command the same authority of elected officials, their "careers" often lead them to acquire forms of influence that contribute to reducing the power gap with formal political institutions.

Finally, and in relation to the two points made above, the dynamics illustrated in this chapter, in resonance with other studies cited throughout (Bob-Milliar, 2012; Brisset-Foucault, 2016; Cante, 2020; Willems & Mano, 2016), serve as a cautionary tale toward tendencies of projecting onto Africa idealized notions of democratic processes, without first developing a fuller understanding of how these processes operate in countries labeled more democratic. As Macnamara (2020) illustrated, even in Australia, the United Kingdom, and the United States, only a small fraction of resources in government institutions are devoted to increasing the capacity to listen to stakeholders. While it is legitimate to posit that institutions in other non-Western contexts may be more interested in or devote more resources toward "listening," this hypothesis should be grounded in a granular understanding of state-society relations in these specific contexts, rather than in well-meaning but often unfounded predictions of the power of technological or institutional innovations to transform societies.

Notes

1 This chapter draws on a larger ethnographic project, the data from which include observations, surveys, interviews, and extensive field notes. In addition to this chapter, interested readers can also find analyses of power, governance, public engagement, and other implications of mobile-radio interactions in Gagliardone (2016) and Stremlau et al. (2015). Some quotes used in this chapter also appear in other published work, though this chapter provides a unique contribution to our understanding of "serial calling."

2 A baraza is a political meeting or council that can be called to discuss any issue considered relevant for/by a community. For more details, see, for example, Haugerud (1997).

References

Bob-Milliar, G. M. (2012). Political party activism in Ghana: Factors influencing the decision of the politically active to join a political party. *Democratization, 19,* 668–689. 10.1080/13510347.2011.605998

Brisset-Foucault, F. (2013). Radio, mobile phones, elite formation and sociability: The case of Uganda's "serial callers." https://papers.ssrn.com/sol3/papers.cfm?abstract_id= 2250539

Brisset-Foucault, F. (2016). Serial callers: Communication technologies as a canvas for political personhood in contemporary Uganda. *Ethnos*, *83*(2), 255–273. 10.1080/ 00141844.2015.1127984

Cante, F. (2018). From 'animation' to encounter: Community radio, sociability and urban life in Abidjan, Côte d'Ivoire. *International Journal of Cultural Studies*, *21*(1), 12–26. 10.1177/1367877917704489

Cante, F. (2020). Mediating anti-political peace in Abidjan: Radio, place and power. *Political Geography*, *83*, 102282. 10.1016/j.polgeo.2020.102282

Chignell, H. (2011). *Public issue radio: Talks, news and current affairs in the twentieth century*. Palgrave Macmillan.

Devas, N., & Grant, U. (2003). Local government decision-making — citizen participation and local accountability: Some evidence from Kenya and Uganda. *Public Administration and Development*, *23*, 307–316. 10.1002/pad.281

Diamond, L. (2010). Liberation technology. *Journal of Democracy*, *2*(3), 69–83. https:// www.journalofdemocracy.org/wp-content/uploads/2012/01/Diamond-21-3.pdf

Dori-Hacohen, G. (2012). Gatekeeping public participation: An ethnographic account of the production process of a radio phone-in programme. *The Radio Journal: International Studies in Broadcast & Audio Media*, *10*(2), 113–129. 10.1386/rjao.10.2.113_1

Fardon, R., & Furniss, G. (Eds.) (2000). *African broadcast cultures: Radio in transition*. Praeger.

Fraser, N. (2007). Transnational public sphere: Transnationalizing the public sphere: On the legitimacy and efficacy of public opinion in a post-Westphalian world. *Theory, Culture & Society*, *24*(4), 7–30. 10.1177/0263276407080090

Gagliardone, I. (2016). 'Can you hear me?' Mobile–radio interactions and governance in Africa. *New Media & Society*, *18*(9), 2080–2095. 10.1177/1461444815581148

Gagliardone, I., Diepeveen, S., Findlay, K., Olaniran, S., Pohjonen, M., & Tallam, E. (2021). Demystifying the COVID-19 infodemic: Conspiracies, context, and the agency of users. *Social Media & Society*, *7*(3), 1–16. 10.1177/20563051211044233

Gaynor, N., & O'Brien, A. (2017). Community radio, democratic participation and the public sphere. *Irish Journal of Sociology*, *25*(1), 29–47. 10.7227/IJS.0002

Gilberds, H., & Myers, M. (2012). Radio, ICT convergence and knowledge brokerage: Lessons from sub-Saharan Africa. *IDS Bulletin*, *43*(5), 76–83. 10.1111/j.1759-5436. 2012.00366.x

Governance Partnership Facility. (2016). *Final report, 2009–2015: Results, lessons, and legacy*. International Bank for Reconstruction and Development/The World Bank. https://documents1.worldbank.org/curated/fr/575891468187475516/pdf/103852-WP-GPFAR14-FINAL-PUBLIC.pdf

Gunner, L., Ligaga, D., Moyo, D., Bosch, T., Chibita, M.B., & Coplan, D.B. (2012). *Radio in Africa: Publics, cultures, communities*. Wits University Press.

Habermas, J. (1991). *The structural transformation of the public sphere: An inquiry into a category of bourgeois society*. MIT press.

Haugerud, A. (1997). *The culture of politics in modern Kenya* (African Studies, Series Number 84) . Cambridge University Press.

Ismail, J. A., & Deane, J. (2008). The 2007 general election in Kenya and its aftermath: The role of local language media. *The International Journal of Press/Politics*, *13*(3), 319–327. 10.1177/1940161208319510

Kellow, C. L., & Steeves, H. L. (1998). The role of radio in the Rwandan genocide. *Journal of Communication, 48*(3), 107–128. 10.1111/j.1460-2466.1998.tb02762.x

Lee, F. L., & Lin, A. M. (2011). Officials' accountability performance on Hong Kong talk radio. The case of the financial secretary hotline. In M. Ekström & M. Patrona (Eds.), *Talking politics in broadcast media: Cross-cultural perspectives on political interviewing* (pp. 223–242). John Benjamins.

Macnamara, J. R. (2016). *Organizational listening: The missing essential in public communication.* Peter Lang.

Macnamara, J. (2020). Listening for healthy democracy. In D. L. Worthington & G. D. Bodie (Eds.), *The handbook of listening* (pp. 385–395). Wiley Blackwell.

Schoemaker, E., & Stremlau, N. (2014). Media and conflict: An assessment of the evidence. *Progress in Development Studies, 14*(2), 181–195. 10.1177/1464993413517790

Selormey, E. E. (2013). *Citizen voice and bureaucratic responsiveness: FM radio phone-ins and the delivery of municipal and local government services in Accra, Ghana.* [Unpublished doctoral thesis]. University of Sussex. http://sro.sussex.ac.uk/46446/

Srinivasan, S., & Lopes, C. A. (2020). Mediated sociability: Audience participation and convened citizen engagement in interactive broadcast shows in Africa. *International Journal of Communication, 14*, 2985–3006. https://ijoc.org/index.php/ijoc/article/view/10571/3106

Stremlau, N., Fantini, E., & Gagliardone, I. (2015). Patronage, politics and performance: Radio call-in programmes and the myth of accountability. *Third World Quarterly, 36*(8), 1510–1526. 10.1080/01436597.2015.1048797

Thompson, M. (2008). ICT and development studies: Towards development 2.0. *Journal of International Development, 20*(6), 821–835. 10.1002/jid.1498

Thornborrow, J., & Fitzgerald, R. (2013). "Grab a pen and paper": Interaction v. interactivity in a political radio phone-in. *Journal of Language and Politics, 12*(1), 1–28. 10.1075/jlp.12.1.01tho

Wainaina, B. (2005). How to write about Africa. *Granta, 92*(1). https://granta.com/how-to-write-about-africa/

Wanjiru-Mwita, M. (2021, May 9). The fascinating history of how residents named their informal settlements in Nairobi. *The Conversation.* http://theconversation.com/the-fascinating-history-of-how-residents-named-their-informal-settlements-in-nairobi-159080

Wasserman, H., & Madrid-Morales, D. (2022). *Disinformation in the Global South.* Wiley-Blackwell.

Willems, W. (2013). Participation–in what? Radio, convergence and the corporate logic of audience input through new media in Zambia. *Telematics and Informatics, 30*(3), 223–231. 10.1016/j.tele.2012.02.006

Willems, W., & Mano, W. (2016). Decolonizing and provincializing audience and internet studies: Contextual approaches from African vantage points. In W. Willems & W. Mano (Eds.), *Everyday media culture in Africa: Audiences and users* (pp. 1–26). Routledge.

Williams, P. D. (2018). Strategic communications for peace operations: The African Union's Information War against al-Shabaab. *Stability: International Journal of Security and Development, 7*(1), 3. 10.5334/sta.606

Ytreberg, E. (2004). Formatting participation within broadcast media production. *Media, Culture & Society, 26*(5), 677–692. 10.1177/0163443704045506

8

LISTENING AND PEACEBUILDING

Nichole Argo and Rachel Brown

OVER ZERO

Broadly, when people refer to peacebuilding, they can mean two things (Schirch, 2013, as cited in Alliance for Peacebuilding, n.d.):

1. "*Peacebuilding as direct processes* that intentionally focus on addressing the factors driving and mitigating conflict"; or
2. "*Peacebuilding as an integral comprehensive set of interrelated efforts* that support peace, including economic development, humanitarian assistance, governance, security, justice, and other sectors where participants may not use the term 'peacebuilding' to describe themselves but that contribute to a broader peace nonetheless."

What separates peacebuilding initiatives from security sector reform or humanitarian aid is that peacebuilding seeks to "transform dynamics between individuals and groups" (Alliance for Peacebuilding, n.d.). Any attempt to transform dynamics between conflicting groups requires extreme context sensitivity to reduce the possibility of unintentional harm that could lead to actual violence or furthered social divisions.

There are two ways in which peacebuilders can maximize context sensitivity. The first is by committing to ongoing, participatory *conflict assessments* that afford understanding of hidden dynamics and the ability to update understandings as elements of the conflict and its setting changes. The second is by making sure projects have *local ownership,* meaning that there is recognition and emphasis on local values, traditions, and practices (Donais, 2012). Design standards for local ownership are the subject of much discussion. While there is consensus that effective peacebuilding requires the inclusion of relevant stakeholders for co-creation in project planning, implementation, and evaluation, not *all* stakeholders

DOI: 10.4324/9781003214465-8

need to be a part of a participatory process for it to be successful, and levels of participation can vary by model (Donais, 2012; see also Bodie et al., Chapter 1). Neither does a fully inclusive, fully participatory model ensure equity, ownership, or satisfaction with outcomes. As Johansson (2017) wrote, "[despite] ... overwhelming normative support, willing partnerships to be equal does not make them so" ¶ 6).

Throughout all of the tasks peacebuilders traverse, they most often use social dialogue processes to build consensus and trust between stakeholders (including, but not limited to, those stakeholders on opposite sides of the conflict). It is within these "difficult dialogues" that "listening across difference" becomes vitally important, or even necessary for the peacebuilding process to continue, and perhaps where it is most intuitive to think about listening. A commitment toward local ownership manifests here, too: It is a best practice to call upon local capacities to manage and resolve conflicts peacefully, often through social dialogue. While a full exploration of all the components of social dialogue is beyond the scope of this chapter, many are highlighted through a focus on the role that listening can play in efforts to enhance understanding and empathy between groups – whether by social contact, dialogue, mediation, or negotiation.

In the sections that follow, we explore the role of social identity and intergroup biases on how groups perceive and behave in conflict and identify ways in which these biases can inform large-scale listening approaches within intergroup interventions. In addition, we examine the role of listening *beyond* intergroup work, looking at its potential for: (a) more effective within-group work (to elevate and amplify group members' acceptance and practice of listening, and to shift group-based norms away from violence), and (b) enhanced cooperation between peacebuilders. Here, we consider the role of listening in relation to building effective "infrastructures for peace" among peacebuilders, conceiving of and implementing "Do No Harm" approaches, and program design. But, first, we turn our attention to our primary term, listening.

What Is listening?

As stated in Chapter 1 of this volume, "good" listening at an interpersonal level can be defined simply as when a single individual attempts to fully understand what another single individual has attempted to communicate. If the listener truly takes in what the speaker shares, they will "understand differently" (Davison, 1998; Johansson, 2017), and this process of understanding will effectuate a deeper relational dynamic (Burleson, 2011). In many ways, the goals of this type of listening are relational (Bodie & Denham, 2017; Rogers & Farson, 1957), where the understanding is marked less by comprehension or evaluation of the information, and more by empathy, sympathy, or compassion (Batson, 2009; Mower, 2020).

In this interpersonal model, empathy involves *feeling as* the other. Specific neural processes are activated as we experience the same (or at least a similar) emotional response as the other person (Lamm et al., 2019) bringing us into a shared mental state (Zaki, 2019). Why is this important to consider in a chapter on listening and peacebuilding? As Epley (2014) wrote, "failing to consider the mind of another and running the risk of treating him or her like a relatively mindless animal or object … are at the heart of dehumanization" (p. 12). In fact, dehumanization is a strong predictor of intergroup hostility (Beyond Conflict, 2019; Bruneau et al., 2018; Giner-Sorolla & Russell, 2019). Perhaps nowhere is it as important to see one another's humanity as in a conflict context, that is, when violence needs to be prevented, halted, or acknowledged, and redressed so that it does not happen again (Wilmer, 2018).

Interpersonal forms of listening, with their focus on comprehension and understanding, can be beneficial in a peacebuilding context – in the alignment processes used to solicit input from multiple stakeholders or when seeking to bring communities together to dialogue across difference (Bodie & Godwin, 2022). However, such approaches do not capture all the complexity of listening at scale (Bodie et al., Chapter 1). For one thing, there are many more stakeholders in peacebuilding than there are in an interpersonal context. This represents a set of complex challenges, including the fact that some stakeholders may not understand the need for receptive listening and may even face strong disincentives to engage in or facilitate listening. For example, while politicians, mediators, and policymakers understand that parties need to have "voice" during or after a conflict, they may not truly understand receptive listening. That is, they might create "channels for voice," such as political listening tours or social media listening tools, but they do not do so in "search of the truth" or to integrate divergent viewpoints; rather, they use what they learn to help them tailor messages or provide strategies to better sell their constituents. When the public voice simply becomes a means of forwarding one's own agenda, it is, in a listening sense, "unheard." As Lewis wrote, "Voice that is unheard is useless to both the speaker and the audience" (Lewis, 2020, p. xiii; see Macnamara, 2016, for a similar argument).

Even international practitioners responsible for encouraging participation from multiple stakeholders may not realize that receptive listening requires an active reflecting back of what has been taken in. There is now ample evidence across national and international NGOs that local peacebuilding partners feel they are not being listened to, even when working with international practitioners who claim a committment to participatory project development and equal partnerships (Anderson & Wallace, 2012; Johansson, 2017). To state it differently, international practitioners often *think* they are listening, but local partners *feel* they are not. Perhaps the design of large-scale listening processes stressing shared discovery and mutual problem solving would enable organizations and their practitioners to break out of communications and power patterns to which they otherwise default (Bodie et al., Chapter 1).

Another challenge to scaling listening practices is that the goals of listening are different in interpersonal and peacebuilding contexts. While individual-level outcomes such as increased understanding or empathy for an outgroup are positive, they cannot be transformative at scale unless they also influence the systems or structures that cause pain in particular communities or with specific groups (Dobson, 2014; Freinacht, 2017). Dialogue is not a panacea for political change, and by pretending it is we "make a shallow call for peace with no justice" (Baron-Cohen, 2012, ¶ 11).

Lastly, where there are a large number of stakeholders, and specifically in conflict contexts, there are usually also issues of power imbalance and trauma (see Sankaranarayan et al., Chapter 9). In cases where there is an unequal distribution of power (such as a conflict rooted in racism or other forms of hatred, or where violence is ongoing), it can be difficult to see how the pre-conditions for receptive listening can be met (e.g., to join a conversation with "open-mindedness," or to create a space for the voices and perspectives of all groups) (Wahl, 2019). A request for a group to listen receptively to another group that wishes them harm will be met with resistance. For these reasons, an examination of "large-scale listening" in a peacebuilding context asks us not just to think about larger-scale effects (within groups, society, organizations, etc.), but also to consider the conditions under which listening is possible (Macnamara, 2016) and the ways in which conflict dynamics influence those conditions (see Beyene & Mengistu Chapter 11; Mugume et al., Chapter 12).

Between-group work and the social psychology of listening in a conflict context

In addition to the more mechanical challenges of "large-scale listening," such as the increased number of stakeholders and the likelihood that there will be knowledge- or power-gaps between them, there are also some psychological challenges to listening within a context of intergroup conflict. Our brains process information differently when we are operating from a *social identity* (when our sense of who we are is based on our group membership, e.g., "Muslim" or "Christian," "Republican," or "Democrat") rather than as an *individual self* (e.g., "Alex") (Tajfel, 1974). This is even more so the case when the group we are attached to, our "ingroup," is in competition with or feels threatened by another group – which is almost always the case when one's group membership is salient in the lead up to, during, or after a violent conflict. Below, we identify how people see the world differently through the lens of their social identities and highlight how these things inform the potential for effective large-scale listening approaches in a conflict context.

Social identity biases and their import for intergroup work

Humans are designed for sociality. Our need to belong is as innate as other basic needs, such as for oxygen, food, or water (Baumeister & Leary, 1995), and individuals attach to groups for self-esteem and a sense of worth (e.g., Smith & Tyler, 1997; Tajfel & Turner, 1979). Our need for attachment grows under conditions of uncertainty or threat (Hogg, 2007). Once attached to a group, often without even realizing it, our perceptions change: We tend to exaggerate the differences between our group (e.g., the "ingroup") and others (the "outgroup/s"), as well as the similarities between the people in our ingroup (Tajfel, 1974). We also tend to favor our own group members over others, often without even knowing it (Tajfel & Turner, 1978). We see our own group members as more human than others, and we believe they are able to feel more complex emotions than members of "other" groups (Demoulin et al., 2009). Further, we perceive the actions of outgroups (Obeid et al., 2017), and feel emotions in reaction to them (Maitner et al., 2016), through the lens of our group. We take greater risks within a group identity than we would as individuals (Gioia, 2017), and we are susceptible to the norms of our social group (norms are what other members or leaders in the group approve of or are doing; Tankard & Paluck, 2016). Indeed, perceived ingroup norms often predict human behavior more than individual beliefs or attitudes (Tankard & Paluck, 2016). For instance, even if a member of Group A does not like Group B, she is more willing to invite a member of Group B to dinner if she thinks others in her community are doing so. Conversely, a person who harbors warm attitudes toward outgroup members is more likely to denigrate them when ingroup members are doing so. Thus, a member of Group A, even if she feels warmly toward members of Group B, might be willing to insult, exclude, or even participate in harming members of Group B if that is what her peers are doing. This is especially the case in situations of inter-group competition or threat – be it real threat such as job or power competition, or symbolic threats to our group identity or values.

Under conditions of threat, our own social identity strengthens and rigidifies, propagating an "us vs. them" lens toward the world (Baron-Cohen, 2012; Sapolsky, 2017; Zeldis, 2018). Our ability to empathize with outgroup members shuts down (Cikara et al., 2011; Zaki & Cikara, 2015), and we tend to denigrate (Sherif, 1956), dehumanize, and even aggress against outgroup members to a greater extent than we would as individuals (Houshmand, 2019). With a focus on protecting our group, we may increasingly perceive outgroup members as suspicious, guilty, or aggressive. Meanwhile, more extreme stances and actions deemed "protective" of the ingroup are rewarded with praise and status within the group.

Because everything from our perceptions to our behaviors are different when we are within a social identity, our social identities – and the biases that stem from them – need to be understood and addressed when we seek to listen, build bridges, or resolve conflicts between groups. Below, we illustrate just a few such biases and offer preliminary thoughts on how a listening approach might take them into account.

Social norms

In the midst or aftermath of conflict, group members may face significant social pressure to not speak to, much less listen to, the "Other." Even if they do not face overt pressure, they may perceive genuine interactions with members from an outgroup to be taboo. Because perceived norms often predict behavior better than individual attitudes, it is important that intervenors consider them explicitly as part of their conflict assessment when planning listening interventions. Moreover, even when "moderate" participants engage in a dialogue (we would call them "moderates," referencing their moderating role against violence and conflict), intervenors must remember that the participants' ingroup norms can influence whether and how much they feel able to share their experience and learnings with the rest of their ingroup. If their ingroups consider engagement with the "Other" to be a form of betrayal, even listening that is successful "in the room" may not translate into a more sustained impact.

Once we are aware of the potential influence of ingroup norms for large-scale listening, we can address them. You can help shape ingroup norms to the extent that you can influence communication or programming (within a group) in a way that identifies, elevates, and amplifies the voices of "ingroup moderates" (Prati et al., 2016; Santos et al., 2002). Ingroup moderates include leaders who support inclusion and tolerance, regardless of their political positions, as well as those who leverage over-arching or cross-cutting identities (showing that they accept, value, and endorse relationships between groups). Peacebuilding institutions can further help by connecting "ingroup moderates" and empowering them with resources to build platforms and coalitions, so that they are not "going it alone" against group norms. Knowing that groups may face pressure *not* to put their new perspectives into action when they return home can also help inform the structure of dialogue programs. For example, they may need to extend programmatic efforts and support beyond the session, invite multiple people from a specific group to encourage support later on, or simply not take the immediate gains made during a dialogue for granted.

Using norms-based approaches can be a way to scale the impacts and reach of listening. Showcasing the listening process, as well as its positive, group-specific results can create positive perceptions of listening while encouraging listening behaviors within groups, and possibly even across them. For example, showing members of a group listening to another group – through stories and even narrative media - can help create an impression that listening is normative.

Meta-perceptions

In recent years, social science has shown that we tend to reciprocate the feelings or perceptions that we think outgroup members have of us. That is, if we think an outgroup dehumanizes our group, we are more likely to dehumanize them (Kteily et al., 2016). Similarly, if we think they hate our culture, we devalue theirs (Gray & Blakey, 2021). However, in some contexts, people overestimate how negatively outgroups feel about them. Science now shows that exposing groups to accurate information about how an outgroup portrays them can lead to greater warmth, cooperation, and hope for a collective future (Lees & Cikara, 2020; Ruggeri et al., 2021).

Indeed, research on meta-perceptions has multiple implications for large-scale listening approaches. First, one might think that the very act of a well-facilitated dialogue with receptive listening would break down meta-perceptions by showing participants that outgroup others are willing to listen and empathize with them. And while that is a potential to be sure, participants could also expect that the progress in the room does not generalize outside of it, and thus continue to believe that outgroup members feel more negatively toward them than they do. More importantly, if meta-perceptions are particularly extreme, participants may not take part in a dialogue at all. That is, it might be useful to identify and counter negative intergroup meta-perceptions as part of the design and initiation of a large-scale listening project. For example, a description of the meta-perceptions at work in a particular conflict can be utilized in the recruitment of prospective participants to illustrate the value and complexity of the process they will encounter. Note that identifying meta-perceptions and providing data to counter them might require research, such as surveys or in-depth interviews designed and executed by neutral and trustworthy parties.

Collective blame

Our brains process groups as entities rather than complicated collections of heterogeneous individuals, meaning that we think of an outgroup as a single actor. Consequently, we have a propensity to blame an entire outgroup for the acts of a few (e.g., the idea that "Muslims" were responsible for the terror attack on the US Pentagon and World Trade Center on 11 September 2001; Lickel et al., 2006). Science has found a way to reduce collective blaming by revealing the hypocrisy of collectively blaming an outgroup for a blameworthy act (e.g., Muslims for acts of terrorism), but not collectively blaming an ingroup for a blameworthy act (e.g., White Americans or Christians for individual acts of violence by members of these groups; Bruneau et al., 2020). By reducing collective blame, negative intergroup attitudes and behavior associated with vicarious retribution are also decreased. In a conflict context, listening efforts that make people aware of this bias and identify examples of the hypocrisy may make it easier for participants and populations to embrace the exercise of listening as well as the other individuals participating in the exercise.

Motive misattribution

Another important intergroup bias is that of motive misattribution. Here, we tend to think that when our own group members harm the other side, even in heinous ways, it is motivated by ingroup love (e.g., to protect); however, we tend to think that the same act by an outgroup member (against our group) is motivated by hate. Importantly, merely activating critical thinking skills – by incentivizing participants to thoughtfully explain what motivated an act – can correct this bias (Waytz et al., 2014). It is also possible that listening to the perspectives and rationales of outgroup members, and drawing universal connections about motives on all sides, would disarm this bias. Either way, listening facilitators should assume that motive misattribution exists on all sides of a conflict until new understandings are made explicit and agreed upon by all parties.

Biases related to intergroup moral perceptions

We distance ourselves from other groups when we think they value harm or fairness differently than our group; unfortunately, we may not always perceive them correctly. Indeed, our perceptions of how much outgroup members value harm or fairness are influenced by whether we see our group as being threatened by them (Obeid et al., 2017). In a conflict context, we almost certainly think that outgroup members are more willing to harm and less likely to be concerned with fairness than members of our own group. By being aware of this bias and naming the intergroup stories or experiences that contradict it, listening efforts may be strengthened.

Sacred values

Sacred values are processed in the brain as moral rules, duties, or obligations rather than choices made by cost-benefit calculations (Baron & Spranca, 1997; Berns et al., 2012; Ginges et al., 2007; Hamid et al., 2018). Sacred values can have their basis in religion, as in the obligation to journey to Mecca if you are Muslim, but they can also be secular, such as a transcendent commitment to security, the welfare of one's children, justice, or nationhood – all likely candidates for sacralization in a conflict context. Understanding sacred values is important for actors designing and implementing listening programs because, once identified, actors must communicate about sacred values differently than other issues. When people perceive that others do not respect a sacred value that they hold, they experience anger, disgust, or moral outrage. These emotions and the destructive, cost-insensitive reactions they manifest have since been coined *the backfire effect*.

For example, in the Palestinian territories, when average Palestinians were asked to evaluate a deal whereby Europe would pay them billions of dollars to give up the right of return, they "quit" negotiations out of disgust (Ginges et al., 2007). The same reaction came from average Iranians who stood to gain a massive economic package were they to give up nuclear energy in 2008 (Dehghani et al., 2010). In Afghanistan, India, Indonesia, Kurdistan, and Ireland attempts to trump a sacred value with material offerings not only triggered negative responses, it sometimes led to an increase in the endorsement of violence (Atran, 2016; Ginges & Atran, 2009; Sheikh et al., 2016). While work on how to communicate around sacred values is still nascent, researchers suggest not invoking a sacralized issue if it is possible to dialogue or negotiate without addressing it (Argo & Ginges, 2015; Atran & Axelrod, 2008). In cases where a sacralized issue must be addressed, it is helpful to understand what is feeling threatened (Argo & Jassin, 2020). Sacred values can be acknowledged and respected; it may also be possible to trade a sacred value for another sacred value. For example, the sacred value of not selling one's children might shift to being acceptable if selling the children meant they could continue to live (Argo & Ginges, 2015).

Status and power differences

Listening is an exercise in perspective giving and perspective taking, and the needs of the parties in such a context differ according to whether they perceive themselves to hold relatively higher or lower power within the conflict. Research shows that low-power actors benefit most from being heard, while high-power actors benefit most from listening (Bruneau & Saxe, 2012). The potential import of this finding for the design of listening initiatives should be understood and considered, even if procedural equity concerns might make one or multiple parties reluctant to engage in such limited listening roles, and even the assignment of high/low power labels could be politically fraught at a negotiation table with diverse actors.

In closing, whether the intergroup intervention be social contact, dialogue, mediation, or negotiation, using the lens of social identity and intergroup dynamics can enable better listening design and implementation in the ways described above. Because, however, our social identities are so influenced by our ingroups, intergroup interventions may be necessary but not sufficient within the larger peacebuilding context. Peacebuilders must be attuned to the dynamics *within* groups as well. In the next section, we look beyond intergroup interventions to discuss the important within-group work that may need to happen in tandem with, or even prior to, intergroup interventions. Further, because peacebuilding contexts involve multiple stakeholders with their own power dynamics – funders, international organizations, grassroots groups, etc. – we next explore how the above insights can apply in peacebuilding beyond intergroup work.

Beyond intergroup work

One of the most critical factors for effectiveness in a peacebuilding context is political will. As Nyheim (2015) wrote, amidst a violent conflict, "technical solutions should not replace political ones" (p. 7). Fortunately, listening-based peacebuilding approaches can help to generate political will by engaging critical stakeholders – including those who are not a part of intergroup work, and might even be contributing to the conflict. Listening can be leveraged to build and shape political will in relation to within-group work (by engaging ingroup members to shift norms and decrease acceptance of violence), and efforts to strengthen cooperation across the peacebuilding field.

Supporting intergroup efforts

Leaders can prepare for or amplify intergroup efforts by beginning to socialize the concept and rationale of listening within their own groups. This might involve priming their people normatively for listening, by modeling the approach in their interactions with other leaders and with their own group members. Leaders within groups who wish to shift their groups' behavior in a conflict can also use listening as a way to understand underlying dynamics – their group's fears, perceptions, the sense of social pressure people are feeling, etc. Done well, listening can help build credibility while also helping identify ways to reach people. This is, in essence, listening to influence norms and listening to inform program design.

In some cases, within group work can be used to increase effectiveness as intergroup work is implemented. It may include communication campaigns and/ or community discussions that reflect on breakthroughs and successes or key insights and stories from the intergroup work within their own group. In both cases, the goal is to prepare groups to engage in listening – with each other and with outgroup members – and to find ways to increase listening behaviors.

Shifting norms away from violence

Another way that "moderate" leaders can leverage listening to promote peace-building efforts within their own groups is by seeking to shift ingroup norms. Leaders are innate referents for normative influence; they can and should be seen talking about their experience of listening to an outgroup member, being listened to, or, ideally, both. Norm-setting work can also be done through fictional media, a method that has proven successful in multiple trials in recent years (Blair et al., 2019; Blair et al., 2021; Paluck, 2009; Paluck & Green, 2009). For example, a character on a TV show representative of a particular group might be shown listening to an outgroup member (or being listened to). These interventions are often most effective when coupled with community discussions around the actions of the characters in the show.

Strengthening cooperation among peacebuilders

In addition to incorporating insights based on social identity biases into listening designs, socializing the importance of listening within stakeholder groups, and generally seeking to shift group norms away from violence, intervenors can employ listening to strengthen cooperation among peacebuilders. Here, we consider its potential for three areas of peacebuilding: building "infrastructures for peace," "Do No Harm" approaches, and peacebuilding design.

Listening to strengthen "infrastructures for peace"

To increase effectiveness, the peacebuilding field has recently emphasized the need to build relationships across the peacebuilding ecosystem, calling this work "Infrastructures for Peace" (Glessmann, 2016; Kumar & de la Haye, 2012; Ryan, 2012). Significant research demonstrates the importance of linking peacebuilders across levels, from the local to the national and even international: "Among the authors who work on subnational peacebuilding, the consensus is that only a combination of top-down and bottom-up efforts can build a sustainable peace" (Autesserre, 2017, p. 118). Autesserre continued noting that this combination allows local and foreign peacebuilders, who typically have differing competencies, to contribute diverse "perspectives, networks, assets, and leverage with particular constituencies," all of which are essential to peacebuilding (Anderson & Olson, 2003, p. 35; as cited in Autesserre, 2017, p. 125–126).

Similarly, research highlights the importance of network heterogeneity, meaning that networks must be built with members from diverse stakeholder groups. Specifically, it is critical to include those most directly affected by violence centrally in these structures. Local communities are often the best positioned to respond to and prevent violence – and are often already taking action, whether it includes prevention or protection. Unfortunately, these actors have sometimes been ignored or not taken seriously. As Autesserre (2017, p. 124) observed:

> In their day-to-day lives, ordinary people engage in actions that researchers often view as banal, mundane, and unimportant, and that are unrelated to formal peacebuilding initiatives, but that in fact help prevent local outbreaks of violence and, at times, even directly deal with conflict and tensions.

It is crucial that peacebuilding efforts are anchored in these communities – both in terms of problem analysis and implementation (e.g., how they ultimately channel resources and support for action). One reason for this is longevity. Saferworld (2016) found that local actors, unlike external actors in some cases, "are likely to stay engaged in conflict prevention and peacebuilding work" over the long term – in part because they will have to live with and uphold the peace and that they are "often not only the most efficient and flexible 'responders' but also potentially the most effective" (p. 4).

Critically, these infrastructures can take many different forms – what is important is including the right constellation of actors to enable information sharing, positive social pressure and support, co-created strategy, and management of conflict dynamics. These networks should be established proactively – and if possible, before a crisis – in order to develop trust, create a sense of unity and belonging, align around risks, and establish a history of getting things done prior to conflict escalation. Below, we offer three central considerations:

1. *Linking efforts across different levels.* As Seibert (2013, pp. 40–41) observed:

> The strength of a peace infrastructure is in fact deeply related to its ability to create direct connections between the participants: top-level political decision-makers in charge of implementing conflict transformation agreements and community members at the local, national, and regional level.

However, the linking of these efforts is often an important gap in peacebuilding. Indeed, there is a lack of knowledge around "how to link bottom-up and top-down efforts effectively, so that individual and grass-roots initiatives contribute to macro-level stability and so that top-down processes do not undermine local achievements" (Autesserre, 2016). For instance, the African Centre for the Constructive Resolution of Disputes seeks further efforts in "mobilising and developing the capacities of local communities, especially those living across and along the borders, to appreciate and utilize intergovernmental structures in peacebuilding, peacemaking and conflict mitigation" (ACCORD, 2016).

2. *Building trust and relationships for real-time information sharing and action.* Efforts should be made to build trust and relationships between those involved in peace infrastructures, and to the relevant groups that need to be influenced. This is critical when it comes to identifying threats – which Cohen argued must "be about more than systems and tools; it needs to be underpinned by the relationships of trust that enable people directly affected by violence to raise their voice and to act" (Saferworld, 2016, p. 3).

Relationships are also essential for enabling information exchange and action. A report on a local peacebuilding project in Timor Leste, for example, noted that "[because] community dynamics can change quickly in a conflict setting, sharing information and learning among team members is essential. This allows all members of the team to respond constructively, in a unified fashion, and with awareness of local sensitivities" (Bolton & Amaral, 2015, p. 9).

It can be harder to build and establish trust within diverse, compared to homogeneous, networks, so it is critical for practitioners to be proactive about building both the relationships and a sense of trust in their work together. In a study of communities across India, Varshney (2003) found that diverse networks where trusted bonds existed across identity groups were able to prevent inter-ethnic violence from escalating once it flared within a community. On the opposite end of the spectrum, in communities characterized by diversity without trust, many cross-group ties can actually impede information flow and cooperation (Larson & Lewis, 2017). By connecting key actors to one another in bonds of mutual dependency and trust, peace networks are able to maintain social pressure for positive action and work adaptively and responsively to emergent dynamics. While they may shift their peacebuilding focus depending on the stage of conflict, they always prioritize the maintenance of relationships – because these determine the infrastructure's capacity for coordination.

It is important that these linkages and relationships are created across different groups within a system – such that those, for example, with high-level access and power are able to trust information that comes from affected communities and are motivated to act; or such that community-level groups are able to respond to trends observed through data analysis; or that those actors who are in affected communities and most equipped and motivated to act supported with necessary resources or cover as needed. The linkages across levels and the cross-cutting nature of relationships can give everyone within the system access to broader knowledge and capacities. Lastly, it is important to note that relationships can be built in atmospheres of distrust – for example those between civil society and security forces – though doing so will require long-term investment and engagement (Saferworld, 2016; Schirch, 2016). These relationships are critical for ongoing action and can outlast even the more formalized structures and processes created.

3. *Specific areas for listening.* Listening is an essential component of "infrastructures for peace." Take, for example, the establishment of conflict assessments and the development of key indicators, triggers, and other dynamics deemed important to peacebuilding. Network systems can create "a basis for shared problem definition" that "sets the stage for improved coherence and response" (Nyheim, 2015, p. 4). This can be done through a participatory process that brings the knowledge and insights of diverse actors to bear (Saferworld, 2016). Different programs do this in different ways. For example, many regional initiatives undertake consultations with actors in different localities as well as at the national level in their process of developing indicators and the set of dynamics that they will monitor. As Saferworld (2016, p. 3) wrote:

> The process for gathering and analyzing data can be as important as the data itself. The inclusion of a wide range of stakeholders in participatory analysis

processes not only contributes to richer analysis but also builds trust, confidence, and the potential for mutually supportive action.

However it is done, all of these processes are built on listening.

Building a peace infrastructure with local and external ties thus requires that those who are supporting violence prevention engage with, listen to, and channel support toward those with the best knowledge of local conflict dynamics and experiences as they play out (Unger et al., 2013). This means working through both formal and informal networks and ties and "[taking] local agency seriously even where it is critical or resistant or seemingly in a different developmental or normative mode" (Richmond, 2013, p. 26). It also requires addressing international dynamics and actors, and their role and responsibilities in contributing to the conflict (Richmond, 2013).

Finally, a peace network can influence a community's ability to cooperate, whether that means public outreach to convene for a vigil or a community celebration, or to support a new norm or policy. As discussed in the previous section, this is because participation behavior depends not only on what people know about an upcoming meeting or initiative, but also their expectations as to what their group members think about it (Chwe, 2000; Siegel, 2009). By establishing an infrastructure for peace, peacebuilding actors and local leaders model engagement and cooperation that can influence their followers.

Listening to "Do No Harm"

All peacebuilding work must take a "Do No Harm" approach (Wallace, 2015). For example, when responding to escalation, Nyheim (2015) wrote that peacebuilders must "ensure that responses are conflict sensitive and do not exacerbate tensions or worsen causes of conflict" (p. 7). Doing so requires thinking across different levels of society and maintaining an immediate and long-term perspective, simultaneously. To do this, peacebuilders need to integrate the wisdom of internal and external stakeholders, even when their perspectives, lived experiences, and even theories of change are in tension with each other; they then need to manage decisions that take these varied perspectives into account. This kind of listening process is even more important in peacebuilding contexts where resources and power are held and used by international institutions.

Processes that can hold both short- and long-term perspectives are essential because (Saferworld, 2016, p. 1):

> long-term conflict prevention processes can also generate further tension, since they involve challenging existing power structures and interests. The key challenge from a developmental and peacebuilding perspective is how to support the management and transformation of these complex social changes without recourse to violence.

Thinking long-term requires reflection on issues of power. Schirch (2018) wrote that peacebuilding must challenge paradigms and structures and that "[structural] changes require dealing with corruption or shifting power balances in societies to address inequalities and disenfranchisement" (¶ 14). Thus, creating long-term peace requires that societies address issues that may be contentious in the short-term. Approaches that seek to simply pacify – and even repress – contentious issues in society can backfire in the long term.

Similarly, linking efforts across levels – local, regional, and national – is critical in order to do no harm. Doing so ensures that actions taken locally do not exacerbate regional tensions and that national attempts to prevent violence do not lead to local violence. It is also critical in order to have an effective impact (as conflict occurs not only at one level but across them). As Autesserre (2017) wrote, "local and subnational conflicts often motivate large parts of civil war violence … peacebuilding success at the macro level does not necessarily constitute peace at the subnational level" (p. 118; see also Mac Ginty et al., 2006). Local and external peacebuilding stakeholders "make the greatest contributions to peace when they work together, each challenging the biases of the other" (Autesserre, 2017, p. 126).

From a "Do No Harm" perspective, then, listening is an essential tool to ensure that multiple, varied perspectives are all brought into play for decision-making. This is especially important because, while local peacebuilders are on the frontlines, national-level institutions and even foreign stakeholders are often making important decisions regarding resourcing. Without truly listening and taking the varied perspectives of one's larger "infrastructure for peace" into account, harm can too easily be done in a conflict context. This is especially the case when those who hold resources and decision-making power at elite or national levels do not "listen" to the local, but simpler harms can occur as a result of a mere lack of coordination across efforts.

Listening to improve peacebuilding design

Audience-centered design has become popular across a range of sectors (Both, 2018) and is equally important in peacebuilding. Designing peacebuilding interventions requires deep listening to understand a context, various audiences, and approaches. Whether understanding local leaders, the pressures they face, and the knowledge they have about their own communities, or listening to learn from those trying to change incentive structures away from violence and toward peace, listening can play important roles in designing peacebuilding interventions. Further, listening and learning from peacebuilding practitioners working at all levels – as described above – is essential for the learning and evaluation needed to continue to improve peacebuilding practice.

Conclusion

This chapter considered the role and potential that listening holds in peace-building work, broadly defined as that "integral comprehensive set of interrelated efforts that support peace" and attempts to transform dynamics between con-flicting groups (Alliance for Peacebuilding, n.d.). It first sought to identify challenges of "listening at scale" within peacebuilding contexts – such as the multitude of stakeholders and the possibility that they do not understand the need for listening or have incentives to participate in it; the fact that individual-level outcomes, such as increased understanding or empathy, are not transformative at scale unless they also are able to influence unjust systems; and the existence of power imbalances and histories of trauma within conflicts, which serve as barriers to effective listening. It then considered how listening can inform some of the more well-known work of peacebuilders – efforts to transform conflict dynamics by *intergroup interventions* such as social contact, dialogue, mediation, or negoti-ation. Specifically, it explored the intergroup dynamics involved in intergroup efforts through the lens of social identity biases (e.g., the influence of within-group norms, meta-perceptions, collective blame, motive misattribution, moral perceptions, sacred values, and status and power differences), and revealed some concrete implications for listening design.

But as important as it is to do between-group work in order to transform conflict dynamics, it is likely not enough. Listening can also play a role in parallel efforts to shift norms away from violence and toward listening practices *within* groups. It can inform the building of relationships across the peacebuilding ecosystem, called "infrastructures for peace," and imbue the way they analyze risk, and design and implement interventions as an ecosystem. Lastly, listening is essential to the conception and implementation of "Do No Harm" approaches in peacebuilding.

References

ACCORD. (2016, May 5). Building regional capacity for conflict prevention and peacebuilding in the Great Lakes Region. *Conflict & Resilience Monitor, 2016/1*. https://www.accord.org.za/conflict-trends/building-regional-capacity-conflict-prevention-peacebuilding-great-lakes-region/

Alliance for Peacebuilding. (n.d.). *What is peacebuilding?* https://www.alliancefor-peacebuilding.org/about-peacebuilding

Anderson, M. B., & Olson, L. (2003). *Confronting war. Critical lessons for peace practitioners.* Collaborative for Development Action. http://hdl.handle.net/1920/12714

Anderson, M. B., & Wallace, M. (2012). *Opting out of war: Strategies to prevent violent conflict.* Lynne Rienner Publishers.

Argo, N., & Ginges, J. (2015). Beyond impasse: Addressing sacred values in international political negotiations. In M. Galluccio (Ed.), *Handbook of international negotiations: Interpersonal, intercultural, and diplomatic perspectives* (pp. 311–327). Springer.

Argo, N., & Jassin, K. (2020). *What immigration issues do Americans hold sacred? A psychological journey into American attitudes toward immigrants.* Over Zero. https://www.americanimmigrationcouncil.org/sites/default/files/research/what_immigration_issues_do_americans_hold_sacred.pdf

Atran, S. (2016). The devoted actor: Unconditional commitment and intractable conflict across cultures. *Current Anthropology, 57*(S13), S192–S203. 10.1086/685495

Atran, S., & Axelrod, R. (2008). Reframing sacred values. *Negotiation Journal, 24*(3), 221–246. 10.1111/j.1571-9979.2008.00182.x

Autesserre, S. (2016, October 19). Here's what Congo can teach the world about peace. *The Washington Post.* https://www.washingtonpost.com/news/monkey-cage/wp/2016/10/19/heres-what-this-island-in-congo-can-teach-the-world-about-peace/

Autesserre, S. (2017). International peacebuilding and local success: Assumptions and effectiveness. *International Studies Review, 19*(1), 114–132. 10.1093/isr/viw054

Baron, J., & Spranca, M. (1997). Protected values. *Organizational Behavior and Human Decision Processes, 70,* 1–16. 10.1006/obhd.1997.2690

Baron-Cohen, S. (2012). *The science of evil: On empathy and the origins of cruelty.* Basic Books.

Batson, C. D. (2009). These things called empathy: Eight related but distinct phenomena. In J. Decety & W. Ickes (Eds.), *The social neuroscience of empathy* (pp. 3–15). MIT Press. 10.7551/mitpress/9780262012973.003.0002

Baumeister, R. F., & Leary, M. R. (1995). The need to belong: Desire for interpersonal attachments as a fundamental human motivation. *Psychological Bulletin, 117*(3), 497–529. https://psycnet.apa.org/doi/10.1037/0033-2909.117.3.497

Berns, G. S., Bell, E., Capra, C. M., Prietula, M. J., Moore, S., Anderson, B., Ginges, J., & Atran, S. (2012). The price of your soul: Neural evidence for the non-utilitarian representation of sacred values. *Philosophical Transactions of the Royal Society B, 367*(1589), 754–762. 10.1098/rstb.2011.0262

Beyond Conflict. (2019, May). *Decoding dehumanization: Policy brief for policymakers and practitioners.* https://beyondconflictint.org/wp-content/uploads/2020/06/Decoding-Dehumanization-Policy-Brief-2019.pdf

Blair, G., Littman, R., Nugent, E., Wolfe, R., Bukar, M., Crisman, B., Etim, A., Hazlett, C., & Kim, J. (2021). Trusted authorities can change minds and shift norms during conflict. *Proceedings of the National Academy of Sciences, 118*(42), e2105570118. 10.1073/pnas.2105570118

Blair, G., Littman, R., & Paluck, E. L. (2019). Motivating the adoption of new community-minded behaviors: An empirical test in Nigeria. *Science Advances, 5*(3). doi: 10.1126/sciadv.aau517

Bodie, G. D., & Denham, J. P. (2017). Listening in(to) close relationships. In M. Stoltz, K. P. Sodowsky, & C. M. Cates (Eds.), *Listening across lives* (pp. 41–61). Kendall Hunt.

Bodie, G. D., & Godwin, P. (2022). On the limits of listening for bridging divides and cross-cultural understanding. In L. Chao & C. Wang (Eds.), *Communication across differences: Negotiating identity, privilege, and marginalization in the 21st century* (pp. 225–243). Cognella.

Bolton, N., & Amaral, L. (2015, July 24). Strategic community peacebuilding in practice. Catholic Relief Services. https://www.crs.org/our-work-overseas/research-publications/strategic-community-peacebuilding-practice

Both, T. (2018, March 9). Human-centered, systems-minded design. *Stanford Social Innovation Review.* https://ssir.org/articles/entry/human_centered_systems_minded_design#

Bruneau, E., Kteily, N., & Laustsen, L. (2018). The unique effects of blatant dehumanization on attitudes and behavior towards Muslim refugees during the European 'refugee crisis' across four countries. *European Journal of Social Psychology, 48*(5), 645–662. doi: 10.1002/ejsp.2357

Bruneau, E., Kteily, N., & Urbiola, A. (2020). A collective blame hypocrisy intervention enduringly reduces hostility towards Muslims. *Nature Human Behaviour, 4,* 45–54. doi: 10.1038/s41562-019-0747-7

Bruneau, E., & Saxe, R. (2012). The power of being heard: The benefits of 'perspective-giving' in the context of intergroup conflict. *Journal of Experimental Social Psychology, 48*(4), 855–866. 10.1016/j.jesp.2012.02.017

Burleson, B. R. (2011). A constructivist approach to listening. *International Journal of Listening, 25,* 27–46. doi: 10.1080/10904018.2011.536470

Chwe, M. S. Y. (2000). Communication and coordination in social networks. *The Review of Economic Studies, 67*(1), 1–16. https://www.jstor.org/stable/2567025

Cikara, M., Bruneau, E. G., & Saxe, R. R. (2011). Us and them: Intergroup failures of empathy. *Current Directions in Psychological Science, 20*(3), 149–153. 10.1177/0963 721411408713

Davison, A. (1998). *Secularism and revivalism in Turkey. A hermeneutic reconsideration.* Yale University Press.

Dehghani, M., Atran, S., Iliev, R., Sachdeva, S., Medin, D., & Ginges, J. (2010). Sacred values and conflict over Iran's nuclear program. *Judgment and Decision Making, 5*(7), 540–546.

Demoulin, S., Cortes, B. P., Viki, T. G., Rodriguez, A. P., Rodriguez, R. T., Paladino, M. P., & Leyens, J. P. (2009). The role of in-group identification in infra-humanization. *International Journal of Psychology, 44*(1), 4–11. 10.1080/00207590802057654

Dobson, A. (2014). *Listening for democracy: Recognition, representation, reconciliation.* Oxford University Press.

Donais, T. (2012). *Peacebuilding and local ownership: Post-conflict consensus-building* (1st ed.). Routledge.

Epley, N. (2014). *Mindwise: How we understand what others think, believe, feel, and want.* Knopf.

Freinacht, H. (2017). *The listening society: A metamodern guide to politics. Book One.* Metamoderna.

Giner-Sorolla, R., & Russell, P. S. (2019). Not just disgust: Fear and anger also relate to intergroup dehumanization. *Collabra: Psychology, 5*(1), Article 56. 10.1525/collabra.211

Ginges, J., & Atran, S. (2009). Noninstrumental reasoning over sacred values: An Indonesian case study. In D. M. Bartels, C. W. Bauman, L. J. Skitka, & D. L. Medin (Eds.), *Moral judgment and decision making* (pp. 193–206). Elsevier Academic Press. 10.1016/ S0079-7421(08)00406-4

Ginges, J., Atran, S., Medin, D., & Shikaki, K. (2007). Sacred bounds on rational resolution of violent political conflict. *Proceedings of the National Academy of Sciences of the United States of America, 104,* 7357–7360. 10.1073/pnas.0701768104

Gioia, F. (2017). Peer effects on risk behaviour: The importance of group identity. *Experimental economics, 20*(1), 100–129. 10.1007/s10683-016-9478-z

Glessmann, H. J. (2016). *Embedded peace: Infrastructures for peace: Approaches and lessons learned.* Berghof Foundation. https://www.undp.org/sites/g/files/zskgke326/files/ publications/Berghof-UNDP_EmbeddedPeaceI4P_2016.pdf

Gray, K., & Blakey, W. (2021). *They hate me: (False) meta-perceptions drive political conflict.* Moral Understanding Blog. https://moralunderstanding.substack.com/p/they-hate-me

Hamid, N., Pretus, C., Sheikh, H., Ginges, J., Tobeña, A., Davis, R., Vilarroya, O., & Atran, S. (2018). Neural and behavioral correlates of sacred values and vulnerability to violent extremism. *Frontiers in Psychology*, *9*, Article 2462. 10.3389/fpsyg.2018.02462

Hogg, M. A. (2007). Uncertainty–identity theory. *Advances in Experimental Social Psychology*, *39*, 69–126. 10.1016/S0065-2601(06)39002-8

Houshmand, Z. (2019, March 13). *The biology of care and conflict in groups*. Mind & Life Institute. https://ubuntudialogue.org/the-biology-of-care-and-conflict-in-groups/

Johansson, P. (2017, May 17). *Feeling for the game: How emotions shape listening in peacebuilding partnerships*. E-International Relations. https://www.e-ir.info/2017/05/17/feeling-for-the-game-how-emotions-shape-listening-in-peacebuilding-partnerships/

Kteily, N., Hodson, G., & Bruneau, E. (2016). They see us as less than human: Meta-dehumanization predicts intergroup conflict via reciprocal dehumanization. *Journal of Personality and Social Psychology*, *110*, 343–370. 10.1037/pspa0000044

Kumar, C., & de la Haye, J. (2012). Hybrid peacemaking: Building national "Infrastructures for Peace." *Global Governance*, *18*(1), 13–20. doi: 10.1163/19426720-01801003

Lamm, C., Rütgen, M., & Wagner, I. C. (2019). Imaging empathy and prosocial emotions. *Neuroscience Letters*, *693*, 49–53. 10.1016/j.neulet.2017.06.054Get

Larson, J. M., & Lewis, J. I. (2017). Ethnic networks. *American Journal of Political Science*, *61*, 350–364. 10.1111/ajps.12282

Lees, J., & Cikara, M. (2020). Inaccurate group meta-perceptions drive negative outgroup attributions in competitive contexts. *Nature Human Behaviour*, *4*(3), 279–286. 10.1038/s41562-019-0766-4

Lewis, L. (2020b). *The power of strategic listening in contemporary organizations*. Rowman & Littlefield.

Lickel, B., Miller, N., Stenstrom, D. M., Denson, T. F., & Schmader, T. (2006). Vicarious retribution: The role of collective blame in intergroup aggression. *Personality and Social Psychology Review*, *10*(4), 372–390. 10.1207/s15327957pspr1004_6

Mac Ginty, R., Muldoon, O. T., & Ferguson, N. (2006). No war, no peace: Northern Ireland after the agreement. *Political psychology*, *28*(1), 1–11. https://www.jstor.org/stable/20447017

Macnamara, J. (2016). *Organizational listening: The missing essential in public communication*. Peter Lang.

Maitner, A., Smith, E., & MacKie, D. (2016). Intergroup emotions theory: Prejudice and differentiated emotional reactions toward outgroups. In C. Sibley & F. Barlow (Eds.), *The Cambridge handbook of the psychology of prejudice* (pp. 111–130). Cambridge University Press. doi: 10.1017/9781316161579.006

Mower, D. S. (2020). Philosophy. In D. L. Worthington, & G. D. Bodie (Eds.), *The handbook of listening* (pp. 217–232). Wiley.

Nyheim, D. (2015, October). *Early warning and response to violent conflict*. Saferworld. https://www.saferworld.org.uk/resources/publications/1009-early-warning-and-response-to-violent-conflict-time-for-a-rethink

Obeid, N., Argo, N., & Ginges, J. (2017). How moral perceptions influence intergroup tolerance: Evidence from Lebanon, Morocco, and the United States. *Personality and Social Psychology Bulletin*, *43*(3), 381–391. 10.1177/0146167216686560

Paluck, E. L. (2009). Reducing intergroup prejudice and conflict using the media: A field experiment in Rwanda. *Journal of Personality and Social Psychology*, *96*(3), 574–587. doi: 10.1037/a0011989. PMID: 19254104.

Paluck, E. L., & Green, D. P. (2009). Deference, dissent, and dispute resolution: A field experiment on a mass media intervention in Rwanda. *American Political Science Review*, *103*(4), 622–644. doi: 10.1017/S0003055409990128

Prati, F., Crisp, R. J., Meleady, R., & Rubini, M. (2016). Humanizing outgroups through multiple categorization: The roles of individuation and threat. *Personality & Social Psychology Bulletin*, *42*(4), 526–539. 10.1177/0146167216636624

Richmond, O. P. (2013). Missing links: Peace infrastructures and peace formation. In B. Unger, S. Lundström, K. Planta, & B. Austin (Eds.), *Peace infrastructures: Assessing concept and practice*. (Berghof Handbook Dialogue Series, No. 10; pp. 21–30). Berghof Foundation. https://berghof-foundation.org/files/publications/dialogue10_peacein-frastructures_complete.pdf

Rogers, C. R., & Farson, R. E. (1957). *Active listening*. University of Chicago.

Ruggeri, K., Većkalov, B., Bojanić, L., Andersen, T. L., Ashcroft-Jones, S., Ayacaxli, N., ... & Folke, T. (2021). The general fault in our fault lines. *Nature Human Behaviour*, *5*(10), 1369–1380. 10.1038/s41562-021-01092-x

Ryan, J. (2012). Infrastructures for peace as a path to resilient societies: An institutional perspective. *Journal of Peacebuilding & Development*, *7*(3), 14–24. 10.1177/154231662 0945681

Saferworld. (2016). Effective local action: From early warning to peacebuilding. https://www.c-r.org/resource/effective-local-action-early-warning-peacebuilding

Santos, L., Voelkel, J., & Zaki, J. (2002). Belief in the utility of cross-partisan empathy reduces partisan animosity and facilitates political persuasion. *Psychological Science*, *33*, 1557–1573. https://journals.sagepub.com/doi/abs/10.1177/09567976221098594

Sapolsky, R. (2017). *Behave: The biology of humans at our best and worst*. Penguin Books.

Schirch, L. (2013). *Conflict assessment and peacebuilding planning: Toward a participatory approach to human security*. Kumarian Press.

Schirch, L. (2016). *Handbook on human security: A civil-military-police curriculum*. GPPAC.

Schirch, L. (2018, November 26). The state of peacebuilding 2018: Twelve observations. *Lisa Schirch: Writing on Human Security Blog*. https://lisaschirch.wordpress.com/2018/11/26/the-state-of-peacebuilding-2018-twelve-observations/

Seibert, H. (2013). National peace and dialogue structures: Strengthening the immune system from within instead of prescribing antibiotics. In B. Unger, S. Lundström, K. Planta, & B. Austin (Eds.), *Peace infrastructures: Assessing concept and practice*. Berghof Handbook Dialogue Series, No. 10 (pp. 30–41). Berghof Foundation. https://berghof-foundation.org/files/publications/dialogue10_peaceinfrastructures_complete.pdf

Sheikh, H., Gómez, Á., & Atran, S. (2016). Empirical evidence for the devoted actor model. *Current Anthropology*, *57*(Suppl 13), S204–S209. https://www.jstor.org/stable/26545630

Sherif, M. (1956). Experiments in group conflict. *Scientific American*, *195*(5), 54–59.

Siegel, D. A. (2009). Social networks and collective action. *American Journal of Political Science*, *53*(1), 122–138. https://www.jstor.org/stable/24941808

Smith, H. J., & Tyler, T. R. (1997). Choosing the right pond: The impact of group membership on self-esteem and group-oriented behavior. *Journal of Experimental Social Psychology*, *33*(2), 146–170. 10.1006/jesp.1996.1318.

Tajfel, H. (1974). Social identity and intergroup behaviour. *Social Science Information*, *13*(2), 65–93. 10.1177/053901847401300204

Tajfel, H., & Turner, J. C. (1978). Intergroup behavior. In H. Tajfel & C. Fraser (Eds.), *Introducing social psychology* (pp. 401–466). Penguin Books.

Tajfel, H., & Turner, J. C. (1979). An integrative theory of intergroup conflict. In W. G. Austin & S. Worchel (Eds.), *The social psychology of intergroup relations* (pp. 33–37). Monterey, CA: Brooks/Cole.

Tankard, M. E., & Paluck, E. L. (2016). Norm perception as a vehicle for social change. *Social Issues and Policy Review*, *10*(1), 181–211. 10.1111/sipr.12022

Unger, B., Lundström, S., Planta, K., & Austin, B. (Eds.). (2013). *Peace infrastructures: Assessing concept and practice*. Berghof Foundation. https://berghof-foundation.org/library/peace-infrastructures-assessing-concept-and-practice

Varshney, A. (2003). *Ethnic conflict and civic life: Hindus and Muslims in India*. Yale University Press.

Wahl, R. (2019). On the ethics of open-mindedness in the age of Trump. *Educational Theory*, *69*, 455–472. 10.1111/edth.12379

Wallace, M. (2015). From principle to practice: A user's guide to do no harm. CDA Collaborative Learning Projects. https://www.cdacollaborative.org/publication/from-principle-to-practice-a-users-guide-to-do-no-harm/

Waytz, A., Young, L. L., & Ginges, J. (2014). Motive attribution asymmetry for love vs. hate drives intractable conflict. *Proceedings of the National Academy of Sciences*, *111*(44), 15687–15692. 10.1073/pnas.1414146111

Wilmer, F. (2018). Empathy as political action: Can empathic engagement disrupt narratives of conflict. *Journal of Social Science Research*, *13*, 2860–2870. 10.24297/jssr.v13i0.7934

Zaki, J. (2019). *The war for kindness: Building empathy in a fractured world*. Crown.

Zaki, J., & Cikara, M. (2015). Addressing empathic failures. *Current Directions in Psychological Science*, *24*(6), 471–476. 10.1177/0963721415599978

Zeldis, K. (2018). *Not our kind*. Harper.

9

LISTENING IN SERVICE OF TRAUMA-INFORMED PEACEBUILDING

Prabha Sankaranarayan, Mary Jo Harwood, and Ginny Morrison

MEDIATORS BEYOND BORDERS INTERNATIONAL

There has been increasing recognition that peacebuilding, conflict transformation, and the field of trauma are interconnected (Reilly et al., 2004) and that collective trauma has its own challenges that must be addressed (Hubl & Auritt, 2020). We, as practitioners, join leading educators and researchers in believing that the role of trauma must be integrated into conflict transformation applications and practitioner education. It is more effective, and it should be an ethical responsibility, to integrate research from multiple fields, particularly psychology, neurobiology, and epigenetics.[1] The peacebuilding field has, thankfully, come a long way in recognizing the impact of empathetic engagement – a practice grounded in deep, effective listening – when working with individuals and communities with a history of traumatic experiences (e.g., John, 2021).

Increasingly, the odds are that those we want to involve in community decision making, consultation, or peacebuilding efforts have also been affected by trauma. This trauma can originate, for example, from mass displacement, torture, rape as a weapon of war, state-sponsored violence against individuals, criminal gang or militia control, kidnapped child soldiers and sex slaves, natural disasters, and living in chaotic, ungoverned spaces. In addition to causing great suffering, these conditions can have lingering, unintended consequences for peacebuilding and governance. Equipped with an understanding of trauma and its impacts, practitioners can design and implement longer-lasting initiatives that more deeply affect the root causes of violence and disorder. Listening, developing narratives, and several complementary practices improve efforts in trauma-affected contexts, whether we are working in state-level negotiations, expanding officials' governance skills, fostering community decision making, addressing historical harms, seeking reconciliation, or supporting community integration. These initiatives may take healing as their primary focus with direct interventions that acknowledge

DOI: 10.4324/9781003214465-9

and address it, or they may be shaped to manage the impact of trauma while not expressly discussing it.

In this chapter, we introduce some common effects of trauma as well as methods that practitioners can integrate into the design and facilitation of processes, trainings, and other engagements – while leaving therapy to other professionals. Nearly all of these methods have listening at their core. Listening is essential to identifying the effects of trauma, and the sources of resilience, in the locations in which the peacebuilder will work; failing to listen can lead us to leave out essential elements of a process or project design and might even cause harm to participants or surrounding communities. Listening allows us to identify those among our participants and colleagues who appear to be struggling with unresolved trauma and gives us clues to the most effective ways to support them. Empathetic listening and validation are an intervention in themselves, rebuilding human connections and trust that have been severed by reactions to trauma. And frequently, peacebuilders will need to develop participants' capacity for listening, so that they may use it to overcome many barriers to collaboration that we see in trauma-affected populations.

What leads to a trauma response?

The term "trauma" has been used in many ways; here, we define it as one or more severe, often life-threatening events that make a person feel overwhelmed and helpless to stop the danger (Herman, 1992). These events may be caused by people or by natural disasters, and people can be affected by trauma as a direct victim or by witnessing a horrific event. They may also be affected by "transgenerational trauma," where trauma-affected elders – consciously or not – pass along fears, suspicions, unusual vigilance, and other impacts to generations who did not experience the traumatic events (McGoldrick & Walsh, 2004). Moreover, epigenetics – the science examining the effects of behavior and environment on genes – is finding that trauma can leave a chemical mark that can affect how some genes are expressed, which may result in higher rates of depression, anxiety, or suicide among the children born later to a trauma-affected person[2] (Centers for Disease Control and Prevention, 2022; Yehuda & Lehrner, 2018).

"Collective trauma" involves traumatic events that affect entire groups or societies, with the trauma living on in the collective memory of generations beyond the direct survivors of the events. Here, we might think of the Rwandan genocide (see Mugume et al., Chapter 12); the conflict among ethnoreligious groups in Bosnia and Hercegovina; the families impacted by genocide in the partition of India and Pakistan; or the effects of slavery on African Americans in the USA. Collective trauma affects, in different ways, the groups that were harmed and those that caused the harms (Hirschberger, 2018).

What effects can trauma have?

Response to trauma depends very much on the individual. Some are sharply affected for decades, some find their reactions recede quickly and without help, while the responses of others can fall anywhere in between these extremes. Indeed, the emotions and physical reactions that occurred during the trauma can be activated by sights, sounds, smells, tactile sensations, and tastes in the current environment, which remind the individual of the traumatic experience. The rational brain could discern that this is a memory, but the emotional brain automatically overrides the rational brain, and the person has physical reactions as if the real event were happening again (Van der Kolk, 2014). This can trigger hyper- or hypo-arousal. With hypo-arousal, we become numb in body and mind. If we are hyper-aroused, we may experience rage or panic, among other possible responses.

Trauma survivors spend inordinate amounts of time working to prevent being hijacked by those intrusive memories, uncomfortable sensations, fear, anxiety, and a profound sense of helplessness. Preoccupation with either the emotions or the attempts to avoid them interferes with survivors' ability to trust, form or sustain bonds, maintain focus, learn from experience, and think of the future. Consequently, the loss of these abilities takes a toll on relationships. The survivor may withdraw, as the promise of closeness can evoke fear of connection and feelings of abandonment and betrayal. People around them may perpetuate a cycle, as they avoid, or don't know how to connect with, someone they perceive as disengaged or volatile. Hyper- or hypo-arousal can be triggered frequently if others involved in the trauma are family or close community members.

Where the trauma is collective, that inability to trust, or to transcend one's own suffering enough to help others, is widespread. This is destabilizing as it rips away a sense of community, both as a source of support and, for many, as an important component of the self (Erikson, 1976). The destabilizing effects of collective trauma is discussed in trauma literature (e.g., Pouligny, 2014; Webb, 2004; Wessels, 2006) and has been apparent in contexts in which we (the authors of this chapter) have worked, such as Liberia and Sri Lanka.

As described by Hirschberger (2018), collective trauma is a dynamic social psychological process that is primarily dedicated to the construction of meaning. For example, descendants of the Holocaust and other genocide survivors may compulsively recreate the trauma in an effort to make sense of it (Yehuda & Lehrner, 2018). For survivors, it is also common to pass down culturally-derived teachings and traditions about threat. As an example, see the story presented by Jones and Neumann to open Chapter 5. Even though this trauma recreation perpetuates suffering, it also increases group cohesion and group identification and strengthens a sense of a transgenerational collective unit that can mitigate the threat and make meaning from it. At the same time, these practices can serve as disincentives to releasing the hold of the trauma on people's lives. Over time, collective trauma can become the epicenter of group identity and the lens through which group members understand their social environment (Hirschberger, 2018).

For the groups who caused the harm, collective trauma represents an identity threat (Branscombe et al., 1999), as it creates tension between the desire to view the group in a positive light (Tajfel & Turner, 1979), and the acknowledgment of severe moral transgressions in its past. Members of the harm-doing group may deny the events, or strongly advance the idea that current group members are unlike their ancestors (Roth et al., 2017). Where they gloss over the destructive actions, it can create a gap in collective memory that can be felt (Imhoff, 2017). Such a group often reconstructs the trauma to make it more palatable and reduce the group's responsibility (Hirschberger, 2018).

It is also important to recognize where the same person may be both victim and perpetrator; for example, if a victim of child abuse goes on to abuse others, or when militias coerce civilians to commit atrocities to save their own lives. Such people may push to have their victimhood recognized and may compete with, or be discriminatory toward, other victims (Noor et al., 2012).

Why address trauma as part of peacebuilding?

Traumatic exposure can undermine collaboration, increase the possibility of further violence, and interfere with processes or project implementation and sustainability. Whether the context is indigenous concerns in a northeastern border state in India or fossil fuel livelihoods in West Virginia in the USA, integrating those with local knowledge of the culture and context, along with those who understand the impact of trauma on individuals and groups, is critical to a practice grounded in the principles of "do no harm" (see Argo & Brown, Chapter 8).

Unresolved trauma leaves people vulnerable to creating further harm. It can be harder for a survivor to feel calm and manage stimuli from the environment. To overcome that fear and sense of being overwhelmed, survivors try to re-establish a sense of agency; stripped of skills, however, they risk doing it harmfully, such as when victim becomes harm-doer, perpetuating the cycle of violence. Indeed, it can be difficult for trauma-affected participants to concentrate or learn new information, and memory can be slowed, all of which can compromise trainings and attempts to foster new outlooks. Discomfort can lead to emotional outbursts, intense fidgeting, fist fights, and other disruptions of meetings and activities. Difficulty in taking initiative, planning, making and keeping commitments, and follow-through can stop a peacebuilding process or project before it is realized and imperil its sustainability.

Conflict, of course, is about relationships. Because trauma affects the capacity to form and maintain relationships, it can compromise any effort that requires collaboration. In addition to heightened distrust, the survivor's need for self-protection can block their ability to listen with empathy to others, limiting perspective-taking and reducing incentives to collaborate, both of which are keys to peacebuilding. Collaboration is necessary for resolving conflicts, community decision making, and civic participation, processes that are further undermined if collective trauma has shredded the fabric of society (Pouligny, 2014; Sesay & Ismail, 2003). Groups may repeatedly recreate forms of the trauma and be unable to participate in unification efforts. Group identity may take on heightened importance and harden into tribalism, locking in place a fractured, volatile state.

In a society with collective trauma, the need to come to terms with a dark past represents a crisis of meaning that must be resolved. Initiatives should integrate means for the society, or key representatives, to deconstruct the current sense of collective self by frankly confronting the past. Failure to do so can threaten fundamental values, ideas of self-worth, and a sense of collective purpose. Beneficial processes then support society in constructing a collective identity that, in healthier ways, provides continuity, coherence, belonging, efficacy, and significance, including valuing the perpetrator group as strong for having overcome past failings (Baumeister, 1991; Vignoles et al., 2006).

What we have just described can be usefully summarized as a process of reconciliation, understood as a means of building relationships today that are not haunted by the violence and hatred of yesterday. From that perspective, the critical questions are not only "what happened?" but also − and above all − "what shall we do with the past?" One of the most fundamental issues for moving forward is not whether to remember *or* forget, but *how* to "remember *and* forget," that is, developing ways to balance the weight of history with the complexity of the present moment − the political context, funders' directives, threat of imminent violence and more − along with all that is evoked for the individuals involved (Zelizer, 2008). It is essential that peacebuilding practitioners have the skills to design such processes, while ensuring that they do no harm.

Empowering individuals to recognize trauma reactions and learn skills to regulate negative reactions enables them to interrupt the cycle of violence. By understanding trauma, they are better equipped to tolerate behavioral differences and employ "trauma-sensitive responses." That, coupled with conflict resolution skills, enhances individuals' capacity for listening, engaging, and building relationships in order to overcome divisions. When trauma is addressed and resolved, or when conflict is transformed, trust is re-established. With trust comes the motivation and capacity to learn, create livelihoods, and build relationships, all of which are components of vital communities and economies.

Methods to address trauma

How exactly might peacebuilders empower people to recognize the effects of trauma and rebuild trust and productive community participation? First, it is important that we do not pathologize reactions to traumatic experience. Instead, we should choose methods of support that acknowledge how common strong reactions are, and through that acknowledgement, help survivors shift so that trauma reactions become part of, but do not dominate, their lives. There are many methods that support these objectives. Here, we will concentrate on four key methods that peacebuilders and community engagement professionals can effectively adopt: reducing reactivity, developing narratives, enhancing human connection, and offering choices. As we will show, effective listening is essential to each of these.

Method 1: reducing reactivity

A key goal of addressing trauma is to repair the traumatized brain's faulty alarm systems and restore the emotional brain to its ordinary job of being a quiet, background presence that takes care of the housekeeping of the body, ensuring that a person eats, sleeps, connects with intimate partners, protects children, and defends against genuine danger (Van der Kolk, 2014). By listening for those triggers that may initiate a trauma response, and directing attention in particular ways, we can widen the window of tolerance for what the traumatized person encounters. This allows the rational brain and emotional brain to work cooperatively (Stanley, 2019). According to neuroscientist Joseph LeDoux (1996), one of the most effective ways to consciously access the emotional brain – reducing how often the emotional brain is activated automatically and overwhelms the rational brain – is through self-awareness. Self-awareness activates the medial prefrontal cortex, the part of the brain that notices what is going on inside us and allows us to feel what we are feeling. This, in turn, allows traumatized individuals to recognize the sensory input that triggers hypo-and hyper-arousal for them, and to do so early enough that they can practice more deliberate reaction – focusing on deep breathing, for example, for its calming effect. Another exercise is to look around and name five things in the room; this helps connect the person with the present and release the sensation that remembered events are recurring.

Method 2: developing narrative

Developing narrative can benefit not only individuals but the larger community, potentially interrupting the cycle of violence. Here, a narrative is both a set of beliefs held by a group and, separately, a healing method that intervenors can use. Hubl and Auritt (2020) advocated examining the narratives being passed from one generation to the next about conflict, war, ethnic difference, and the like, and identifying whether those narratives are toxic. If so, they suggest using narrative as a method to surface those beliefs; identify the ways those beliefs continue to harm society; and acknowledge, honor, and let go of those beliefs. This leaves us better able to connect, contribute, and thrive within the larger community.

When working with individuals, there are at least six benefits of supporting narrative development and sharing (Gillihan, 2019). By developing the narrative more fully, the memory can become less triggering, the survivor gains a sense of mastery, the trauma memory can become more organized, and the survivor can begin to make sense of the trauma.

Feelings of shame subside

One benefit of developing narrative is helping feelings of shame subside. Many survivors report they feel responsible for what happened to them (Herman, 1992). Many talk about feeling alone with their trauma, which may be driven by shame or fears to which others cannot relate. When survivors share their stories in the presence of supportive listening, and are not blamed, they can feel less isolated, more empowered, and better able to release their shame and perseveration on the events (Gillihan, 2019).

Discussion, however, can also be a mixed experience; it can bring to light the phenomenon of emotional contagion, which drives some individuals to group behavior contrary to their own values and normal behavior (Fitzduff, 2021). This can exacerbate feelings of shame, regret, anger, and sadness. Helpers must take care to support the expression of these feelings as one common healing step, but not feelings the survivor should hold on to.

Unhelpful beliefs about the event are corrected

Gillihan (2019) noted that a second benefit of developing narratives is that survivors may learn new information that corrects beliefs they held while keeping the experience a secret. For example, survivors often think they were targeted, but later learn that crimes against them were random. Insights often emerge just by talking through the experience, and that can be empowering.

The memory becomes less triggering

Developing narratives can also lead to the trauma memories becoming less triggering (Gillihan, 2019). By sharing the experience with safe listeners, it begins to lose its intensity, and the duration of discomfort lessens. Uncomfortable emotions and sensations weaken as the survivor learns to regulate the discomfort. This builds new neural pathways that help them trust again and develop "new normal" behaviors. Healing integrates the trauma so it becomes one of many life components, not the main story. While peacebuilding projects may not be able to offer this sustained engagement, they can provide initial opportunities and should be structured to set survivors on the path to continue practicing self-regulation and seeking and receiving supportive listening from mental health professionals, family, and/or community.

The survivor finds a sense of mastery

An additional benefit of developing narratives is that it can help the survivor find a sense of mastery. Survivors expend much effort to keep memories at bay, but this can never be fully successful; thus, survivors are left feeling out of control and subject to false alarms of danger, poorer quality relationships, and a disrupted life (Gillihan, 2019). They can become so preoccupied with managing intrusive thoughts, and lost in depression or shame, that they lose sight of their own strengths.

Consequently, a key practice for trauma-informed peacebuilders is to help survivors recall their own skills, assets, and resilience, and to tap back into them. Gillihan (2019) explained that helping a survivor build the ability to tell their story, and manage the intense feelings that accompany it, is an excellent way for a survivor to recognize a strength they hold and gain confidence that they can control the reactions (see also Zachariah et al., Chapter 4).

Trauma memory becomes more organized

Developing narratives can also help the trauma memories, which are often stored in fragments, become more organized (Gillihan, 2019). This is evident in brain imaging; when thinking about unprocessed trauma memories, the hippocampus – the part of the brain that provides context to memories – appears to be less activated (Brewin et al., 2010). By putting a narrative around trauma memories, it provides a beginning, middle, and end and helps the survivor contain the trauma to a specific time and place, thus making it more manageable and less disruptive.[3]

The survivor begins to make sense of the trauma

A further benefit of developing narratives is for a survivor to begin to make sense of the trauma, which can help release some of its power. We are hardwired to make sense of our experiences, and survivors often get stuck in asking "why?" As Tedeschi et al. (2020) explained, struggling with highly challenging, highly stressful life circumstances can lead to "posttraumatic growth." Improved self-regulation, retraining the mind, and creating new neural pathways are all ways this growth can manifest.

Supportive listening is a key component of survivor sense making.-Peacebuilders with a direct trauma healing role can listen to survivors' stories, observe the storyteller's feelings and help to name them, assist survivors to develop a fuller narrative, and guide survivors to practice techniques to regulate big emotions. We should never insist that survivors tell these stories, but rather create safe environments that encourage sharing as much as they wish – which also has the healing power of making choices (see below) – while truly listening to the narratives they offer (Siegel, 1999). Trauma potentially affects everyone in a context, and we should offer these supports to host country colleagues, as well as participants. Even when work is not expressly a trauma healing intervention, meetings and other activities can be structured so that content is exchanged in storytelling form, serving similar purposes.

These supports assist in widening a survivor's window of tolerance, which reduces aggressive, fear-based reactions and creates more openness to collaboration. When people feel in control of their emotions, they are better able to access the brain's executive functioning, which enables us to generate solutions; problem-solve; make decisions; and create, and follow through on, any type of plan (Center on the Developing Child, 2022).

Method 3: enhancing human connection

Many survivors have lost human connection; deliberately rebuilding it is essential. Humans are hardwired for connection and attunement with others, and listening is a primary means by which we connect to others (Lipari, 2014). Peacebuilders help survivors reconnect when they listen with a compassionate ear, engage without judgment, and create opportunities for peers to do the same. Practitioners should take care not to diminish perceived inequities or ignore histories. Rebuilding connection is not only a matter of kindness, but also an essential component for survivors to actively participate in peacebuilding and community engagement.

Method 4: offering choices

Survivors lacked control during the traumatic experience, and this often leaves them with generalized, lasting feelings of powerlessness, being out of control, and a belief they cannot keep themselves or their loved ones safe (Hicks-Ray, 2004). Peacebuilders can contribute to restoring survivors' sense of agency and power by introducing choices at various stages (Van der Kolk et al., 1996). Choices may be simple or complicated. The choices of whether to share a story; where to sit, stand, or walk; and whether to join a group, seek professional help, or engage with justice systems are all examples that provide opportunities to regain a sense of agency.

Integrating trauma understanding in practice

Trauma-informed peacebuilding has taken place in diverse settings; this chapter's authors have employed these practices in Sri Lanka, Indonesia, Liberia, South Sudan, USA, Ghana, Kenya, Sierra Leone, Nigeria, and Rwanda. Below, we discuss practice components we see as important to peacebuilding effectiveness, and how they naturally address, or can be shaped to address, the effects of trauma.

While we will discuss an illustrative project in Liberia, we encourage readers to look for implementation opportunities in their home countries as well as abroad.

Practice components

In community-level projects, we find the following components are usually essential. First, team members are identified and assembled. For a multi-national team, we identify peacebuilders in the host area who are interested in collaborating – whether they be professionals or community members known for these skills and outlook. We identify key stakeholders through the team's[4] relationships and mapping of community conflicts and sources of resilience. Where possible, the team makes multiple informal visits to build relationships, begin to fit in to the community, and observe dynamics.

Next, the team designs the project collaboratively; careful listening is essential to understanding what is important to various collaborators and what concerns must be accommodated. If we propose to use trainings or other material that have been used previously, the team adapts them to the local context. When possible, we pilot the material so that local people experience it before giving feedback. We adapt for consistency with cultural values, unfamiliar references, relatability, and language choices; to accomplish that, one must set up a listening environment where all believe their insights are welcomed and will be respected, and designers listen closely for necessary changes. Joint decision making on content, strategy, and relationships continues throughout the intervention.

We find many initiatives benefit from several content elements as well. Peacebuilding activities should be embedded in activities relevant to participants – livelihood, other development, or religious activity, as examples. Initiatives should employ a relationship-building form of dialogue, usually held serially with a diverse group, that aims to increase perspective-taking, self-disclosure, and empathy. Some or all activities should be designed to expressly, or in effect, build participants' trauma resilience. It is ideal if the project employs opportunity for joint action and decision making by participants.

Women Hold Up Half the Sky: an application

One such project was *Women Hold Up Half the Sky*, in which Mediators Beyond Borders International (MBBI), National Ex-Combatant Peacebuilding Initiatives, RECEIVE, and Peacebuilding Resource Center contributed to rebuilding community after Liberia's civil wars. These wars spanned from 1989 to 2003, and involved atrocities, child soldiers, displacement of one-quarter of the population, rape as a weapon, and the betrayals and destabilizing effect of shifting militia alliances. The project took place in Gba town, Bomi County, a former stronghold for waves of fighting forces, which left the area with a newly multi-ethnic make-up and tremendous scars. Women of nine tribes and two religions came together to move beyond this devastation to build trust and social cohesion.

The project was built on the complementary strengths of Liberian peace-builders, community women, and MBBI conflict and trauma specialists. The peacebuilders brought a deep understanding of the effects of the war; knowledge of the social practices and structures through which change occurs; experience in promoting community acceptance of ex-combatants; and an appreciation of the deep connection between community trauma, development, and national healing. The trauma specialists brought different approaches to conflict trans-formation, building trauma resilience, dialogue, project design, and data gathering and analysis. Some community women brought influence, some brought farming experience, and others resilience from surviving atrocities.

The team jointly designed the interventions, mapping and data tools, and reporting formats. In addition, trainings and communications were adapted to the Liberian context. Liberian peacebuilders conducted mapping, which provides an early opportunity to listen for what is meaningful to the community and demonstrate empathy and collaboration. Surveyors should be coached to make their interest and partnership evident, and steer away from survey techniques that seem extractive and objectifying. Mapping can directly ask about trauma's impact and sources of resilience, and, even if frank answers are not forthcoming, surveyors can listen for clues suggestive of traumatic response that can be tested once sufficient trust is established. Teams should keep in mind that the extent of conflict and traumatic experience may not surface for months.

Before initiating work in the community, Liberian team members were trained in methods to facilitate trust-building dialogue. The training incorporated exercises to increase self-awareness, listening, openness, interest in others, empathy, connection, and identity as a source of reactivity and prejudice. Trainees learned to foster each of these practices in dialogue participants. All staff experienced this type of dialogue as a participant or as a facilitator and then organized dialogues in their home community with trauma specialists present to provide support, answer questions, and debrief. The team deepened these understandings and skills in further trainings during the project.

Additionally, Liberian team members were trained in trauma awareness and resilience. They learned to recognize behavioral indicators of traumatic experiences and practiced simple techniques that help people regulate their reactions and stay present in the moment when traumatic memories were activated. Exercises emphasized the importance of empathetic engagement and validating survivor experiences. The group also explored cultural rituals and activities that enhance resilience, and all of these practices serve to address some effects of trauma, as summarized in Box 9.1.

The Liberian peacebuilders moved to become embedded in the community. The core participants included the most influential women in the town – the Town Chief, Chairlady, mosque chairlady, market superintendent, and a midwife –

BOX 9.1   *HOW THIS PROJECT PREPARATION ADDRESSES TRAUMA*

The mapping began to surface information that enabled the team to work with community members to help **feelings of shame subside, correct unhelpful beliefs** about the traumatic experiences, and begin to have **trauma memories become more organized**.

We must not mistakenly assume that accomplished and well-functioning people are void unresolved trauma. The Liberian peacebuilders had lived through the same horrendous conditions as the communities. Some had been child soldiers and may have carried out atrocities; others lived with terror and loss and witnessed horrors. The project design must build in some methods to help address trauma's impact on staff as well.

Centering Liberian staff's expertise and *joint decision making* are not only respectful, but they also help expand traumatized staff's own **sense of mastery.**

Working through Liberian's staff's networks **enhanced human connection**. So, too, did having *staff experience trust-building dialogue* as a participant before they led dialogues.

Staff training about trauma helped them to **make sense of the trauma**. For some, the exercises provided opportunities for **feelings of shame to subside** and for **unhelpful beliefs about the events to be corrected.**

---

and members of a variety of ethnic groups, ages, and religions. They committed to participating in these complementary activities throughout the year:

- running a collective farm using new, sustainable farming techniques to grow saleable crops,
- participating in a series of trust-building dialogues,
- deepening understanding about the impact of exposure to violence, and
- building skills to increase resilience to traumatic experience.

The multimodal nature of the design is key to sustained peacebuilding. Not only was larger scale farming a new means of income generation, but it also acted as a laboratory in which to practice interdependence and trust. It was a visible, concrete space where relational and practical transformations were possible. When trust was built at that practical level, it created a willingness to talk, and listen, during dialogues. As dialogue over time generated more meaningful conversation, people connected and felt safe to offer stories of trauma and recovery and to listen and offer the support they learned in workshops. When a

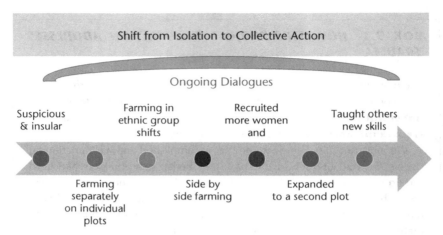

FIGURE 9.1   Shift from isolation to collective action

husband died, or long-held, silent grief surfaced, the women talked about it as they pulled weeds. Each component of the intervention strengthened the others, and the combination allowed participants the time, trust, and familiarity to become more vulnerable and forthcoming, to be more attuned to the others, and to build deeper connections (see also Mugume et al., Chapter 12).

At the time, it was common for men to dominate production for the market, so this project newly opened the possibility of farming for profit to women. Area ethnic groups were not outright hostile, but harbored prejudices that kept them insular. Kissi and Gola women, for example, initially refused to farm jointly because the Gola were thought to be lazy and likely to take advantage of the Kissi women's work. Over time, however, they evolved from their original insistence on farming individual plots, to farming in ethnic group-specific shifts, to side-by-side farming. Ultimately, women spoke of forgiving grievances they had carried for years. Because they felt connected, the women began recruiting more female farmers and expanded to a second plot, and some taught family to use these farming techniques in home gardens.

Figure 9.1 depicts the progression from refusal of working with "them" to increasing notions of working alongside "others" to working together. We also summarize in Box 9.2 how this part of the project design addressed some effects of trauma.

As an addition to joint farm work, women also said the dialogues allowed them to shift angry conversations to ones that promoted a sense of connection, community, caring, and compassion. Some key goals of these dialogues were to increase empathy and perspective-taking. Can I see the events from someone else's position? Can she hear my experience and understand why I did what I did? This occurred because active listening and validation generated an environment of trust, group belonging, and safety, in which all stories were welcomed. While

---

**BOX 9.2 *HOW THE SUSTAINED COMBINATION OF COLLA-
BORATIVE DEVELOPMENT, DIALOGUE, AND TRAUMA AWARE-
NESS ADDRESSES THE EFFECTS OF TRAUMA***

Regularly spending time in a productive activity **enhanced human connection**, especially for those who had been isolating. It provided time for trust to
grow at its own pace, and the listening and mutual support created the
possibility for more openness.

When the team supported the *evolution* of the ethnic groups' willingness
to farm together, this **provided choices** that supported participants' sense
of control.

The women **found a sense of mastery** when they were newly able to
farm for income and teach others.

---

trauma-associated feelings can arise and be uncomfortable, they also are opportunities to practice widening the window of tolerance for them.

The women noticed that the dialogues reduced their reactivity and temper
and created a sense of responsibility about their own harmful behavior. Women
felt empowered to "talk to people to understand you," to "speak our mind," and
they experienced other people being interested in listening to them. As one
participant captured it:

> *I learned we need to respect each other because in trust there is a lot of respect. They
> need to respect you for what you are. We need to respect them for what they are
> because they have their own experience in life.*

Women also reported improved psychosocial functioning. Several said they
began to feel at peace about feelings that had tormented them. Women whose
depression had caused them to withdraw and feel unworthy to speak came to feel
"free" and "brave" to offer their perspectives and take action, as expressed by this
program participant:

> *When the program start, I happy. The reason why: I not used to go among women.
> I used to be ashamed. When women would get together, they would call me, and I
> would say no. But now, they make me feel free. I can talk with my friend-woman. If
> they're wrong, I say what they are doing wrong. I feel to myself: I am a woman. I
> can stand among public and talk. I happy for what they do for me. For them to do
> something that I feel heard.*

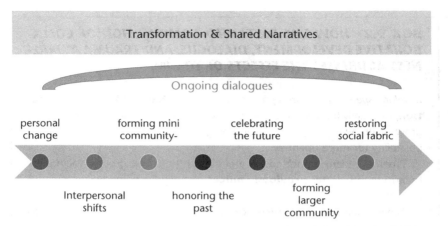

FIGURE 9.2 Dialog transformation trajectory from personal change to social fabric restoration. The image depicts a linear shift from personal change driven by interpersonal shifts to forming mini community and celebrating the future driven by honoring the past. At the end is the forming of larger community and a resulting restoration of a cohesive social fabric

The quality of playfulness in their interactions was one of the most remarkable differences. During the war, one participant was forced to braid the hair on her decapitated husband's head, yet she could be seen joking and laughing in the farm. The rains washing away crops became a shared challenge, not a cause for blame or abandoning the project; and the women joined in laughter at the first sight of renewed green growth. By helping each other through the sudden death of a spouse during the project, and telling of losses never before shared, the women created a true community of support. They went on to create rituals for honoring the past and celebrating the future.

As shown in Figure 9.2, personal change can often generate societal change. In this project, the connection among participants rippled outward. Participants who initially said they had been indifferent to the fights around them felt newly connected to neighbors and responsible to help them resolve conflicts. Women's association meetings were previously suspended because of conflict, but women participating in the project used the dialogue techniques to resume and run these meetings, as well as mosque meetings, helping all of the town's women have more peaceful interactions, and contributing to restoring the social fabric. Box 9.3 summarizes how these outcomes also functioned to address some effects of trauma.

Vicarious trauma

As we work side by side with trauma-affected colleagues, spend time where violence is unpredictable and atrocities continue, and immerse ourselves in

---

BOX 9.3   *HOW ADDRESSING TRAUMA LED TO THE IMPACTS OUTLINED ABOVE*

When the women noted having less anger and more perspective-taking, this likely reflects the **memory becoming less triggering**; this also occurred for the women who shared their stories, yet later were able to be playful.

Their rituals showed the women's progress on **making sense of the trauma.** It is likely that, in their facilitated conversations, common experiences surfaced, and **unhelpful beliefs about the events were corrected.**

The woman newly expressing her freedom to speak and join others in activity, as well as inviting her co-wives, clearly illustrated **feelings of shame subsiding**.

These each were made possible by the sustained, **enhanced human connection** and the **development** and telling **of narratives**, some of which the women said they had never before shared.

---

listening to participants' great suffering and helping them develop narratives about it, it is inevitable that we will be affected. As Rothschild (2006) pointed out, there are advantages and risks of empathetic engagement. Both pleasant and unpleasant emotions are contagious (Rothschild, 2006). Listening empathically builds emotional connection and greater ability to see similarities between us, which puts us at greater risk for internalizing stories and concomitant emotions. We may respond anywhere along a continuum from sadness or rage at injustice to experiencing some of the same issues – some might say symptoms – as our participants.

The Antares Foundation (2012) indicated that nearly one out of three humanitarian aid workers report significant symptoms of post-traumatic stress disorder (PTSD), and no doubt it is little different for peacebuilders. For those professionals, sometimes intense and powerful images, sounds, smells, and tactile experiences can become intrusive in everyday life. Another hallmark of vicarious trauma is a disrupted sense of hope and meaning (Saakvitne & Pearlman, 1996). We refer to these reactions as vicarious trauma, the negative changes in a helper resulting from empathically engaging with, and feeling responsible for, traumatized individuals.

To prevent and manage these reactions, it is both a personal and an organizational responsibility for peacebuilders to understand trauma and their response to it. Most organizations brief staff on the purpose of the mission, logistics, cultural awareness, and other key information, but as far as we know, few prepare team members for exposure to the intense suffering, deprivation, and harsh environments that contribute to traumatic reactions and vicarious trauma. It can be challenging to prepare people for this exposure because those settings can be unstable and unpredictable. However, this is all the more reason to develop staff members' skills to remain healthy and functional under such conditions.

Peacebuilders should be guided to understand the neurobiology of trauma and the effects of listening empathically on the capacity to responsibly manage trauma exposure. We should learn to identify and acknowledge our own trauma responses. We must learn techniques that allow us to remain present and helpful, hearing stories of pain without taking on that pain (van Dernoot Lipsky & Burk, 2009). Self-care and emotional regulation open the doors to our own resilience and enable us to continue being truly empathetic, compassionate, and useful to those in need (Rothschild, 2006).

In the language of van Dernoot Lipsky and Burk (2009), microculture is particularly important to preventing and managing reactions to trauma exposure. The microculture should support us in two ways: by showering us with encouragement and by holding us accountable. The *Women Hold Up Half the Sky* team became a microculture that adopted these principles. At the end of each training day, trainers offered encouragement by recapping all that the Liberian colleagues accomplished and acknowledging the bravery involved in sharing and listening to each other's stories. Then there was an exercise requiring empathetic listening and engagement that employed four questions:

1. What impact did hearing today's stories have on you?
2. What were your feelings when hearing those stories?
3. Where did you feel it in your body?
4. What can you do to reduce how big those feelings are?

All were encouraged, but not required, to share. We closed with an activity that stimulated the "happy hormones" – endorphins, oxytocin, and dopamine – such as dancing, singing, storytelling, or joking.

We also provided accountability by reminding the team of simple grounding techniques and the importance of reaching out to another team member or another trusted person if big feelings persisted. Because team members had utilized empathetic listening to validate each other's emotions and experiences, they built trust. Consequently, it was less risky to reach out to each other. Individuals, then, became accountable to each other for their personal healing and the healing of the team. The team was encouraged to continue these practices throughout the project and in their future professional lives.

Conclusion

Where peacebuilders and community engagement professionals have reason to believe they are working in a context that has been exposed to trauma, a trauma-informed approach is essential to our commitment to do no harm. This approach does not require psychology or social work licensure, and everyone can integrate into their practice simple approaches that have a significant impact. Even so, it does require anticipating where traumatic responses may be present, both through traditional research and discussions with people holding local knowledge. It requires training to understand more fully the principles and practices laid out in this chapter, to be able to spot signs that trauma may be affecting program participants, their communities, or the agencies involved in the peacebuilding work. We also want to keep these ideas in mind to prevent vicarious trauma for ourselves and our colleagues. Because trauma responses vary so widely, practitioners must prepare to recognize when participants or colleagues need more help than we can provide, identify (in advance) local resources for professional support, and make those referrals when needed. In settings without mental health professionals, peacebuilders should help participants identify a source of support and, on days where we see heightened distress, make our best efforts to ensure that the person connects with that support upon leaving our activities.

When the time comes to design the project, trauma-informed practitioners explore what adaptations may accommodate people with ongoing trauma responses and what interventions may be needed, in addition to traditional peacebuilding methods. Trauma-informed peacebuilding recognizes the individual behaviors that may occur, acknowledges the relational difficulties that hamper collaboration and collective action, and acknowledges the potential effect trauma may have on the social fabric. Peacebuilders help individuals and improve outcomes by empathetic listening and validation, and by helping trauma survivors become more aware of their own trauma reactions, develop and share stories, build human connection, and regain the ability to recognize and tap into their own strengths. Peacebuilders help trauma-affected societies by designing processes that integrate these features, such as serial dialogues where participants can move toward self-disclosure, trust, and human connection at their own pace. Reconciliation work is sorely in need of carefully facilitated processes in which groups directly take on understanding the past and deciding how to balance it with current needs.

In many conflict contexts, unaddressed trauma can keep a society fractured despite the best designed peacebuilding or community engagement initiatives. A trauma-informed approach is essential, allowing peacebuilders to address a key conflict driver, break recurrent cycles of violence, and foster the trust and collaboration necessary for stable societies.

Notes

1 Trauma effects and interventions, neurobiology, and epigenetics are highly detailed, nuanced fields. This chapter introduces some key concepts broadly with the understanding that readers would look to the source material for a fuller discussion of these complex topics.
2 Studies show that survivors of Cambodia's genocide by the Khmer Rouge tend to have children with depression and anxiety, for example, and children of Australian veterans

of the Vietnam War were found to have higher rates of suicide than the general population.
3 A similar line of work on "writing therapy" also shows significant decreases in post-traumatic stress and comorbid depressive symptoms for patients who may not otherwise respond to traditional psychotherapy or other treatments (Gerger et al., 2021).
4 This always refers to the host country peacebuilders and any outside peacebuilders, such as this chapter's authors.

References

Antares Foundation. (2012). *Managing stress in humanitarian workers.* Antares Foundation.
Baumeister, R. F. (1991). *Meanings of life.* Guilford Press.
Branscombe, N. R., Ellemers, N., Spears, R., & Doosje, B. (Eds.) (1999). The context and content of social identity threat. In N. Ellemers, R. Spears & B. Doosje (Eds.), *Social identity: Context, commitment, content* (pp. 35–58). Blackwell.
Brewin, C. R., Gregory, J. D., Lipton, M., & Burgess, N. (2010). Intrusive images in psychological disorders: Characteristics, neural mechanisms, and treatment implications. *Psychological Review, 117*(1), 210–232. 10.1037/a0018113
Center on the Developing Child. (2022). *The science of adult capabilities.* Harvard University. https://developingchild.harvard.edu/science/deep-dives/adult-capabilities/
Centers for Disease Control and Prevention. (2022, May 18). *Genomics and precision health.* https://www.cdc.gov/genomics/disease/epigenetics.htm
Erikson, K. T. (1976). *Everything in its path.* Simon and Schuster.
Fitzduff, M. (2021). *Our brains at war: The neuroscience of conflict and peacebuilding.* Oxford University Press.
Gerger, H., Werner, C., Gaab, J., & Cuijpers, P. (2021). Comparative efficacy and acceptability of expressive writing treatments compared with psychotherapy, other writing treatments, and waiting list control for adult trauma survivors: A systematic review and network meta-analysis. *Psychological Medicine, 52*, 1–13. doi:10.1017/S0033291721000143
Gillihan, S. G. (2019, March 6). The healing power of telling your trauma story: Six ways revisiting painful memories can loosen their grip. *Psychology Today.* https://www.psychologytoday.com/us/blog/think-act-be/201903/the-healing-power-telling-your-trauma-story
Herman, J. (1992). *Trauma and recovery: The aftermath of violence.* Basic Books.
Hicks-Ray, D. (2004). *The pain didn't start here: Trauma and violence in the African American community.* TSA Communications.
Hirschberger, G. (2018). Collective trauma and the social construction of meaning. *Frontiers in Psychology, 9*, 1441. 10.3389/fpsyg.2018.01441
Hubl, T., & Auritt, J. J. (2020). *Healing collective trauma: A process for integrating our intergenerational and cultural wounds.* Sounds True.
Imhoff, R., Bilewicz, M., Hanke, K., Kahn, D.T., Henkel-Guembel, N., & Halabi, S. (2017). Explaining the inexplicable: Differences in attributions for the holocaust in Germany, Israel, and Poland. *Political Psychology, 38*, 907–924. 10.1111/pops.12348
John, V. M. (2021). Supporting trauma recovery, healing, and peacebuilding with the Alternatives to Violence Project. *Peace and Conflict: Journal of Peace Psychology, 27*(2), 182–190. 10.1037/pac0000532

LeDoux, J. (1996). *The emotional brain: The mysterious underpinnings of emotional life.* Simon & Shuster.

Lipari, L. (2014). *Listening, thinking, being: Toward an ethics of attunement.* Penn State University Press.

McGoldrick, M., & Walsh, F. (2004). *Living with loss.* Norton.

Noor, M., Shnabel, N., Halabi, S., & Nadler, A. (2012). When suffering begets suffering: The psychology of competitive victimhood between adversarial groups in violent conflicts. *Personality and Social Psychology Review, 16,* 351–374. doi:10.1177/1088868312440048

Pouligny, B. (2014, May 6). The impact of individual traumas on communities and societies. In *Invisible wounds: A practitioner's dialogue in improving development outcomes through psychosocial support.* World Bank Group. https://acrobat.adobe.com/link/track?uri=urn:aaid:scds:US:1f22ccf8-285e-3ec2-9e86-78954cb87508

Reilly, I., McDermott, M., & Coulter, S. (2004). Living in the shadow of community violence in Northern Ireland: A therapeutic response In N. B. Webb (Ed.), *Mass trauma and violence: Helping families and children cope* (pp. 304–326). Guilford Press.

Roth J., Huber M., Juenger, A., & Liu, J. H. (2017). It's about valence: Historical continuity or historical discontinuity as a threat to social identity. *Journal of Social and Political Psychology, 5,* 320–341. doi: 10.5964/jspp.v5i2.677

Rothschild, B. (2006). *Help for the helper: The psychophysiology of compassion fatigue and vicarious trauma.* W.W. Norton & Company.

Saakvitne, K., & Pearlman, L. A. (1996). *Transforming the pain: A workbook on vicarious transformation.* W.W. Norton.

Sesay, A., & Ismail, W. (2003). Conflict and post war trauma among child soldiers in Liberia and Sierra Leone civil wars. In A. Sasay (Ed.), *Child wars, child soldiers and post conflict peacebuilding in West Africa* (pp. 160–194). College Press.

Siegel, D. J. (1999). *The developing mind: Toward a neurobiology of interpersonal experience.* Guilford Press.

Stanley, E. A. (2019). *Widen the window of tolerance: Training your brain and body to thrive during stress and recover from trauma.* Avery.

Tajfel, H., & Turner, J. C. (1979). An integrative theory of intergroup conflict. In S. Worchel & W. G. Austin (Eds.), *The social psychology of intergroup relations* (pp. 33–47). Brooks/Cole.

Tedeschi, R. G., Moore, B. A., Flake, K., & Goldberg, J. (2020). *Transformed by trauma: Stories of posttraumatic growth.* Boulder Crest Institute.

Van Dernoot Lipsky, L., & Burk, C. (2009). *Trauma stewardship: An everyday guide to caring for self while caring for others.* Bernett-Koehler.

Van der Kolk, B. A. (2014). *The body keeps the score: Brain, mind, and body in the healing of trauma.* Penguin Books.

Van der Kolk, B. A., McFarlane, A. C., & Weisaeth, L. (1996). *Traumatic stress: The effects of overwhelming experience on mind, body and society.* Guilford Press.

Vignoles, V. L., Regalia, C., Manzi, C., Golledge, J., & Scabini, E. (2006). Beyond self-esteem: Influence of multiple motives on identity construction. *Journal of Personality and Social Psychology, 90,* 308–333. doi: 10.1037/0022-3514.90.2.308

Webb, N. B. (2004). *Mass trauma and violence: Helping families and children cope.* Guilford Press.

Wessels, M. (2006). *Child soldiers: From violence to protection.* Harvard University Press.

Yehuda, R., & Lehrner, A. (2018). Intergenerational transmission of trauma effects: Putative role of epigenetic mechanisms. *World Psychiatry*, *17*(3), 243–257. 10.1002/wps.20568

Zelizer, C. (2008). Trauma-sensitive peace-building: Lessons for theory and practice. *Africa Peace and Conflict Journal*, *1*, 81–94. http://www.apcj.upeace.org/issues/APCJ_Dec2008_Vol1_Num1.pdf

10

LISTENING PERFORMANCES AS TRANSFORMATIVE MECHANISMS IN THE CONTEXT OF RESTORATIVE TRANSITIONAL JUSTICE SCENARIOS

The Colombian case

Luis Carlos Sotelo Castro

DEPARTMENT OF THEATRE, CONCORDIA UNIVERSITY, MONTREAL, QC H3G 1M8, CANADA

In 2016, President Juan Manuel Santos (in office between 2010 and 2018) and the Revolutionary Armed Forces of Colombia (hereafter FARC) officially ended an internal war that had lasted more than five decades by signing "The Final Agreement for Ending the Conflict and Building a Stable and Lasting Peace" (hereafter Peace Agreement). The Peace Agreement introduced a restorative transitional justice model. Restorative transitional justice, broadly speaking, is the application of restorative justice in transitional, peacebuilding settings, often through mechanisms such as a Truth Commission or a War Crimes Tribunal. The Colombian "Comprehensive System of Truth, Justice, Reparation and Non-Repetition"[1] is a two-track model, including the Truth, Coexistence and Non-Repetition Commission (hereafter Truth Commission), which acted from 2018 to 2022, and the Special Peace Jurisdiction, a War Crimes Tribunal whose mandate will end in 2038. Bueno (2014) described restorative transitional justice as "the variety of processes and *mechanisms* established to restore, to the extent possible, the individual and social harm caused by mass abuses" (*emphasis* added; p. 99).

The term mechanism is typically used in transitional justice literature in an everyday life sense, without any explicit attempt to explain what a mechanism is and what exactly makes it work as such. At times, mechanism is used as synonymous with policy, as when Hayner (2011) stated, "Likewise, there are a

DOI: 10.4324/9781003214465-10

variety of mechanisms or policies to reach these [post-conflict justice] objectives: holding trials; purging perpetrators from public or security posts; etc." (p. 8). Whether a policy or a process, a transitional justice mechanism is considered a practical means for achieving post-conflict goals. After examining the charters of 40 truth commissions established between 1970 and 2010, Guthrey (2015, p. 19) concluded that there are five recurrent primary goals: truth, reconciliation, reparations, preventing recurrence, and healing. Guthrey's finding partially confirms Parmentier's (2003) TARR model, according to which the building blocks and key issues of transitional justice are Truth, Accountability, Reparation, and Reconciliation (TARR). Accountability is a particularly relevant goal in connection with restorative justice. In fact, in transitional justice settings in which restorative justice principles are applied, such as the ongoing Colombian model, accountability is an explicit goal, coupled with truth-seeking, reparation of the harms suffered by victims, and reintegration of offenders into civil life (Acto Legislativo, 2017).

Drawing on social mechanisms theory (Hedström & Swedberg, 1998a), positioning theory (Harré & Slocum, 2003), and performance studies (Schechner, 2002; Sotelo Castro, 2020; see also McRae et al., Chapter 3), I conceptualize the Colombian restorative transitional justice model as a social mechanism facilitating the emergence of repositioning performances by former violent actors in a public scenario. Overall, I describe the current Colombian restorative transitional model as comprising four main interconnected elementary mechanisms. Together, if they achieve intended or unintended transitional justice and post-conflict outcomes at a macro level, they form a transformative, post-conflict social mechanism.[2] The four elementary mechanisms are: (1) facilitated, structured, and supported Private Gatherings (PGs) between a relatively small group of victims, offenders, and community members (i.e., primary stakeholders); (2) a Public Act (PA) representing some of the victims' narratives and listening performances by offenders that occurred during the PGs; (3) the Amplification of the Stakeholders' (AoS) performances through social and mass media; and (4) the facilitation of a Public Conversation (PC) about the issues raised by the primary stakeholders' performances and, in particular, by the offenders' admission of responsibility; that is, their responsive listening performance. In formal terms, the mechanism may be described as:

$$PG + PA + AoS + PC = \text{Restorative transitional justice as social mechanism.}$$

These four main processes happen stepwise, in a particular sequence to achieve the specified restorative transitional justice outcomes. The case studies will illustrate those steps. However, the chapter will focus on characterizing listening in the PGs and the subsequent PAs. More research is needed to test how the PG, the PA, the AoS performances, and the PC combine to produce intended or unintended social outcomes.

This chapter proceeds by, first, defining key concepts and outlining an analytical, abstract model for understanding the link between listening to victims' narratives and the emergence in a perpetrator's mind of the commitment to making themselves accountable and responsible in a restorative transitional justice context. The second section uses two admission of responsibility acts co-organized by the Colombian Truth Commission and the Special Peace Jurisdiction in 2021 as case studies. The third section elaborates the argument in more detail, and the last section draws some conclusions and gives some directions for future research.

Concepts and analytical model

Listening as transformative

In the context of restorative transitional justice, listening might be described as a mode of attending with a specified social purpose. The purpose is to achieve social outcomes and outcomes for the individual stakeholders participating in the restorative process. The primary stakeholders in such a process are victims, offenders, and their communities, along with the state, as represented by the transitional justice authorities facilitating or conducting the process. These outcomes intersect with peacebuilding and a restorative approach to justice.

More concretely, echoing Stauffer's (2015) contribution to the study of why listening matters for survivors of severe mass violence in a transitional justice context, listening in this context might be described as a mode that aims at transforming and, thus, repairing violent attitudes and discourses, moral positionings justifying violence, lies and manipulated versions of the past, and the sense of detachment some may feel due to not being directly implicated in the conflict (e.g., those who observed it indifferently or from a distance). Importantly, this type of listening is also aimed at correcting the deep sense of social abandonment survivors feel as a lasting effect of having been subject to inhumane abuse (Stauffer, 2015). In that sense, listening is supposed to act as a mechanism to generate transformations at a relational, political, and social level in the present and future lives of all stakeholders, including the wider society of which they are a part.

Although these transformations go beyond the individual cognitive, affective, and behavioral dimensions often described as key components of listening, such an instrumental approach to listening does align with the perspective of "listening as competent behavior" (Worthington & Bodie, 2018, p. 8). For example, a central claim in this perspective is that "the competency resides in the eye of the beholder" (p. 8). In the context under study, this perspective implies that the perpetrator's listening performance needs to become, quite literally, observable, and assessable in terms of the specified post-conflict goals.

Accountability

The primary focus of this chapter is on accountability, as accountability is the first step for restoration and all other outcomes that follow. Victims need to feel heard and attended by those who caused them harm, transitional justice authorities need to be able to assess the offenders' listening performance, and the wider public needs to witness and discuss their performance as effective or ineffective as well.

Thus, there needs to be a mechanism to turn listening into an observable, archivable practice, a performance upon which the listening subject and others offering feedback and support to them can act, and which can be assessed now and, in the future, to inform public discussions. As Bickford (1996) asked, "How can listening itself be made visible or audible? How can it appear in public?" (p. 153). What mechanism facilitates an effective, transformative listening performance in a restorative transitional justice context?

Transformative social mechanisms

In social theory, social mechanisms have been defined as "social processes having designated consequences for designated parts of the social structure" (Merton, 1968, p. 43). Social mechanisms theory distinguishes between psychological or sociopsychological and transformative social mechanisms (Hedström & Swedberg, 1998b). While the former mechanisms are internal, the latter are external. According to Hedström and Swedberg (1998b), a transformative (or transformational) social mechanism is such that a number of individuals interact with one another, "and the specific mechanism explains or shows how these individual actions are transformed into some kind of collective outcome, be it intended or unintended" (p. 23). As several authors in Hedström and Swedberg's (1998a) book, *Social Mechanisms,* pointed out, one single mechanism is not enough to cause transformational social outcomes (see especially chapters by Hedström & Swedberg, Schelling, Elster, and Gambetta). Rather, "several elementary mechanisms" interact and work together to develop into a larger social mechanism (Hedström & Swedberg, 1998b, p. 21). The important point for social mechanisms as explanatory models, according to Hedström and Swedberg (1998b), is that changes at a macro-level influence actions and changes at a micro-level; in turn, changes at the micro-level influence transformations at a macro-level (see also Zachariah et al., Chapter 4). This implies that the "several elementary mechanisms" need to be all part of the wider restorative transitional justice mechanism to produce, together, the intended or unintended social outcomes. It is thus important to understand what restorative justice is and how it works in a transitional justice context.

Restorative justice

Restorative justice introduced a "change of lenses" in how crime and other painful conflicts in Western democracies were approached (Zehr, 2015). At the same time, different "lenses" have been developed. For example, while the Maximalist model (Bazemore & Walgrave, 1999) acknowledges the importance of a process between victims, offenders, and communities to get to a restorative sanction (i.e., the one that will repair the harms caused), it does not consider the process as necessarily one in which the parties come together in face-to-face dialogue.

This perspective is criticized by advocates of the Purist model to restorative justice, who believe that a distinguishing characteristic of restorative justice is "the concern about [what] the injury crime/harmful wrongdoing does to personal relationships" (McCold, 2000, p. 393). They suggest that it is not just the individual harm caused to victims that needs to be repaired, but, importantly, also the offenders' standing in their community and the relationships between all the stakeholders involved (i.e., the victims, the offenders, and their communities). As McCold observed, those taking a Purist approach cannot understand "how the relational aspects of restorative justice can be addressed without the primary stakeholders coming together" (p. 393). Central to this approach is the belief that restorative justice is "essentially about engaging offenders, victims, and their communities in a [voluntary] process where they define the harm and determine the obligations of the offender" (McCold, 2000, p. 393).

From the Purist perspective, listening to the victims' narratives in the context of a restorative justice process is a crucial sociopsychological mechanism for achieving restorative truth *and* reintegrative outcomes simultaneously. The key for understanding the function of listening to victims' narratives in such contexts has to do with the notion of accountability. This approach helps us distinguish between criminal or legal accountability (guilt) and what Bueno et al. (2016) have termed "restorative accountability." Criminal liability is defined as lawbreaking. In criminal law, accountability is defined in purely legal terms. As a result, "Moral and social issues become not only secondary but irrelevant. The context of the action is not considered except to the extent that they have legal implications" (Zehr, 2015, p. 83). Restorative accountability, on the other hand, which McCold (2000) called "true accountability" and Zehr (2015) called "real accountability," requires the offender to acknowledge and understand the victims' emotional needs and what, from their perspective, needs repair. The process of understanding or learning of victims' needs requires offenders to listen to the victims' directly. As McCold (2000) wrote, "How can offenders understand what to be remorseful about *if they have not heard* the effects directly from the victims?" (p. 393; italics added).

The Purist model provides a basis for an initial proposition about what makes restorative justice work − as a sociopsychological mechanism for achieving reconciliation of relationships; as a means of reintegration of offenders; and as a pursuit of truth, repair, and eventually even healing of all those affected by a specific crime. It is through the "coming together," in a properly facilitated dialogic process, where all the stakeholders impacted by a crime/wrongdoing have the chance to listen to each other, in particular to the victims' narratives of harms and needs. Listening allows for the possibility of achieving the desired outcome, what McCold (2000) called "the healing of the relational injuries among the affected parties" (p. 393). The facilitator's role is to actively support accurate, effective listening and mutual comprehension by always asking precise questions that enable the parties *to show*, in the public context of the restorative encounter (Barter, 2012), that they feel heard, acknowledged, and understood. How does that Purist approach to restorative justice work in a transitional justice context, where victims are in the thousands, and where perpetrators are not individuals but significantly large armed groups?

The transitional justice authorities must select, by necessity, small groups of victims and perpetrators to facilitate their interaction in small groups in the Private Gatherings (PGs) and subsequent Public Acts (PAs). In the Colombian context, the system offers various opportunities for victims to participate in other hearings and procedures. The discussion of their efficacy is beyond the scope of this chapter, and other authors have started to address it (Aranguren Romero, 2017; Britto Diaz et al., 2021; Pearson, 2017). The selection process highlights the symbolic and performative nature of each victim's narrative and perpetrator's admission of responsibility. The need to make such selections opens the process to numerous criticisms. For instance, some scholars question the extent to which restorative justice is applicable to a transitional context (Clamp & Doak, 2012; Rohne et al., 2008; Uprimny & Saffon, 2006). While I acknowledge that the implementation of restorative justice in a transitional scenario faces significant challenges, I nevertheless think that the current Colombian system is showing results that illustrate the power of properly facilitated and supported listening performances as transformative social mechanisms.

Self-positioning analytical model

I argue that the sociopsychological mechanism mediating the offender's involvement in violent actions is their self-positioning. The analytical model I propose suggests that an offender's self-positioning and their consequent positioning of others determines whom they listen to and whom they harm during a war. Similarly, a repositioning of the self may determine a transformed approach to listening to those to whom they previously refused to listen and that they victimized. Drawing on positioning theory (Harré & Slocum, 2003), I define a positioning act as an embodiment (a performance) of what the actor believes are their rights and duties in a specific spatio-temporal situation. Positioning theory takes doing something and referring to what one does in words as an articulation of a moral framework. This articulation is called a positioning. There are three elements to a positioning act: (1) an action in the context of a social interaction or in the context of a situation in space and time; (2) narratives describing or referring to the entitlements for doing the action there and then, including attributes of those against whom the action is addressed; and (3) a storyline, that is, a story making sense of what the person is doing and how the person who does the action got to the point of undertaking that action there and then.

Applied to the study of listening, positionings determine what and to whom someone can and will actually listen in a given situation. As Harré and Slocum (2003) observed, "Positions constrain what one may say and do" (p. 106). By making evident how positioning and listening are entwined, this analytical approach places listening within a moral sociopsychological realm.

Previous research on ethical listening has focused on proposing models to justify why one should listen ethically and what that might mean (Beard, 2009; Lipari, 2009; Makau, 2018). For instance, drawing on Gadamer's concept of openness, Macnamara (2016) argued that a prerequisite to listening is that "one must want to know what others have to say" (p. 136). Another common argument is that the listening subject needs to "still" the self to "open up" an ability to truly hear the other from the other's standpoint. It is a strand that Bickford (1996) called an "understanding of listening as a self-annulling openness" (p. 145). While the concept of openness is indeed of crucial significance for understanding listening from a moral, ethical, and political standpoint (Dreher & Mondal, 2018; Gadamer, 2004; Stauffer, 2015), there is a question that this strand of literature overlooks. Gadamer (2004) argued that fundamental openness "involves recognizing that I myself must accept some things that are against me, even though no one else forces me to do so" (p. 355). That statement is directly relevant to a perpetrator's listening situation. The perpetrator is required to let victims say very serious accusations against them, and to listen attentively to what they say against them, even in the public setting of a transitional justice scenario. Thus, the question that needs to be addressed first is, why would someone want to voluntarily place themself in such a shameful position? What is the prerequisite for an offender of very serious crimes, a former combatant and proud rebel or Army officer, to step forward and position themself physically and morally on that stage?

I argue that positioning is a sociopsychological, often unconscious dynamic, determining and constraining listening performances. Rather than annulling the self, the task for the listening subject is to become aware and communicate the positioning from which they are performing listening in a given situation. In that sense, the path for the listening subject to open up to the other's narratives starts with disclosing autobiographical or, more broadly, personal information making sense of their current and past positionings relevant for the task at hand. Such a process, however, implies revealing sensitive information, namely the storyline informing the positioning; it implies a disclosure and a sociopsychological task that are an emotional challenge and involve many risks too at a social level. Often, the individual cannot do it alone. One needs support and ultimately to participate in a Private Gathering (PG) to become aware of hidden socio-psychological mechanisms prompting one's self-positioning, particularly when silenced by years of violence or when violent forces are still acting against that disclosure.

The case studies

In 2021, two offenders from the two main conflict groups (the Army and FARC) reported a similar experience after meeting victims in a PG co-organized by the Truth Commission and the Special Peace Jurisdiction. In each of the two cases presented below, there was a victim whose narrative the two offenders reported as particularly instrumental in helping them understand the impact of their wrongdoing on the victim's personal life and, by extension, on other victims' lives. In the pages that follow, I focus on describing the impact of that specific victim's narrative on the two offenders. First, I provide a context for understanding the victimizations and the offenders' role in each case. Then, I trace the emergence of his transformed approach to listening to victims' narratives during the PG.

Background

During the war, 'Alberto' and Captain 'Ricardo' played an important military role within their respective groups.[3] Alberto (not his real name) became one of FARC's top regional leaders for the Medium Magdalena Bloc, whose task was to control a strategic part of the Colombian territory along the upstream Magdalena River. Between 1982 and 2012, FARC committed over 21,000 kidnappings. According to the Special Peace Jurisdiction (SPJ) investigations (JEP, 2021 June; Lina Rondón, personal communication, 30 June 2021), their kidnapping served three main strategic purposes:

1.   They took hundreds of police, armed forces personnel, politicians, and even foreign citizens to manipulate the government into an exchange of prisoners.
2.   They did kidnap for ransom to fund their activities.
3.   By kidnapping, they showed their factual control over specific territories and, thus, created an image of being in charge.

Ricardo (not his real name), a former Captain of the Armed Forces, was the intelligence chief of a special military unit called GAULA in another region, the Department of Casanare in eastern Colombia. GAULA aimed to counteract drug trafficking and money laundering activities. However, because of how FARC was enmeshed with drug trafficking across Colombia, GAULA units also ended up carrying out activities against FARC. As criminal investigations and research have shown, some of those activities were made in collaboration with the paramilitary (CEV, 2022a). Innocent, young, impoverished, or otherwise vulnerable civilians were killed, their papers disappeared, and their bodies were falsely labeled as enemy combatants that had been killed in combat. They would become known as "false positives" (Palau, 2020). The numbers of false positives inflated the achievements of Mr. Alvaro Uribe's (Colombian President between

2002 and 2008) so-called antiterror *Defense and Democratic Security* policy, by generating the perception that his policy was more successful than it was.[4] Mr. Uribe's defense strategy "hinged on encouraging soldiers with vacation time, promotion, and other prizes to kill guerrilla fighters" (Deadly incentives, 2020). Mr. Uribe denies any responsibility for what the officers under his command did. The official version of Mr. Uribe and the Armed Forces is that those who committed those crimes are "rotten apples" (*manzanas podridas*). They deny any systematic responsibility of the Army or the government for those crimes.

Two families illustrate the victimizations suffered by many at the hands of both FARC and members of the Armed Forces in alliance with paramilitary. In October 1989, a FARC front kidnapped Roberto Lacouture, a landowner and wealthy farmer. He was held for 87 days, most of the time tied to a tree.[5] He was released when the family paid the ransom. His was a comparatively short-lasting kidnapping, yet it left enduring consequences for him and his family. How much the family paid for his release is not publicly known, but even after his release, FARC continued targeting his family. Mr. Lacouture reported during the Public Act that 15 of his close relatives, including cousins and uncles, were kidnapped for ransom. Two of his uncles were killed in captivity.

In Lacouture's view, as stated during the PA in 2021, FARC leaders need to be punished with severe sanctions, not with "restorative sanctions," which give the top leaders the chance to become congressmen and women. At the same time, he accepts that because transitional justice is already in place, he prefers to make sure that FARC leaders tell the truth and commit to doing their part so similar things do not happen again. At his request, his wife Diana Daza accompanied him to the Private Gathering (PG) and the subsequent PA with ex-FARC top leaders. Diana Daza's words, as I will explain below, were instrumental in catalyzing a "deeply personal" reflection in Alberto, which he reports during the PA (CEV, 2021a) as a turning point for him.

In 2006 and 2007, two brothers, Yuri Achagua Reyes and Abelardo Achagua Reyes, were killed by members of the GAULA unit based in Casanare. In contrast to Mr. Lacouture's kidnapping, there is little available information about their case. Their death is one of 6,402 extrajudicial killings that, according to the SPJ investigations, occurred between 2002 and 2008 (Daniels, 2021). The lack of public information about their case probably evidences the much humbler origin of the Achagua family. Deyanira Achagua, who is also Yuri and Abelardo's sister, has become the family's spokesperson in the hearings and activities organized by the SPJ and the Truth Commission.[6] In a statement before the SPJ, Deyanira Achagua, observed that while the transitional justice system grants the killers of her brothers benefits such as parole, they - the victims - do not get anything. She stated, "Who has ever listened to us?", adding, "My brother Abelardo's daughter [who was born two months after his death] is now eleven years old. We have not been able to get her legally acknowledged as his daughter because we do not have the money to pay for a DNA test." As we will see below, her participation in the

PG led by a Truth Commission facilitators' team, where she and her sister met Captain Ricardo, had a transformative impact on him.

The phases of a transformed approach to listening to victims' narratives

Both Alberto, the FARC ex-top rebel, and Ricardo, the retired Army Captain, attended a PG with victims in 2021. The meetings were planned and facilitated by a Truth Commission *Engine Team* (*Equipo Motor*) (CEV, 2022a). The meetings took place behind closed doors. In each case, there was a small group of other offenders and approximately seven victims, some of whom were accompanied by a relative for support. The *Engine Team* was transdisciplinary, including psychologists, anthropologists, and Truth Commission facilitators. In both cases, the PGs were followed by a public Admission of Responsibility Act (a PA) to make public some of the victims' narratives and the offenders' admission of responsibility. Not all the participants in the PG attended the PA (A. Cruz, personal communication, 22 July 2022).

The first PA, titled *Liberating Truths: FARC Admits Responsibility for the Kidnappings They Committed,* was on 23 June 2021.[7] The COVID-19 pandemic slowed down the Truth Commission's work. For that reason, and because of the complexity of the process, its preparation lasted two years (2019–2021) (A. Cruz, personal communication, 22 July 2022). The PG took place a few days prior to the PA. While the Public Performance was live streamed and for all to witness, there is not a public video of the private meeting.[8]

The second PA, *Admission of Responsibility for Extrajudicial Killings in Casanare,* occurred on 10 November 2021.[9] Similarly, it took more than two years for the *Engine Team* to prepare this act. A PG between three offenders and victims took place prior to the PA. As in the previous act, this one was live streamed via social media platforms. The video is still available on YouTube. In both cases, it is possible to read the comments posted on the chat by those following the Acts. I will come back to this point later.

In each of the above-mentioned public Admission of Responsibility Acts, both Alberto and Captain Ricardo gave an insight into what happened during the PGs with victims. Both men indicated they were greatly impacted by what they heard from victims. Alberto stated (CEV, 2021a):

> In my case, it is thanks to Mrs. Diana … whom I met here in Bogota two days ago during a meeting at the Truth Commission. Her words, testimony, and story illustrate the suffering of many whose relatives were kidnapped. That was, for me, the catalyst of a deeply personal reflection about the harm caused to the relatives of the victims who suffered kidnapping. I have a sincere desire to contribute to the search for the truth. I want to contribute to the healing of so much suffering.

Captain Ricardo expressed a similar response (CEV, 2021b):

> ... at the first hearing, we saw these people initially and listened to some of their testimonies. That changed my judgment, my determination to be here and advance all these processes to take responsibility and understand the magnitude of these acts.

For the analysis, I will not question the credibility of either statement. The assumption is that both are genuine expressions of a transformed approach to their participation in these crimes. Captain Ricardo and Alberto expressed either a "change of judgment" or having been prompted to go through a "deeply personal reflection," leading them toward a willingness to admit responsibility or contribute to the victims' healing and search for the truth.[10] In interviews with me, both men confirmed the sincerity of their statements. After all, it takes courage to step forward and publicly acknowledge, as they did, that the acts they had committed were wrong and that they are willing to admit their responsibility, in 2021, before the Truth Commission, and, more significantly, before the Special Peace Jurisdiction (in 2023), with legal consequences for them.

So, why would Alberto, a top regional FARC rebel during the war, and Captain Ricardo, a proud Army officer, want to voluntarily place themselves in the extremely shameful and dishonorable position of someone who is responsible for war crimes and crimes against humanity? What is the prerequisite for an offender of very serious crimes to become willing to listen to victims' narratives? Narratives that say serious things against them and their organizations? Narratives that begin in a PG and are followed by a PA for all to see and talk about? To answer these questions, it is necessary to listen to how Alberto and Captain Ricardo narrated their storyline concerning their willingness to participate in the restorative transitional justice scenarios of the PGs and the PAs. The inclusive nature of the 2012–2016 peace dialogues seem to have contributed to their repositioning process.

Inclusive peace dialogues

In 2014, the FARC and government delegations sitting at the negotiating table heard five groups of 12 victims each. The 60 victims represented the diversity of victimizations caused by the main key armed actors: FARC and other guerrilla groups, the Army, paramilitary, and drug trafficking. Listening to the victims' narratives "ended up transforming in an irreversible way the peace dialogues" (Brett, 2017, p. 16). It substantially informed the shape that the transitional justice model was going to take. According to Brett (2017), their voices "introduced a human face to the negotiations, making the human suffering caused by the conflict evident" (p. 16).

Bickford (1996) characterized political listening as listening that "takes conflict and differences seriously and yet allows for joint action" (p. 2) This implies that the new, post-conflict FARC, in its form of the COMUNES political party, does not need to give up its conviction that there is structural violence that needs to be addressed, even though elites may resist their arguments. The conflict and the differences persist. Yet, joint action with those elites, some of whom they victimized in the past, is possible if there is political listening on both sides. Further, action, not just reception of information, defines political listening. It is also a core element of what Dreher and Mondal (2018) termed "responsive listening." They argued that responsive listening is one in which the ethical and the political intersect. The powerful, or previously powerful (FARC or the Army), in its encounter with the powerless, must now respond "more ethically to the voices of the disempowered, that is, to respond to them on their own terms rather than on terms dictated by established elites" (Dreher & Mondal, 2018, p. 10). A response, then, implies an ethical act in relation to what the powerful have heard the disempowered requesting from them.

Strategically, ethically, and politically, FARC's path toward becoming legitimate actors (a political party) within the new peacebuilding landscape requires them to listen to victims' narratives. More concretely, it requires FARC top leaders to be seen publicly as effective, responsive listening subjects in the Admission of Responsibility Acts. Strategically, what is at stake, primarily, is the organization's image. Thus, the presence of top leaders as symbols of the new FARC (now called the COMUNES political party) in Admission of Responsibility Acts becomes crucial.

The peace dialogues also created a new opportunity for Captain Ricardo and all Army personnel involved in extrajudicial killings. For political reasons, President Santos included, for the first time in a peace process in Colombia, active and retired Armed Forces representatives in his negotiating team (Illera & Ruiz, 2018). Captain Ricardo said he and other officials talked directly with the retired general representing the Army at the negotiating table about putting pressure on one issue: that Armed Forces and Police officers responsible for extrajudicial killings and other abuses would be considered for benefits on equal terms with ex-rebels. In Ricardo's words, "We wanted our voice to be heard" (Ricardo, personal communication, 26 August 2022). They succeeded.

As outlined above, Armed Forces personnel and FARC ex-rebels appear to share a prerequisite that bolsters their willingness to listen to victims' narratives, even when those narratives express serious things against them and their organizations, in a PG and in a subsequent PA. They both have strategic reasons and necessities to do so. It seems a repositioning in Alberto and FARC started to take place in the context of the inclusive peace dialogues model of 2012–2016. From positioning their struggle as a violent revolution, FARC started to see the option of a new political revolution. They intended to continue playing a role within Colombia's political landscape. This new self-positioning started to open the doors for them to collectively listen to victims' narratives. In that sense, listening to victims' narratives of suffering was a strategic move. For example, Captain Ricardo's concern at that time was not to listen to victims' narratives, but to be heard first and positioned as a person eligible for the future benefits of a restorative transitional justice scenario. That strategic positioning became the condition for him to be open to listen to victims' narratives.

The personal is political: full and half truths

Diana Daza, Roberto Lacouture's wife, attended the PG with him. Both spoke. Yet, Diana's narrative was a strong(er) "catalyst" of Alberto's deeply personal reflection, a reflection that led to his transformed, more committed, perhaps less strategic and more ethical approach to "wanting to contribute to the search for truth" and to say, as he did publicly in the subsequent Admission of Responsibility Act, "There are too many things that should not have happened during this conflict; many. One of them, and the most painful, is kidnapping. I regret deeply to have committed that practice" (CEV, 2021a).

Diana Daza spoke in the PG from a different position than her husband, Roberto. While Roberto was the direct victim (the kidnapped person), Diana positioned herself as the voice of the direct victims' relatives. In the words of Cruz, a social psychologist facilitating the PG (A. Cruz, personal communication, 22 July 2022):

> Diana placed the conversation in a different site. Her talk was about how the [close] relative experiences the kidnapping. What she wanted FARC to acknowledge is that the family's suffering is more or at least as grave as that experienced by the kidnapped person.

During the PA, Diana shared a version of what she said to Alberto and other FARC perpetrators. Cruz confirmed that the public version is the same as what she shared in the PG. It is worth noting that the position from which Diana speaks, as well as the content of her narrative, its structure, and its delivery (performance) differed significantly from that of her husband.[11]

Roberto Lacouture started his presentation by positioning himself politically (CEV, 2021a):

> My name is Roberto Lacouture. I am Catholic, conservative, Uribist. [a follower of ex-President Alvaro Uribe's political party] and I am here … [he struggles to speak, drinks water, seems to be about to cry but controls himself] … . I am here so that those who did so much violence on us tell us the truth.

In contrast, Diana Daza, after calmly positioning herself as Roberto's wife, sharing that they have been married for 34 years, and that they have three children and one granddaughter, "who is our happiness," started with a, perhaps unexpected personal statement:

> I am here because I want to heal my heart. I seek to forgive those who caused this suffering ... . [she cries] ... that deed, leaving so many consequence on us. And after 31 years, we still wonder why?

She continued by giving details of how the kidnapping impacted her life. A moment that Alberto found particularly striking was when she described how confounding it was for her when their two-year-old son asked her about his dad. She stated, "How does a two-year-old son interpret the father's absence? As abandonment. Each time I talk about it, I cry" (CEV, 2021a).

Alberto acknowledged that her narrative was strong(er) because it triggered a "deeply personal reflection." As he disclosed (Alberto, personal communication, 21 September 2022):

> I didn't know those cases. Roberto was very direct. I don't think that is bad. But Diana marked me because now, after starting all this process, there is a little child where I live, he is our son, I am very afraid that something happens to me, or the family, or to him. When Diana told the story about her child, I felt it was me now.

While Roberto Lacouture addressed FARC members with anger, which is completely understandable, and typical of restorative justice dynamics, Diana Daza spoke from her heart and to their hearts as human beings. She asked them a direct and open question: *why?* She did not demand them to tell "*the* truth;" rather, her question prompted a deeper, personal questioning of the subject-who-listens. She wanted to know their personal truth as well as the strategic truth. Unintendedly, she prompted Alberto to position the Self mentally as a parent whose child feels abandoned. In his current positioning, he can feel compassion for her, whereas, in the past, he could not. His new positioning allows him to feel the child's suffering with her. He realizes that this harm is irreparable and extremely painful. Alberto did not know about his harm. He is now becoming aware of the consequences of their deeds (Alberto, personal communication, 21 September 2022). Echoing feminist stances, Diana Daza does not separate the private from the political. Telling the truth from FARC's strategic point of view would only tell half of the story.[12]

The argument: preparation, support, and rehearsal for a listening performance

In the PGs under study here, neither Alberto nor Captain Ricardo met victims directly affected by their acts but by acts committed by their armed groups, and similar to the ones for which they are responsible. Yet, listening to them is challenging for perpetrators. Alberto confirmed this challenge, saying: "All the versions I heard were hard to hear. I think, only us who have been in those acts can say how hard it is" (Alberto, personal communication, 21 September 2022).

Gadamer's (2004) notion that a fundamental openness is required for listening needs to be seen under a different light when what is said against us is a deep trauma caused by acts in which the listener participated. Alberto shared that to place himself there physically is a very hard task, hard in a way only those in that situation know. Similarly, Captain Ricardo shared that in the PG he attended with the Achagua sisters, the facilitators asked them to close their eyes while listening to the victims' narratives (Ricardo, personal communication, 26 August 2022):

> I started to imagine what they were narrating and to tell you the truth, I could not, I started crying and could not stop the emotion of listening and imagining what they could have felt, what their kids could have felt, their mothers … .

Three elements stand out from Alberto's and Ricardo's statements. First, their experience of positioning the self as a perpetrator who listens to victims' narratives saying things against them is a significant physical and sociopsychological stressor. No doubt, the victim narrating their story is in a vulnerable position (Chaitin, 2014). However, paradoxically, perpetrators, once positioned as a listener in this context, place themselves in a position of serious yet necessary vulnerability. The listening subject may be grabbed by the victims' "nervous system"[13] as strong emotions, such as anger, sorrow, and resentment are expressed. Such situations within restorative justice encounters have been described as an "emotional dynamic" (Rodogno, 2008).

Without the skillful intervention of a facilitator, or adequate preparation, however, the emotional dynamic runs the risk of sparking a shame-rage spiral (rage on the side of the victim, shame on the side of the perpetrator-who-listens). The risk is that perpetrators thrown into a shame corner are likely to perceive victim statements as an attack, and most probably will respond defensively. They will not be open to listen. Similarly, victims will feel revictimized by the defensive response. The restorative encounter may go badly, deepening the sense of ethical loneliness victims feel. Ethical loneliness was described by Stauffer (2015) as "the experience of having been abandoned by humanity compounded by the experience of not being heard" (pp. 15–16). To a large extent, the effectiveness of the listening process within the described emotional dynamic lies on how well the parties are emotionally prepared for the meeting, and how it is facilitated and supported. Alberto confirmed this insight. I asked him how he had perceived Roberto's positioning as Catholic, conservative, and Uribist, and whether he had perceived Roberto's positioning as a critic of the Peace Accord as an attack. He said, "No, I did not feel defensive. That was part of the preparation;, the psychologists helped me to understand that issue" (Alberto, personal communication, 21 September 2022).

In a restorative transitional justice context, prerequisites of speaking and listening include preparation, facilitation, and support. For example, Captain Ricardo, when asked about the preparation he received from social psychologists before meeting the Achagua sisters, said, "the preparation goes toward you becoming aware that you will stand there badly, it will look bad for you" (Ricardo, personal communication, 26 August 2022).

In the context under study, the listening subject needs to mobilize resources to cope with the stress and strong emotions proper of the emotional dynamic they are co-creating as participants. Pernilla (2022) called this form of listening "receptive listening," that is a listening in peacebuilding partnerships where the speaker feels heard and perceives the listener to be open to "understand differently." Pernilla argued that emotions shape attention and that they are typically neglected in peacebuilding partnerships. I add that emotions shape positionings, and positionings enable or constrain listening. Receptive listening would be receptive to emotions. By framing listening as responsive performance, and as a transformative sociopsychological elementary mechanism within the larger social mechanism (the transitional justice model), I argue for the need to be receptive for the repositionings that emerge among participants as the restorative dynamics unfold in the PG and PAs.

In the case of offenders, two strong emotions are typically shame and guilt. The dynamic needs to unfold in such a way that participants feel safe enough (Richardson & Reynolds, 2014) and equipped enough to regulate their emotions to listen and speak effectively. However, they may not know how to effectively regulate these and other emotions. As a result, they need preparation, support, and facilitation to accomplish that task.

The act of facing those suffering as a perpetrator-who-listens *for* is central to accountability, as learning what to admit responsibility for is a completely new task for combatants who have refused to listen to victims for decades and who have engaged in silence, denial, and other defense mechanisms against accusations. As Captain Ricardo acknowledged, "I faced criminal investigations for ten years. I never met a victim directly. I had built a wall to negate the victims' humanity and to negate any wrongdoing (Ricardo, personal communication, 26 August 2022).

Thus, the prerequisite to be open to listen to victims' narratives for a perpetrator is to demolish that wall. In fact, both the speaker and the listener need emotional support and preparation to accomplish that difficult task. Social psychologist Angela Cruz, reflecting on this preparation, noted that, "We helped the victims prepare for how to communicate their story, and to reflect on – 'What do I want them to hear from me?', 'How will I look to him?," "What questions will I ask?'" (A. Cruz, personal communication, 22 July 2022).

In performance studies, this preparation is called rehearsal, "the phase of the performance process where the specific details of a performance are shaped, repeated, and made ready for a public showing" (Schechner, 2002, p. 202). In a restorative justice context, the rehearsal process is much less rigorous than in the performing arts. A proper rehearsal process would make the process much slower and cost intensive. Nevertheless, a contribution this chapter makes is to demonstrate that a transdisciplinary approach to performance combining socio-psychological, listening, performative, and dramaturgical techniques, have a crucial role to play in this context (see also McRae et el., Chapter 3). I elaborate on this idea below.[14]

Second, by Alberto saying that only those in that situation know how hard it is, he is suggesting that he cannot find the words to communicate what he feels in such a listening situation. Yet, the situation's purpose is precisely to give the perpetrator the historic opportunity to communicate to the victims and the world how he feels in the present about what he now knows are the consequences of his past actions. He needs to be able to find the way to communicate, as he did in the PA, that kidnapping is one of the most painful things that should have never happened and that "I regret deeply to have committed that practice" (CEV, 2021a). Note that he did not say "that crime," but rather called it "a practice." The words that he chose in his response to the victims' narratives by naming what he did in the past and acknowledging what they suffered, makes his listening evident and accessible.

Indeed, during the conflict, FARC refused to name that practice "kidnapping," preferring instead to name it "retentions." A recurrent demand by victims is to hear FARC ex-rebels naming what they did to them a "kidnapping," which Colombians popularly understand as being a crime (JEP, 2021 January). To be able to perform that response, Alberto received significant emotional and "dramaturgical" support to find and utter the right words, in the right tone, addressing the right people and even wearing the right outfit. One of his advisors (an anthropologist) said, "We don't advise them to wear anything resembling a military outfit. We advise them to wear something in line with peacebuilding symbols, white for instance" (G. A. Perez, personal communication, 21 September 2022). The conversation between the advisor and Alberto about what to wear is, again, a rehearsal for his listening performance.

Additionally, the perpetrator's listening performance needs to use techniques that are sometimes called active or reflective listening (McConville & Bryson, 2014). Perpetrators need to show the victims that they are trying to understand them. They also need to build trust in the context of a relationship marked by a history of violence. Importantly, from the restorative perspective, they need to show victims that they are trying to understand their pain, that is, the harm caused, and that they now care about that pain and harm, where they did not care in the past. One such technique is paraphrasing, or a short summary of what the victim has said, ideally using their own words or, in any case, showing that they have listened. For instance, during the PA, Alberto said (CEV, 2021a):

> I say to the families that I have understood they carried the heaviest load; I have understood their biggest suffering …*not to know about their beloved ones: had they had something to eat, how were they doing, were they alive?* (emphasis added)

The added italics are examples of Alberto's paraphrasing of Diana Daza's narrative. However, McConville and Bryson (2014) described active listening as an advanced, "highly developed skill demanding full concentration," which goes well beyond hearing (p. 68). Active listening also goes beyond responding with words, as in paraphrasing. It takes much training in areas such as counseling, oral history research, and even investigative criminal interviewing to develop adequate active listening skills (Bull, 2014). The physical bodily positioning of the listener in relation to the speaker, eye contact, gestures such as nodding, facial expressions, and even the use of silence to give time to the speaker to continue narrating, are all means to show active listening. The listener needs to listen "not just to the words, but also to the tone, to silences, implied references, and what is not said" (McConville & Bryson, 2014, p. 68). A restorative transitional justice mechanism cannot assume that perpetrators bring this skill to their activities. Developing this technique by all stakeholders in a restorative justice process is crucial for the achievement of the specified and desired outcomes, yet is often taken for granted; training is rarely offered.

Third, art-based approaches and local cultural practices are integral to the facilitation techniques that helped Alberto and Ricardo listen and respond to the victims' narratives in the PG they attended. When Ricardo was asked to close his eyes and focus on listening to the victims' narratives, that action was part of a ritualistic atmosphere created by the facilitators. The Truth Commission's methodological guidelines state that the admissions of responsibility are situated at a deep humane level (harms to human dignity). In consequence, they paid great attention to symbolic elements including religious and cultural practices. They also paid great attention to the space where the gatherings took place, and to the spatial configuration of the bodies within that space. For instance, participants typically sat in a circle (CEV, 2022b).

The symbolic quality of the listening situation shapes the participants' attention. Captain Ricardo used the term "transportation" to describe his experience: "We were listening with closed eyes as if they were transporting us to that moment they were telling in their story" (Ricardo, personal communication, 26 August 2022). In this case, listening is more than receiving, processing, and responding (Wolvin, 2011). Here, listening is an integral part of participating in a ritual designed to remember the listener's own trajectories across a space and time previously perceived as separate from the victims' life story. The listener is set in motion subjectively across a space and time where his and the victims' life stories intersect. The use of participatory and ritualistic activities enables embodied engagements with potentially deep emotional effects and responses. As trauma research has demonstrated, "trauma is not just an event that took place sometime in the past; it is also the imprint left by that experience on mind, brain, and body" (Van der Kolk, 2014, p. 21). Both victims and perpetrators have deep imprints of the violence they have suffered and caused in their bodies. Captain Ricardo shared how powerful it was for him to be listening to victims' narratives with closed eyes, saying, "I started crying and could not stop the emotion of listening and imagining what they could have felt, what their kids could have felt, their mothers …" (Ricardo, personal communication, 26 August 2022).

Physical proximity

Victims may play a crucial role in deactivating the defensive and silencing walls perpetrators may bring to the PG. As I previously illustrated with Diana Daza's narrative, the content, structure, and delivery of what victims say impact how perpetrators listen to them. I want to add that the physical proximity of victims and perpetrators in the PG is also an integral element of the transformative power of the mechanism.

In the PG, Deyanira Achagua, a sister of two brothers killed by Captain Ricardo's colleagues, sat next to him. She must have seen him in distress as he listened with closed eyes and could not stop crying. As he shared, "She holds my hand, hanging on the side of the chair, squeezes it and tells me 'be calm, nothing will happen'." He described the effect of the gesture on him: "Imagine, they are supporting me. These are the kind of things that have torn the wall of denial down that I had built." The gesture seemed to have made him feel something that he thought was impossible, to be approached by those suffering from his deeds, not as a monster, but as a human being. In his words, "It made me feel that I can be again the person I was before I had committed all that. That is what I call self-reconstruction (*reconstruirse*)" (Ricardo, personal communication, 26 August 2022).

Captain Ricardo acknowledged that his superiors and colleagues had built an image of the victims as a threat and as criminals, which he had not questioned before. After being in direct contact with victims and having learned that all they want is to hear the truth from them, he realized that his previous ideas were completely wrong. What made him "change his judgment" and commit at a deeper level "to be here and advance all these processes to take responsibility and understand the magnitude of these acts" is having been physically repositioned, through touch, as a fellow human being who is trusted to be able to admit his responsibility after listening to victims' narratives of suffering.

Final words and future research

This chapter has demonstrated that for perpetrators to be ready and willing to listen to victims' narratives in a restorative transitional justice scenario, there must first be a strategic repositioning. While the chapter focused on micro-level reposition, a change at a macro-level needs to take place initially, which then leads to changes at the micro level. At the macro level, the armed groups' strategic repositioning in Colombia was part of the wider 2016 Peace Accord. A repositioning from violent actor to political actor makes it necessary for members of these groups to listen to victims' narratives and position themselves in the vulnerable position of a perpetrator, who listens and responds to the victims' demands. As individuals, they need to perform responsive and active or reflective listening acts that show to the victims and the wider public that they now realize that (a) their past positionings caused the victims' sufferings, (b) they regret them, and (c) they are willing to repair and contribute to the pursuit of the truth. This repositioning is both strategic and personal.

The PG within the Colombian Restorative transitional justice model works as a sociopsychological elementary mechanism. It embraces a Purist approach to restorative justice which includes facilitating small group PGs between victims, their relatives (community members), and offenders. For offenders to perform a kind of responsive and active listening, they are expected to perform in response to the victims' narratives in Admission of Responsibility Acts, both private and public. To do this, they need adequate preparation. That preparation includes becoming aware and, whenever safe, to communicate the positioning from which they listen. But to do that, they need to apply emotional, "dramaturgical," and listening techniques, all of which require rehearsal. In addition, the PG with victims requires skillful facilitation to moderate the emotional dynamic, particularly to avoid participants falling into a rage-shame spiral. Without adequate, transdisciplinary preparation, skillful facilitation, and support, they may not be open to listening to victims' narratives. Skillful facilitation may include arts-based methodologies and local cultural practices. Defensive and silencing forces must be deactivated before the perpetrator is fully open to listening compassionately and in restorative terms to the victims' narratives.

The PAs amplified the Stakeholder's performances through social media platforms and mass media. The legacy of the Commission includes an extensive testimonial and documentary archive, multiple databases, and artistic products that resulted from the broad dialogue promoted during the Commission's mandate. One of its core mandates was to "contribute to the construction of a peace based on truth, knowledge and recognition of a bloody past that must be accepted in order to be overcome" (Dec. 588 de 2017). Performing active listening acts in response to victims' demands, it seems, is the route that enables achieving that goal.

More research is needed to establish the extent to which PGs, subsequent PAs, the AoS Listening Performances (in particular of perpetrators' admission of responsibility acts), and the broad PC that followed worked together to produce social outcomes at the macro-level. It is still too early to know if the restorative sanctions that the Special Peace Jurisdiction will issue will achieve that goal. Even so, a recent historic social outcome occurred. For the first time, a former rebel of another guerrilla group (M-19), and an active defender of the 2016 Peace Accord, was elected President. Gustavo Petro based his campaign on his promise to fully implement the Peace Accord and the Truth Commission's final recommendations. It does not seem arbitrary to believe that listening performances by perpetrators have contributed to this unintended social outcome. More research is needed to test that claim.

Notes

1 The translation into English of the current Colombian transitional justice system is taken from Bustamante-Reyes (2017). All other translations of personal communications, laws, and testimonies from Spanish into English are made by the author.
2 The idea of "intended" and "unintended" outcomes is part of the definition of social mechanism provided by Hedstrom & Swedenberg. As such, the outcomes that fit into those categories are dependent on the case under consideration. For this project, intended outcomes might include admissions of accountability by the top leaders of FARC or by army officials responsible of extrajudicial killings. An unintended outcome might be that because of the public becoming aware of the number of extrajudicial killings by Armed Forces personnel, fewer people are inclined to vote for right wing political parties supporting a negationist stand. Or, perhaps, if the admission of responsibility acts by FARC ex-top leaders are not convincing, victims' organizations may start to campaign for the attribution of retributive sanctions (jail), putting a core intention of the peace accord at risk.
3 The name of the two perpetrators have been changed yet they are aware that they can be identified by watching the videos documenting the PAs discussed in this chapter. Their petitions when I interviewed them (separately) were to avoid mentioning their names in the body of the chapter.
4 It is important to note that false positives as a criminal practice was not exclusively committed during Alvaro Uribe's presidency. However, the SPJ investigations show that during his presidency, the number of extrajudicial killings by military personnel increased dramatically. See Jurisdicción Especial para la Paz, Auto 125 de 2021.
5 This description is my translation of his narrative during the Public Act (PA) facilitated by the Truth Commission, see: https://youtu.be/DsZntZZvsxE
6 All the quoted testimonies by Deyanira Achagua are publicly available in a YouTube video documenting the hearing Audiencia de Régimen de Condicionalidad, Caso Gaula Casanare, Agosto 30 de 2018. https://youtu.be/ZKeyTjuj05k. See also https://www.eltiempo.com/politica/proceso-de-paz/militares-y-victimas-de-falsos-positivos-en-casanare-se-vieron-en-la-jep-262510
7 The Public Act, Verdades que liberen: Reconocimiento de responsabilidades de secuestro por parte de Farc, can be viewed online at https://youtu.be/DsZntZZvsxE.
8 However, the *Engine Team* wrote a report of all the private encounters that it facilitated. It is included in the document Hallazgos y Recomendaciones, which is part of

the final report of the Truth Commission. See: https://www.comisiondelaverdad.co/hay-futuro-si-hay-verdad.

9 This act, Reconocimiento de responsabilidades sobre las ejecuciones extrajudiciales en Casanare, can be viewed online at https://youtu.be/vUmKMg–lhk.

10 It is important to note that there are different degrees of admission of responsibility. The first level is a generic admission of responsibility for the wrongdoing. This generic admission is an important first step towards full and detailed admission of responsibility, which is a later, more advanced step that is expected to take place before the Special Peace Jurisdiction in 2023. Certainly, without the first, generic step, it is less likely that more detailed admissions would follow.

11 See Verdades que liberen: Reconocimiento de responsabilidades de secuestro por parte de Farc, beginning at 1:02:00 minutes, https://www.youtube.com/watch?v=DsZntZZvsxE&list=PL-3wmKKHWMwssPYefyZtBw_GHhNGTTCQ1&index=21&t=1682s.

12 See, for instance, Tamale and Oloka-Onyango (1995).

13 I borrow this expression from Daniel N Stern, cited in Rothschild B., & Rand M. L. (2006). *Help for the helper: the psychophysiology of compassion fatigue and vicarious trauma* (1st ed., Chapter 1). W.W. Norton.

14 There is an increasing interest in how performance can contribute to transitional justice (see, for example, Cohen, 2020; Cole, 2010; Ramirez-Barat, 2014). However, the role of listening is to a large extent overlooked in the said literature. For a consideration of listening in post-conflict performance, see Sotelo Castro (2019, 2021).

References

Acto Legislativo (2017). *Of the standards for the termination of the armed conflict and the construction of a stable and lasting peace.* https://www.funcionpublica.gov.co/eva/gestornormativo/norma.php?i=80615

Aranguren Romero, J. P. (2017). *Managing testimony and administrating victims: Colombia's transitional scenario under the Justice and Peace Act.* Palgrave Macmillan.

Barter, D. (2012, January 9). Walking toward conflict. *Tikkun, 27*(1), 21–70. https://www.tikkun.org/walking-toward-conflict/

Bazemore, G., & Walgrave, L. (1999). Restorative juvenile justice: In search of fundamentals and an outline for systemic reform. In G. Bazemore & L. Walgrave (Eds.), *Restorative juvenile justice: Repairing the harm of youth crime* (pp. 45–74). Criminal Justice Press.

Beard, D. (2009). A broader understanding of the ethics of listening: Philosophy, cultural studies, media studies and the ethical listening subject. *International Journal of Listening, 23*(1), 7–20. 10.1080/10904010802591771

Bickford, S. (1996). *The dissonance of democracy: Listening, conflict, and citizenship.* Cornell University Press.

Brett, R. (2017). *La voz de las víctimas en la negociación: Sistematización de una experiencia.* [The voice of the victims in the negotiation: Systematization of an experience]. Programa de las Naciones Unidas para el Desarrollo. https://www.undp.org/es/latin-america/publicaciones/la-voz-de-las-victimas-en-la-negociacion-sistematizacion-de-una-experiencia.

Britto Diaz, D., Aponte Castro, D., & Escobar Zamora, D. (2021). *Justicia restaurativa en contextos de transición. Colombia, 15 años de implementación.* [Restorative justice in transition contexts. Colombia, 15 years of implementation]. Universidad de San Buenaventura Cali.

Bueno, I. (2014). *Mass victimization and restorative justice in Colombia. Pathways towards peace and reconciliation?* Scholars' Press.

Bueno, I., Parmentier, S., & Weitekamp, E. (2016). Exploring restorative justice in situations of political violence. The case of Colombia. In K. Clamp (Ed.), *Restorative justice in transitional settings* (Chapter 3). Routledge. DOI: 10.4324/9781315723860-3

Bull, R. (Ed.). (2014). *Investigative interviewing.* Springer.

Bustamante-Reyes, J. (2017). Colombia's path to peace. *New Zealand International Review*, *42*(1), 14–17. https://www.jstor.org/stable/48551969

CEV (2021a, June 23). Verdades que liberen: Reconocimiento de responsabilidades de secuestro por parte de FARC [Truths that liberate: Acknowledgment of kidnapping responsibilities by the FARC]. https://youtu.be/DsZntZZvsxE

CEV (2021b, November 10). *Reconocimiento de responsabilidades sobre las ejecuciones extrajudiciales en Casanare* [Acknowledgment of responsibility for extrajudicial executions in Casanare]. https://youtu.be/vUmKMg–lhk

CEV (2022a). *Hay futuro si hay verdad. [There is future if there is truth].* Truth Commission. https://www.comisiondelaverdad.co/hay-futuro-si-hay-verdad

CEV (2022b, June 17). *Enfoque conceptual y metodológico para los procesos de promoción y contribución al reconocimiento de lo ocurrido en el marco del conflicto armado* [Methodology for the processes of promotion and contribution to the recognition of what happened in the context of the armed conflict]. Truth Commission. https://www.comisiondelaverdad. co/enfoque-conceptual-y-metodologico-para-los-procesos-de-promocion-y-contribucion-al-reconocimiento

Chaitin, J. (2014). "I need you to listen to what happened to me": Personal narratives of social trauma in research and peace-building. *American Journal of Orthopsychiatry, 84*(5), 475–486. DOI: 10.1037/ort0000023

Clamp, K., & Doak, J. (2012). More than words: Restorative justice concepts in transitional justice settings. *International Criminal Law Review, 12*, 339–360. DOI: 10.11 63/157181212X648824

Cohen, C. E. (2020). Reimagining transitional justice. *International Journal of Transitional Justice, 14*(1), 1–13. 10.1093/ijtj/ijaa001

Cole, C. M. (2010). *Performing South Africa's truth commission: Stages of transition.* Indiana University Press.

Daniels, J. P. (2021, February 19). Colombian tribunal reveals at least 6,402 people were killed by army to boost body count. *The Guardian.* https://www.theguardian.com/ global-development/2021/feb/19/colombia-farc-tribunal-false-positives

Deadly incentives. (2020, October 26). American Economic Association. https://www. aeaweb.org/research/charts/high-powered-incentives-false-positives-colombia.

Dreher, T., & Mondal, A. A. (2018). *Ethical responsiveness and the politics of difference.* Palgrave.

Gadamer, H.-G. (2004). *Truth and method* (2nd rev. ed.). (J. Weinsheimer & D. G. Marshall, Trans. Rev.). Continuum.

Guthrey, H. L. (2015). *Victim healing and truth commissions: Transforming pain through voice in Solomon Islands and Timor-Leste.* Springer.

Harré, R., & Slocum, N. (2003). Disputes as complex social events: On the uses of positioning theory. *Common Knowledge, 9*(1), 100–118. DOI: 10.1215/0961754X-9-1-100

Hayner, P. B. (2011). *Unspeakable truths: Confronting state terror and atrocity.* Routledge.

Hedström P., & Swedberg, R. (1998a). *Social mechanisms: An analytical approach to social theory.* Cambridge University Press.

Hedström, P., & Swedberg, R. (1998b). Social mechanisms: An introductory essay. In P. Hedström & R. Swedberg (Eds.), *Social mechanisms: An analytical approach to social theory*. Cambridge University Press.

Illera, O., & Ruiz, J. C.. (2018). Entre la política y la paz: Las fuerzas militares tras la firma del Acuerdo de Paz. [Between politics and peace: The armed forces after the signing of the Peace Agreement]. *Araucaria*, *20*(39), 509–533. https://revistascientificas.us.es/index.php/araucaria/article/view/4917

Jurisdicción Especial para la Paz (JEP) (2021, January 26). Caso 01. Auto 019 (2021). Caso 01: Toma de rehenes y graves privaciones de la libertad cometidas por las FARC-EP. Auto de determinación de hechos y conductas atribuibles a los antiguos miembros del Secretariado de las FARC-EP. (Jurisdicción Especial para la Paz). [Case No. 01. Decision No. 19, 2021. Case 01: Taking of hostages and serious deprivation of liberty committed by the FARC-EP. Decision by which the facts and conducts attributable to former members of the FARC-EP Secretariat are determined. (Special Peace Jurisdiction) https://www.jep.gov.co/Sala-de-Prensa/Documents/CASO%2001%20TOMA%20DE%20REHENES/Auto%20No.%2019%20de%202021.pdf?csf=1&e=16bYs0

Jurisdicción Especial para la Paz (JEP). (2021, June 30). Despacho de la Magistrada Julieta Lemaitre. Caracterización del sufrimiento y del daño moral asociados con los hechos y conductas investigados denro del Caso 0. Elaborado por Lina Rondón Daza.

Lipari, L. (2009). Listening otherwise: The voice of ethics. *International Journal of Listening*, *23*(1), 44–59. 10.1080/10904010802591888

Macnamara, J. (2016). The work and 'architecture of listening': Addressing gaps in organization-public communication. *International Journal of Strategic Communication*, *10*(2), 133–148. 10.1080/1553118X.2016.1147043

Makau, J. M. (2018). Dialogue, listening, and ethics. *Oxford research encyclopedia of communication*. 10.1093/acrefore/9780190228613.013.629

McCold, P. (2000). Toward a holistic vision of restorative juvenile justice: A reply to the maximalist model. *Contemporary Justice Review*, *3*(4), 357–414.

McConville, S., & Bryson, A. (2014). *The Routledge guide to interviewing: Oral history, social enquiry and investigation*. Taylor & Francis.

Merton, R. K. (1968). *Social theory and social structure*. Free Press.

Palau, M. (2020, November 19). The 'false positives' scandal that felled Colombia's military hero. *The Guardian*. https://www.theguardian.com/world/2020/nov/19/colombia-false-positives-killings-general-mario-montoya-trial

Parmentier, S. (2003). Global justice in the aftermath of mass violence. The role of the International Criminal Court in dealing with political crimes. In G. Kellens (Ed.), *Annales internationales de criminologie* [*International annals of criminology*], *41*(1/2), pp. 203–224). International Society of Criminology.

Pearson, A. (2017). Is restorative justice a piece of the Colombian transitional justice puzzle? *Restorative Justice*, *5*(2), 293–308. 10.1080/20504721.2017.1343419

Pernilla, J. (2022). *Emotional practices and listening in peacebuilding partnerships: The invisibility cloak* (1st ed.). Routledge.

Ramirez-Barat, C. (2014). *Transitional justice, culture, and society: Beyond outreach*. Social Science Research Council.

Richardson C., & Reynolds V. (2014). Structuring safety in therapeutic work alongside indigenous survivors of residential schools. *Canadian Journal of Native Studies*, *34*(2), 147–164.

Rodogno, R. (2008). Shame and guilt in restorative justice. *Psychology, Public Policy, and Law, 14*(2), 142–176. 10.1037/a0013474

Rohne, H., Arsovska, J., & Aertsen, I. (2008). Challenging restorative justice - State-based conflict, mass victimisation and the changing nature of warfare. In I. Aertsen, J. Arsovska, H. Rohne, M. Valiñas, & K. Vanspauwen (Eds.), *Restoring justice after large-scale violent conflicts: Kosovo, DR Congo and the Israeli-Palestinian case* (pp. 3–45). Willan Publisher.

Schechner, R. (2002). *Performance studies: An introduction* (3rd ed.). Routledge.

Sotelo Castro, L. C. (2020). Not being able to speak is torture: Performing listening to painful narratives. *International Journal of Transitional Justice, 14*(1), 220–231. 10.1093/ijtj/ijz033

Sotelo Castro, L. C. (2021). Facilitating voicing and listening in the context of post-conflict performances of memory. The Colombian scenario. In S. De Nardi, H. Orange, S. High, & E. Koskinen-Koivisto (Eds.), *Routledge handbook of memory and place* (pp. 277–286). Routledge.

Stauffer, J. (2015). *Ethical loneliness: The injustice of not being heard.* Columbia University Press.

Tamale, S., & Oloka-Onyango, J. (1995). The personal is political, or why women's rights are indeed human rights: An African perspective on international feminism. *Human Rights Quarterly, 17*(4), 691–731. DOI: 10.1353/hrq.1995.0037

Uprimny, R., & Saffon, M. P. (2006). Transitional Justice, Restorative Justice and Reconciliation: Some Insights from the Colombian Case. *Coming to Terms' with Reconciliation–Working Paper Library.* Dejusticia. https://www.dejusticia.org/wp-content/uploads/2017/04/fi_name_recurso_55.pdf

Van der Kolk, B. A. (2014). *The body keeps the score: Brain, mind, and body in the healing of trauma.* Viking.

Wolvin, A. D. (2011). *Listening and human communication in the 21st century.* John Wiley.

Worthington, D. L., & Bodie, G. D. (2018). *The sourcebook of listening research: Methodology and measures.* John Wiley.

Zehr, H. (2015). *Changing lenses: Restorative justice for our times* (25th anniversary ed.). Herald Press.

11

THE ROLE OF LISTENING IN THE TRANSFORMATION OF CONFLICT

Implications for peacemaking and peacebuilding in Ethiopia

Zenebe Beyene[1] and Berhanu Mengistu[2]

[1]SCHOOL OF JOURNALISM AND NEW MEDIA, UNIVERSITY OF MISSISSIPPI
[2]SCHOOL OF PUBLIC SERVICE, OLD DOMINION UNIVERSITY

Communication theorists have proposed that conflict is the result of poorly framed or incomplete exchanges between and among contending parties to a presenting conflict. For instance, Christopher Moore (1996) observed that "… if the right quality of communication can be attained, the quality of the information exchanged can be improved, and if this information is put into mutually accepted form, the causes of the disputes will be addressed, and the participants will move toward resolutions" (p. 62). Moore is not suggesting, of course, that quality, defined as clear and appropriate communication, guarantees a resolution of conflict much less a transformation to peacemaking and peacebuilding. Rather, what he is suggesting is that the right quality, quantity, and forms of communication moves the conflict towards resolution. Furthermore, "the right quality" and framing of the communication depends on the interpersonal skills, sometimes referred to as "soft skills" (e.g., effective speaking and listening), of the individuals responsible for managing conflict.

The purpose of this chapter is to describe and analyze listening skills as one of the critical aspects of communication and explore the role it plays in transforming conflict in the process of peacemaking and peacebuilding. The context for the analysis is peacemaking and peacebuilding in Ethiopia, an important and historically meaningful country located in the Horn of Africa. Although others have written about various elements of conflict in Ethiopia (e.g., Abbink, 2006; Beyene, 2012; Gebre Selassie, 2003; Kebede, 2008, 2011; Yared, 2022), little has been directly written on listening skills that is both reflective of a) empirical findings from communication science and b) the rich Ethiopian traditions and history surrounding

DOI: 10.4324/9781003214465-11

conflicts resulting from thousands of years of ethnic-based tensions. To this end, we organize this chapter as follows: The first part of the chapter provides a brief and focused history of conflict in Ethiopia. Given its richness and complexity, our review will be necessarily incomplete. Nevertheless, it is important that we highlight a few key characteristics that enable an analysis of the types of communication and listening models and skills that can help teach and train peacemakers and others desiring to work in this region. We then explore listening in the context of conflict resolution and peacemaking and provide brief strategic steps in learning and developing active, critical, and empathic listening skills for dialogue in the discourse of disagreements. The chapter concludes with a brief "how to" for practitioners that can provide a viable starting point for this important work.

Conflict in Ethiopia and the imperative for listening skills

There are several reasons why we chose Ethiopia as a case study for listening and its implication for peacemaking and peacebuilding.[1] First, as a multi-ethnic, multilingual, and multi-religious country, Ethiopia needs to bring its people together in the spirit of national unity. Ethnic and linguistic diversity calls for competence in cross-cultural communication. While cross-cultural communication can be challenging in and of itself, excessive attention to ethnic differences and cleavages can make communication across cultural boundaries challenging, hence making listening more difficult. Ethnic entrepreneurs use ethnic cleavages and ethnic identity to mobilize their ethnic kinship to advance their own political and economic goals (Mengie, 2015), adding to polarizing dynamics. In this context, achieving national unity, advancing a common vision, and building common national identity can appear, at first, a daunting task. Designing ways and policies to bridge differences and bring people together is critical for the future of Ethiopia. And, listening plays an important role in the process.

Second, Ethiopia can be considered a center of gravity for the region. As the second most populous nation in Africa, and strategically located in the Horn of Africa, Ethiopia's stability is vital to the stability of the Horn and Africa at large. Given the instability in the region (Sudan, South Sudan and Somalia), Ethiopia's stability is critical for the region. Along those lines, Kłosowicz (2015) noted that "Ethiopia lies in a neighborhood which is exceptionally unstable in security terms" (p. 87).

Third, because Ethiopia hosts hundreds of thousands of refugees from various countries in the region and beyond, Ethiopia's stability does not only affect Ethiopians, but also those refugees who sought shelter in the country. In this regard, a comparison can be made between Ethiopia's case with that of Syria. For a long time, Syria was considered home for refugees from Palestine (Al-Mawed, 1999). Al-Mawed predicted the number of Palestinians will exceed 460,000 in 2005. Due the conflict in Syria, millions of Syrians have become refugees all over the world. According to World Vision, "in 2021, more than 6.8 million refugees were from Syria – more than any other country in the world." One can note that a country that was home for refugees has become the largest producer of refugees due to the violence in the country.

The fourth and final reason for selecting Ethiopia is that the ongoing violence in different parts of the country requires an immediate solution (Mengie, 2015; Yared, 2022). According to Mengie (2015), "Ethnic groups are now competing with each other over the power at the center, and several inter-ethnic conflicts have arisen across boundaries of regional government that are drawn along ethnic lines" (p. 463). The ongoing conflict, if left unresolved, will make the future of Ethiopia uncertain and the Horn of Africa more insecure (Mengie, 2015). Along the same line, Yared (2022; para. 1) argued that:

> Ethiopia's 2018 transition failed to bring stability to the country. On the contrary, sporadic ethnic and political violence since then has brought the nation to its knees. And its war in the north with the Tigray People's Liberation Front (TPLF) that started in November 2020 has tipped the country into further crisis.

Unless Ethiopia gets its acts together and addresses these crises, such ongoing violence will make the country vulnerable to civil war. At the center of a solution to such grave challenges is the willingness of various actors to sit together and sort out their differences through peaceful means (Yared, 2022). It is also hoped that the insights gained from Ethiopia will be relevant when addressing ongoing conflicts in other societies in the region and across the globe.

Defining listening

In his explanation of the transactional model of communication, Barnlund (1970) wrote the following; "Communication seems more accurately described as a circular process in which the words 'sender' and 'receiver,' when they have to be used at all, serve only to fix the point of view of the analyst who uses them" (p. 50). To date, the majority of our scholarly attention has fixed our point of view toward the speaker, with listening receiving much less attention (e.g., Bodie, 2012; Macnamara, 2016). A common misunderstanding surrounding the concept is that it merely describes a cognitive process, one that deals with pro-cesses like attention, comprehension, and memory (Worthington, 2018). Although hundreds of definitions of listening have been offered in the literature (Worthington & Bodie, 2018), two elements common to most are particularly relevant for this chapter: "giving attention and recognition to others" (Husband, 2009, p. 441; Macnamara, 2016, p. 136).

Husband (2009) noted that "listening is an act of attention, a willingness to focus on the other, to heed both their presence and their communication"

(p. 441). For Hoffman (2012), listening is "non-judgmental, non-adversarial, and seeks the truth of the person questioned" (p. 4). As he wrote (p. 4):

> I'm not talking about listening with the 'human ear.' I am talking about discerning. To discern means to perceive something hidden or obscure. We must listen with our 'spiritual ear.' This is very different from deciding in advance who is right and who is wrong, and then seeking to rectify it.

In fact, it is that ability to stay away from being judgmental or adversarial and to embrace a willingness to listen to all parties in conflict that contributes to reconciliation and effective peacemaking.

Listening's role in peacemaking

Regardless of the communication channels chosen, social conflicts, for the most part, involve misunderstandings of both what was said and was left unsaid. What was said, the verbal messages, often comprise three parts: Content, feelings, and relationships (Patterson et al., 2012; Reece & Reece, 2017). These three social-psychological concepts help us understand why conflict in general is complex. Content complexity refers to the immediate and historical, as well as the dynamic nature of the underlying issues in conflict situations. Feeling complexity, on the other hand, refers to how the parties to the conflict perceive each other, including the power balance between and among the contending parties. It also refers to the attributes and personality-like characteristics of the parties to the conflict. Relationship dynamics, whether in their historical or current context, strongly influence the negotiation process for peacemaking and peacebuilding. Do, for example, the parties to the conflict see each other as mortal enemies or just individuals and groups with differences of interests and values? Are they willing to engage emotionally and cognitively in complex dialogues? As Kriesberg (2007) suggested, the answers to such questions help determine the dynamic complexity of the negotiated settlements and the viability of the efforts in peacemaking and peacebuilding. To help effectively address such dynamics in communication, several soft skills are suggested, including empathic listening. Before we outline those, however, we present brief descriptions of three Ethiopian communities and draw implications for resolving disputes between individuals and among groups given the political culture within which individuals from these communities are called to make meaning together.

Indigenous models of communication

Even though studies exploring the role of listening in peacebuilding in Africa are limited (Beyene, 2020), Ethiopia's political culture seems to be deprived of compassionate listening, a striking contrast to its social culture, showing high levels of a willingness to listen to and understand the concerns and aspirations of others. Indeed, one of the trademarks of traditional societies is that they have "a rich communication environment that predates modern electronic media by many, many years" (FAO 2009, as cited in Mohammed, 2016, p. 1). As ancient as many of the Ethiopian communities are, they share a rich communication tradition. Even so, elites tend to remain in their echo chambers and engage in deliberations with people who share their views and ideologies. Isolation and rejection of 'others' with opposing views can be described as the hallmark of Ethiopia's recent political culture (Beyene, 2020; Kebede, 2008). Glaringly absent from the political culture of elites is a willingness to engage in civil discourse, debate over issues of national importance, and narrow down differences for building consensus. And yet, listening and open debate for building consensus is practiced among many communities in Ethiopia. The three cases from Hamar, Gurage, and Afar show that members of those communities use traditional systems of communication that allow sharing information by engaging in open, (at times) debate, and (often) dialogue, to address differences and arrive at consensus.

The Hamar

The first ethnic group selected for this study is Hamar. Located in the Southern part of Ethiopia, Hamars are mainly pastoralist communities. As Strecker (2011) described, "Hamar political discourse moves from an open form in which differences, insecurities, and alternatives are expressed and discussed to more and more closed forms in which differences are narrowed down and funneled as it were towards a consensus" (p. 131). Strecker's extensive studies in Hamar indicate the communities are committed to open debate to address differences no matter how long settling the issues might take. Clearly, this is a stark example of major differences between the present political culture of Ethiopia and the traditions of its communities. While communities such as those in Hamar show a willingness to express and discuss issues and narrow down differences through debate in an open forum, the political elites seem to be unable to replicate such rich tradition in their consensus building efforts. Instead, different factions resort to violence. The inability of elites to find common ground in addressing Ethiopia's fundamental and structural problems peacefully has made the country prone to violence during recent successive governments. What the tradition of this community suggests to the elites of Ethiopia is that cultivating the culture of listening to address the fundamental challenges the country is facing is one possible intervention to help Ethiopia break the cycle of violence.

The Gurages

The second ethnic group, the Gurage, is one of the Semitic groups in Southern Ethiopia with a rich history of engaging in dialogue and open debate to address differences. As described in Bitew et al. (2021, p. 2):

Historically, the Gurage people gathered in a specific place, such as around big trees, to discuss issues. Customary laws were enacted and modified in meetings that directly involved the local people. Inter-Clan and intra-tribal conflicts were also resolved through meetings of all mature members of the local community.

This is an important feature of Gurages that makes them an exemplary community for what it means to employ listening and open debate to address differences. Their primary platform to enact these modes of communication is called "Yajoka" (Engdawork, 2013). Similar to a modern court system, disputants have unconditional right to present their case and to be heard (Bitew et al., 2021). According to Bitew et al. (2021, p. 2):

> In settling conflicts, disputants have the unconditional right to present their case to Yejoka Elders. Every participant in the conflict resolution process has the right to raise concerns that may mediate the dispute. Finally, the Elders make a decision after analyzing the case presented by the conflicting parties.

As seen above, the decision is not made arbitrarily; rather, it is based on agreed upon cultural values. While this is an important tradition, which resembles both Western democratic practices and elements of a modern court system, it is not unique to the Gurages. Many other local communities, such as the Shekacho people, also practice similar traditions (Bekele & Akako, 2022; see also Mugume et al., Chapter 12).

The Afar

The third example is from Afar. Located in Northeastern Ethiopia, Afar is a pastoral community situated in a very hostile area (Morell, 2005). The community has enjoyed a traditional communication system called Dagu, which could be translated to mean 'news' (Menbere & Skjerdal, 2008, p. 1). Dagu "is a form of traditional oral communication system by the Afar society" mainly dependent on observation and memory (Mohammed, 2016, p. 24). According to Parker (1971, pp. 231–232):

> The Afra are expert at observation and will make a mental note of everything in detail. When one is asked about his movements and to recount the things which befell him on his journey from A to B, it is quite illuminating to see the detail which have been registered.

Ultimately, Dagu centers on the ability to observe, remember, and recount events. It is the encounter of people that kick starts the news cycle. When meeting someone on a journey, Afars find it customary to stop and exchange news. They exchange news right after exchanging greetings. In Afar, this is how news is passed.

According to Haile Mohammed (2016), the main feature of this exchange lies in the ability and willingness of the listener (A) to remain attentive to the narrator (B) without interference. Once the reporting is done, it is up to the listener (A) to ask for clarity, attribution, verification, or any other inquiry that is related to the news. Once this cycle of news reporting is done, they change turns. The one who was listening (A) to the news reporting will share what they have seen. In this round, the listener (A) will be a narrator and report what they have observed. Once the reporting is done, it is up to the listener (B) to ask for clarity, attribution, verification, etc.

Included in this news swap is the issue of source attribution and accountability. If someone is not the direct source of information, they should attribute their sources. In effect, this resembles modern news reporting when the latter is done appropriately. In Afar, people acknowledge their sources while sharing the information. Source attribution will add value to this rich tradition mainly in terms of trustworthiness and accountability (Mohammed, 2016; Menbere & Skjerdal, 2008). Indeed, as Mohammed (2016) noted, "What is more, as it is commonly true of the mass media, Dagu too pays great attention to the trustworthiness of a story" (p. 32). Reliability of Dagu is usually secured through attribution. That is, if a narrator is not an eyewitness, he or she must disclose the source of information, which normally goes back to at least two chains of narration. It should be noted that citation in Dagu includes the person's name, clan, and locality (Mohammed, 2016, p. 33). Credibility in news sharing is extremely important as failing to do so will be considered as cheating or misleading. In Afar, cheating results in condemnation. As the Afar proverb says, "he who cheats his neighbor will get an evil reward" (Parker, 1971, p. 235).

Summary

What is common among the three communities is the practice of listening. Albeit for various reasons, the Hamar, Gurages, and Afar communities engage in listening and show a willingness to attune to what others have to say. Unfortunately, one cannot say the same about the political elites of Ethiopia. In other words, these examples reveal a practice and tradition that is not strong in Ethiopia's recent political culture – the ability of communities to debate issues openly, address differences peacefully, and build consensus. One might wonder why local communities show grace and patience to deal with their differences peacefully, while the political elites fail to replicate similar practices at the national level and engage in "nip it in the bud."

Kebede's (2008) analysis of the impact of Marxism on what he called "cultural dislocation" in Ethiopia can provide a possible explanation. Zewde (2014) wrote that "the Ethiopian student movement produced many militant adherents of Marxism-Leninism" (p. 138). The result of this militant mindset appeared to pave the way for an era that has witnessed assassination of opponents as a technique of eliminating enemies. The Marxist government that came to power in 1974 took this militant mindset to the next level "by launching the Red Terror campaign to wipe out their opponents" (Kebede, 2011, p. 261). This campaign "lasted until late 1978 and brought about the end of The Ethiopian People's Revolutionary Party (EPRP) at the cost of thousands of its members being either killed, imprisoned, or forced to flee the country" (p. 261). EPRP also contributed to the toxic political culture, which, according to Kebede, initiated a campaign of assassination of opponents, which mainly targeted the rival civilian faction that had supported Mengistu, the leader of the Dergue. Zewde's assessment perhaps is an excellent description of what has become Ethiopia's political culture. According to Zewde (2014), "the country's political culture, which made the [student] movement inevitable, also conditioned their behavior. Dogmatic belief, rather than seasoned debate and a spirit of compromise, became the norm" (pp. 279–280).

The above description of the genesis of the "my way or the highway" mindset in Ethiopia's recent political culture makes sense to those who study the issues rather carefully. This is not, however, to suggest here that Ethiopia's political culture in the past was completely peaceful and inclusive. What we are pointing out is that the use of violence as the primary and structural means of eliminating groups was not a common practice in the Ethiopian political culture. What Ethiopians are witnessing in subsequent years after the fall of Emperor Hailesillasie's government can only be considered as one of the darkest moments in its recent history. Introducing a culture of listening to promote mutual understanding in addressing old and present political issues is the context for building lasting peace. That should be considered the top priority.

Implications for peacemaking in Ethiopia

As even those who are vaguely familiar with Ethiopia know, it is a country of many customs, traditions, and communication styles. It is also the home of two major religions, Christianity and Islam. The communication styles vary according to ethnic orientation as well as by regions of the country. Some of the communication styles are direct and to the point, while others are vague, indirect, and, at times, even polite in verbal and nonverbal ways. Clearly, such cultural differences in style make the communication process difficult at times. It can be challenging to quickly decipher meaning, and, more importantly in the context of a conflict situation, the communication may become susceptible to misunderstandings and misinterpretations. This is where developing effective listening skills, especially in managing, resolving, and transforming conflicts, becomes essential. But developing effective listening skills is not automatic; it starts with awareness and commitment to acquire the skill sets. As Reece and Reece (2017) observed, "We may be born with the ability to hear, but we have to learn to listen" (p. 33).

Unfortunately, in academia, we typically emphasize speaking skills over listening skills. This lack of education for listening is further complicated by cultural differences even when offered through other means of learning such as in

communication workshops. And yet, evidence from the communication literature suggests that if there is awareness of the problem and willingness to learn,
even people with different styles of communications and deep cultural differences
can learn to more effectively negotiate across global cultures (Augsberger, 1992),
much less in a country where there are shared values and traditions. The effective
listening skills in this regard include active listening, critical listening, and empathic listening, among others.

Important listening skills

Active listening is fueled by a positive and constructive engagement with a speaker.
As listeners, we should seek first to learn what the speaker is saying, rather than
engaging in the typical propensity to judge what is being shared. Studies in effective
communication suggest that taking the following steps during a conversation,
particularly where there is conflict that is complicated by cultural differences, will
improve listening skills (Reece & Reece, 2017; Shellengarger, 2014):

- Taking note of what is being said;
- Using paraphrasing and perception checking;
- Asking clarifying questions such as "please tell me more about this or that;"
- Noticing the body language of the speaker (i.e., nonverbal and para-verbal
  channels of communications); and,
- Summarizing what the speaker shared in the conversation until he/she agrees
  with the content and meaning.

In addition to the above basic listening skills, empathic and critical listening, we
believe, are even more imperative in peacemaking and peacebuilding in Ethiopia.
As Tom Bruneau (1993, pp. 194–195) noted:

> Empathic listening is to be respectful of the dignity of others. Empathic
> listening is a caring, a love of the wisdom to be found in others whoever they
> may be. It is to be open to the work and others as unique and separate reality.

Added to this is what Hoffman (2008) observed, that we should understand that
everyone has a partial truth: "Everyone has a partial truth, and we must listen,
discern, acknowledge this partial truth in everyone – particularly those with whom
we disagree" (p. 2). Unfortunately, the current governance system of Ethiopia has
spent over three decades emphasizing differences, when it could have instead
employed an open communication environment to safely share feelings, stressed the
nationalistic bonds of its people (both mutual private as well as national interests),
and worked toward rebuilding national social capital. Empathic listening, which is
understanding another person's feelings, is one such rebuilding skill of listening.

Another way of adding depth to such active listening skills is to improve one's critical listening skills. As Reece and Reece (2017) wrote, "Critical listening is the attempt to see the topic of discussion from the speaker's point of view and to consider how the speaker's perception of the situation may be different from your own" (p. 34). The way to improve such a skill is to be sure when listening to others, to look for and consider the evidence that is being offered by the speaker, particularly that which challenges one's assumptions and perspectives.

In short, in a conflict situation, the ability and willingness to listen to others with compassion and open mindedness will contribute to mutual understanding. Knowing more about the concerns of others, particularly those that one is in conflict with, has evidence-based potential to transform the perceptions of each other for mutual good. It can also change social narratives (Rosoux, 2009), narratives that political merchants use to divide and control the political agenda of a given nation such as Ethiopia. In every nation where there is civil disorder and violence, the masses are often only part of the process by way of their victimization. As Longfellow (in Hoffman, 1997) noted, "If we could read the secret history of our enemies, we should find in each person's life sorrow and suffering enough to disarm all hostility" (p. 4).

Compassionate and empathic, as well as critical listening, we believe, will help transcend the "enemy vs. perpetrator" narrative and emphasize treating others, instead, as fellow humans (see Argo et al., Chapter 8). Such new narratives, in turn, will allow the creation of opportunities for forgiveness, encourage the transformation of the conflict, and contribute to the much-needed healing that Ethiopia needs. In short, embracing one another with forgiveness and creating a sense of national unity will be consistent with the African philosophy of Ubuntu, "I am" because "you are." As human beings sharing this world, we have a common destiny. We enjoy peace together and suffer from injustice together. The "us versus them" dichotomy is a recipe for mutual destruction. As Nepo (2020, p. xvii) succinctly put it:

> Still every life, every generation, every age takes its turn at pushing each other away, only to be loved and worn back to the one tribe we belong to. This seems even more relevant in our tense, modern world. For there is no "they." We are they. We are each other. And, there is a deep unity that always waits below our righteous insistence that we know they.

Clearly, such a national social narrative will be a foundation for building bridges and windows instead of walls, kililization, to use the Ethiopian word. And the means in this case is active, empathetic, and critical listening.

Conclusion: empathic listening for constructive dialogues

The purpose of this chapter was to explore listening skills as key to transforming conflict in Ethiopia. This section concludes with a brief "how to" for practitioners that can provide a viable starting point for this important work. As the above sections demonstrated, local communities rely on open debate and listening to resolve their differences peacefully. However, unless the political elites translate traditional forms of communication at community levels into the political culture, addressing century old and current issues will remain elusive. It is in this context we propose promoting a culture of listening as a solution that gets at the core of the problem. Failure to do so will result in inevitable misunderstandings and create concomitant frustration. Those negative interpersonal dynamics that lead to "us vs them" eventuate to the types of societal and national disharmonies that ultimately lead to civil wars.

As we argue above, engaging in constructive dialogue where people listen to each other without judgment can promote mutual understanding. One of the core values of engaging in constructive dialogue is to communicate with the goal of bridging differences, even radical differences. The communication tool for this is empathic listening which is a way of listening and responding for mutual understanding and initiating conversation in the building of trust. The psychological perspective of effective communication, especially when the stakes are high, suggests the "how of listening empathically" as follows:

- Create a safe, a trusting, environment to talk;
- Acknowledge each other as human beings with problems to solve, but not as if the speaker or anyone else present is the problem;
- Listen to the information without passing judgment.

When it comes to withholding judgment to help build a constructive dialogue, Patterson et al. (2012, p. 162) described the AMPP process. In this process, listeners begin by Asking questions. This process starts the conversation, especially if framed with a genuine interest to hear, reflect on, and learn. Agreeing with what the speaker is sharing is not the point currently, as the goal is mutual understanding of the problem for the conflict. The "M" stands for mirroring, as the metaphor represents the listener making genuine efforts to reflect the speaker's emotions and feelings, which is followed by more extensive Paraphrasing of what one is hearing. This listening technique serves several purposes, especially if framed with opening statements such as "Let me see if I heard you right." The last "P" represents the notion of "priming." Despite efforts to make the meeting environment both physically and psychologically safe, individuals may still feel unsafe to openly speak and share their respective truths. In this case, listeners might effectively "prime the pump" by offering gentle guesses of what the speaker might be thinking or feeling, serving to move the conversation forward.

In short, empathic and active listening require learnable and teachable skills such as creating a positive and inviting social environment, a somewhat neutral meeting place, showing interest in what the other person has to say, being attentive and alert, and allowing the other person to bounce perspectives and ideas for mutual gains. The benefits of such empathic listening include un-covering true feelings about the conflict situation, allowing venting (emotional release), clarifying miscommunication breakdown, and reducing tensions. In short, the process builds trust and, in turn, creates the foundation for common ground in resolving and transforming the conflict.

Finally, a commitment to listening (empathic and compassionate listening) will also help us break the cycle of violence and trauma in each society, as "a great source of violence stems from our unhealed wounds" (Hoffman, 2008). Sankaranarayan et al. (Chapter 9) also discuss the fact that "violence and trauma can fuel each other, and this traumatic exposure can undermine collaboration and also increases the possibility of further violence." Similarly, a study by World Bank Group (2014, p. 10) indicated that:

> a potential cycle of violence and trauma [exists] if trauma is not addressed … . [these cycles] are seen as inward and outward expressions of reactive violence in which victims can become perpetrators and vice versa. However, it is important to note that this is not a mechanical result, but untreated trauma increases the risk of this pattern.

In other words, victims of violence/traumatic experience are more likely to perpetuate the violence and trauma they have experienced, and this leaves people vulnerable to creating further harm (Sankaranarayan et al., Chapter 9). Thus, breaking such a cycle is in the best interest of any forward-looking society, and compassionate listening contributes to that effort (Green, 2008; Hoffman, 2008). Compassionate listening assumes that "both sides to any violence are wounded, and their wounds are unhealed … and unhealed wounds are a great source of violence" (Hoffman, 2008, p. 2).

The last few decades of Ethiopian politics are a clear testament to the danger of the growing trends of violence, and business as usual has continued to inflict more pain. The cycle of violence and retribution in search of "justice" will remain a major hurdle blocking any peace initiative in the country. The trend of increasing violence will continue to cause more damage to the fabric of the nation. Before it is too late, "the country has to come to grips with and move beyond this legacy if it is to have any hope of redemption" (Zewde, 2014, p. 280). To move beyond its history of political violence, a more coordinated policy to cure unhealed wounds will usher in a new era. Focusing on healing is what is at the heart of compassionate listening. In the absence of genuine efforts to understand and help groups who are suffering, initiatives to bring lasting peace to Ethiopia will remain a daunting task. What is missing in Ethiopia's ongoing violence is an effort to move beyond a victim mentality and an acknowledgment of the suffering of others. Focusing on others, giving them attention, and making them a part of the healing process will help rebuild relationships as well as restore trust and har-mony. The cumulative effect of such an undertaking will create an environment for collective healing from collective suffering. That, in turn, will help break the cycle of violence and bring about much-needed redemption.

Note

1 In addition to these more formal reasons establishing Ethiopia as a compelling case study for listening, we (the authors) are also from Ethiopia and have each spent decades working to bring peace to our homeland. We thus have compelling personal reasons to introduce others to the need for peace in Ethiopia, and we hope this chapter is one way we are giving back to a place that continues to mean so much to us both.

References

Abbink, J. (2006). Ethnicity and conflict generation in Ethiopia: Some problems and prospects of ethno-regional federalism. *Journal of Contemporary African Studies, 24*(3), 389–414. 10.1080/02589000600976729

Al-Mawed, H. S. (1999). *The Palestinian refugees in Syria their past, present and future.* The Expert and Advisory Services Fund International Development Research Centre. http://prrn.mcgill.ca/prrn/al-mawed.pdf

Augsberger, D. (1992). *Conflict mediation across cultures: Pathways and patterns.* Westminster/ John Knox Press.

Barnlund, D. (1970). A transactional model of communication. In J. Akin, A. Goldberg, G. Myers & J. Steward (Eds.), *Language behavior: A book of readings in communication. For Elwood Murray on the occasion of his retirement* (pp. 43–62). De Gruyter Mouton.

Bekele, W. B., & Akako, A. A. (2022). Ethiopia: Indigenous conflict resolution mechanism of Shekacho people and its role in promoting peace and good governance. *Conflict Studies Quarterly, 38*, 3–22. 10.24193/csq.38.1

Beyene, Z. (2012). *The role of media in ethnic violence during political transition in Africa: The case of Rwanda and Kenya.* [Doctoral dissertation, University of Nebraska, Lincoln]. Digital Commons at University of Nebraska-Lincoln. https://digitalcommons.unl.edu/dissertations/AAI3522072/

Beyene, Z. (2020). Building peace through listening. In D. L. Worthington & G. D. Bodie (Eds.), *The handbook of listening* (pp. 419–426). Wiley.

Bitew, B., Sewenet, A., & Fentahun, G. (2021). Indigenous governance systems and democracy in Ethiopia: Yejoka Qicha system of the Gurage people. *The International Indigenous Policy Journal, 12*(3). 10.18584/iipj.2021.12.3.10969

Bodie, G. D. (2012). Listening as positive communication. In T. Socha & M. Pitts (Eds.), *The positive side of interpersonal communication* (pp. 109–125). Peter Lang.

Bruneau, T. (1993). Empathy and listening. In A. D. Wolvin & C. G. Coakley (Eds.), *Perspectives on listening* (pp. 185–200). Ablex.

Engdawork, N. (2013). *Yajoka: Council of Sabat-Bet Clan Chiefs and Notables.* Lambert Academic Publishing.

Gebre Selassie, A. (2003). Ethnic federalism: Its promise and pitfalls forAfrica. *The Yale Journal of International Law, 28*(51), 51–107. https://scholarship.law.wm.edu/cgi/viewcontent.cgi?article=1088&context=facpubs

Green, L. (2008, January). Compassionate listening in the Middle East. In D. Rivers (Ed.), *Compassionate Listening! An exploratory sourcebook about conflict transformation* (pp. 5–8). https://newconversations.net/

Hoffman, G. K. (1997, November 25). *Compassionate listening – First step to reconciliation?* Speech transcript. https://newconversations.net/communication-skills-library-of-articles-and-teaching-materials/gene-knudsen-hoffman-articles/compassionate-listening-first-step-to-reconciliation/

Hoffman, G. K. (2008, January). Compassionate listening: A first step toward reconciliation. In D. Rivers (Ed.), *Compassionate listening! An exploratory sourcebook about conflict transformation* (pp. 2–4). https://newconversations.net/

Husband, C. (2009). Commentary between listening and understanding. *Journal of Media and Cultural Studies, 23*(4), 441–443. 10.1080/10304310903026602

Kebede, M. (2008). *Radicalism and cultural dislocation in Ethiopia, 1960–1974.* University of Rochester Press.

Kebede, M. (2011). *Ideology and elite conflict: Autopsy of the Ethiopian revolution.* Lexington Books.

Kriesberg, L. (2007). *Constructive conflicts: From escalation to resolution.* Rowman & Littlefield.

Kłosowicz, R. (2015). The role of Ethiopia in the regional security complex of the Horn of Africa. *Ethiopian Journal of Social Sciences and Language Studies, 2*(2), 83–97. https://ejhs.ju.edu.et/index.php/ejssls/article/view/742

Macnamara, J. (2016). The work and 'architecture of listening': Addressing gaps in organization-public communication. *International Journal of Strategic Communication, 10*(2), 133–148. 10.1080/1553118X.2016.1147043

Menbere, G., & Skjerdal, T. (2008). The potential of Dagu communication in North-Eastern Ethiopia. *Media Development, 55*(1), 19–21.

Mengie, L. T. (2015). Ethnic federalism and conflict in Ethiopia: What lessons can other jurisdictions draw? *Africa Journal of International and Comparative Law, 23*(3), 462–475. doi: 10.3366/ajicl.2015.0131

Mohammed, J. (2016). Dagu: Its nature, attributes and reporting praxis. *Ethiopian Journal of Language, Culture and Communication, 1*, 24–50. https://journals.bdu.edu.et/index.php/EJLCC/article/view/347

Moore, C. (1996). *The mediation process: Practical strategies for resolving conflict* (2nd ed.). Jossey-Bass.

Morell, V. (2005, October). Africa's Danakil desert: Cruelest place on earth. *National Geographic*, pp. 34–53.

Nepo, M. (2020). *The book of soul: 52 paths to living what matters.* St. Martin's Essentials.

Parker, E. (1971). Afar stories, riddles and proverbs. *Journal of Ethiopian Studies, 9*(2), 219–287. https://www.jstor.org/stable/41967477

Patterson, K., Grenny, J., McMillan, R., & Switzler, A. (2012). *Crucial conversations: Tools for talking when the stakes are high.* McGraw-Hill.

Reece, B. L., & Reece, M. (2017). *Effective human relations: Interpersonal and organizational applications.* Cengage.

Rosoux, V. (2009). Reconciliation as a peace-building process: Scope and limits. In J. Bercovitch, V. Kremenyuk, and I. W. Zartman, (Eds.), *The SAGE handbook of conflict resolution* (pp. 543–560). SAGE.

Shellengarger, S. (2014, July). Tuning in: Improving your listening skills. *The Wallstreet Journal.* https://www.wsj.com/articles/tuning-in-how-to-listen-better-1406070727

Strecker, I. (2011). *Ethnographic chiasmus: Essays on culture, conflict, and rhetoric.* Michigan State University Press.

World Bank Group. (2014). *Invisible wounds: A practitioner's dialogue in improving development outcomes through psychosocial support.* https://acrobat.adobe.com/link/track?uri= urn:aaid:scds:US:1f22ccf8-285e-3ec2-9e86-78954cb87508

World Vision. (2022, July 12). *Syrian refugee crisis: Facts, FAQs, and how to help.* https:// www.worldvision.org/refugees-news-stories/syrian-refugee-crisis-facts

Worthington, D. L. (2018). Modeling and measuring cognitive components of listening. In D. L. Worthington & G. D. Bodie (Eds.), *Sourcebook of listening research: Methodology & measurement* (pp. 70–96). Wiley.

Worthington, D. L., & Bodie, G. D. (2018). Defining listening: A historical, theoretical, and pragmatic assessment. In D. L. Worthington & G. D. Bodie (Eds.), *Sourcebook of listening research: Methodology & measurement* (pp. 3–17). Wiley.

Yared, T. (2022, January 17). *Getting to grips with Ethiopia's ethnic and political violence is vital for stability. Institute for Security Studies (ISS).* https://issafrica.org/iss-today/getting-to-grips-with-ethiopias-ethnic-and-political-violence-is-vital-for-stability

Zewde, B. (2014). *The quest for socialist utopia: The Ethiopian student movement, 1960–1974.* Boydell & Brewer.

12

LISTENING AND PEACEBUILDING IN RWANDA

Perspective of homegrown approaches

Peter John Mugume[1], Josephine Mukabera[2], and Jane Umutoni[2]

[1]COLLEGE OF ARTS AND SOCIAL SCIENCES/CENTRE FOR CONFLICT MANAGEMENT, UNIVERSITY OF RWANDA
[2]COLLEGE OF ARTS AND SOCIAL SCIENCES/CENTRE FOR GENDER STUDIES, UNIVERSITY OF RWANDA

Although the country known as modern-day Rwanda has a rich history, dating back to at least 3,000 BC, most readers are likely more familiar with Rwanda because of the 1994 genocide against the Tutsis. Justified as a response to the downing of a plane carrying then-President Juvenal Habyarimana on 6 April 1994, Hutu extremists launched a months-long campaign targeting government opponents (mainly Tutsis but also their sympathizers regardless of ethnicity) that eventuated in the execution of over 1,000,000 Rwandans and that left millions more either displaced or physically and psychologically traumatized. Although the Rwandan Patriotic Front took control of the capital, Kigali, by 4 July 1994, putting an official end to the genocide, conflict in the region continued through the early 2000s. These conflicts, like those pre-dating the genocide, involved multiple countries and ethnic and militia groups. Indeed, the 1994 genocide might best be cast as the climax of decades of ethnic tension, largely between the Hutu and Tutsis who, to this day, disagree on the origin and antecedents of their conflict (Corey & Joireman, 2004).

The purpose of this chapter is not to settle on a single, all encompassing "truth" regarding the history of violence, conflict, and genocide in Rwanda. Rather, it is to analyze how three homegrown approaches to peacebuilding in post-genocide Rwanda provided an alternative to attempts by international actors and entities. While international aid and interventions can be important contributors to peacebuilding in a post-conflict society like Rwanda, it is the "challenge and responsibility ... [of] the citizens of the countries where peacebuilding is underway, with support from their governments, who assume the responsibility for laying the foundations of lasting peace" (Peacebuilding Support Office, 2010, p. 5). Of particular interest in this chapter is unpacking the various

DOI: 10.4324/9781003214465-12

modes and models of listening that underlie *Gacaca, Umuganda,* and *Umugoroba w'Imiryango.* While scholars have certainly published on these forms of community engagement and explored their implications for peacebuilding (e.g., Nyseth Brehm et al., 2014; Uwihangana et al., 2020), the specific roles that listening has played remain unclear. It is toward conceptual clarity of listening and its role in homegrown approaches to peacebuilding in Rwanda that this chapter is concerned. To provide the context for that clarity, we first offer a brief history of post-independence Rwanda.

Post-independence Rwanda: a brief history

Some (e.g., Lemarchand, 1970; Mamdani, 2001; Prunier, 1995) have argued that the violence in Rwanda was a consequence of mostly colonial administrative policies, particularly the Belgian system of divide and conquer, and post-colonial Rwanda's subsequent administrative system. In the 1950s, Rwanda experienced several political events including the so-called 1959 revolution (Hutu emancipation) and the colonialists' switching of allegiances in support of the majority Hutus who took power from the Tutsi monarchy (Lemarchand, 1970; Newbury, 1995). In 1961, a Belgian-organized referendum abolished the monarchical system of administration in Rwanda. This process was violent and led to massacres against the Tutsis (Boudreaux, 2009; Mamdani, 2001; Melvern, 2006). In 1962, Rwanda gained its independence from Belgium and was declared a republic under a Hutu government led by President Gregoire Kayibanda. Prior to independence, however, the Tutsi massacre had already been instigated. Clashes in 1959 had led to the displacement of many Tutsis fleeing Rwanda.

President Kayibanda's government was characterized by ethnic violence. In 1963, the Tutsis, who fled Rwanda in fear of the massacre, launched an incursion against President Kayibanda's regime. Their attack was not successful; government forces defeated and killed many of them. Meanwhile, the Tutsi massacre continued in different parts of Rwanda like Gikongoro (Chrétien, 2006; Reyntjens, 2013), and many people, particularly Tutsis, fled to neighboring countries. In 1973, the then-Minister of Defense, major General Juvenal Habyarimana, in a *coup d'etat*, overthrew President Kayibanda's regime. This political process involved widespread persecution and more killings, including that of President Kayibanda. After the coup, Habyarimana became the Rwandan President and subsequently became the sole candidate for the National Revolutionary Movement for Development Party (*Mouvement Revolutionnaire National pour le Development*). In 1990, President Habyarimana's regime was confronted with pressure from the Rwandese Patriotic Front/Army, donors, and opposition from within the country and urged to allow the political opposition to exercise its democratic rights. There were also other demands including the return of refugees who had fled the country from 1959 through the 1970s and the end of ethnic discrimination. Towards the end of 1990, the pressure intensified, and in 1991, the government of Kigali accepted a multi-party government, which led to the formation of a coalition government in 1992 under the Republican Democratic Party (MDR) Prime Minister. It was this government that partici-pated in the Arusha Peace Accords with the intent to end the war with the Rwanda Patriotic Front who were composed primarily of those who had fled the country between the 1950s and 1970s.

The Arusha Accords were negotiated and ultimately overseen by the UN Security Council and Belgian troops operating as peacekeepers. Despite the presence of the Arusha Peace Accords, however, the then-Rwandan government organized and perpetrated genocide against the Tutsis (Corey & Joireman, 2004). The genocide culminated in the early 1993 massacres against the Tutsis in northern Rwanda (Bideri, 2009) and prompted the Rwanda Patriotic Front/ Army (RPF/A) to resume their fight against the government. Indeed, the signing of the Accords led to further disagreements among the Hutu extremists who saw the Arusha Agreement as favoring the RPF/A, which they perceived to be a Tutsi group that wanted to restore Tutsi aristocracy. The discontent among Hutus extremists was, in this regard, a threat to the Arusha Accords. This opposition was especially concerning because some of the extremist Hutus were powerful in the government and could influence the implementation of the peace agreement.

The political consequences of violence in Rwanda are enormous and range from issues related to administration and identity politics to Rwanda's colonial and post-colonial history. These issues have also influenced the management of identity-related issues that have plagued Rwanda for decades. After the 1994 genocide against the Tutsis, there was an urgent need to rebuild peace for Rwanda through different ways including diplomacy, peacemaking, peace-keeping, and peacebuilding.

Peacebuilding in Rwanda

According to Sezibera (2012), "peacebuilding is meant to make peace last" and is based on the recognition that "peace, development, and democracy are inter-dependent" (p. 2). Efforts to build sustainable peace in post-conflict Rwanda started early and were initiated by both international and local actors to focus on a range of activities (e.g., rebuilding trust in institutions, creating an equitable justice system; Eriksson, 1996). The scope of this chapter does not extend to the more formal or international peacebuilding efforts except to agree with some prior critiques that these efforts largely failed, perhaps because they were not grounded in the type of ideological clarity that marks local/homegrown ap-proaches (Clark, 2012). The United Nations (UN) Office of the High Commissioner for Human Rights argued vehemently that community-based courts were ill-equipped to handle complex genocide cases, and Amnesty International Human Rights Watch and a host of legal commentators waged a concerted campaign against one such homegrown approach, *Gacaca*, on grounds that it falls short of international standards of due process for the prosecution of serious crimes (cited by Clark, 2012). From the judgment of these organizations, it was not possible for the homegrown approaches such as the *Gacaca* court system to handle the cases of genocide crimes.

As others have noted (e.g., Karimunda, 2019; Ndahinda & Muleefu, 2012), however, approaches that provide for 1) a critical examination of our society's history, 2) the cultural values that cemented an evolving Rwandan polity over time, and 3) the deficits of leadership and governance that brought the country to the brink of extinction are more likely to generate the kind of sustained peace required after the deep-seated and violent conflict precipitated by the genocide. Indeed, in the immediate aftermath of the genocide, international experts gave little hope for the peaceful, long-term development of Rwanda (Eriksson, 1996). Local leaders in Rwanda, however, were not in universal consensus and decided to focus on returning to normalcy through national unity and reconstruction, national sovereignty, and human security.

In addition to a focus on sustainability, successful peacebuilding also requires development that is always unique and, thus, context based (Sezibera, 2012). For Rwanda, these efforts involved ensuring basic but necessary tasks were done. First, Rwandan peacebuilding efforts were based on intense negotiations and discussions, such as the Arusha Peace Accords. The Accords clearly defined the acceptable polity, including the emphasis on national unity and reconciliation, power sharing, integration of warring forces, and a political code of conduct for political parties. Peacebuilding in this transitional period was based on the principles agreed on at Arusha. In this vein, institutions, such as the National Unity and Reconciliation Commission (NURC) whose purpose is "to promote unity, reconciliation, and social cohesion among Rwandans and build a country in which everyone has equal rights and contributing to good governance," were established (Mission of NURC, n.d.). From April to June 2001, NURC initiated a series of consultations that sought to deeply listen to the Rwandan people about their hopes and fears for the possibility of reconciliation. The resulting report included numerous recommendations including the establishment of various homegrown approaches to peacebuilding (NURC, 2012).

Homegrown approaches to peace

As a post-conflict nation, Rwanda has heavily invested in homegrown solutions that have been used to address community issues and support the nation to preserve social cohesion, harmony, and overall community wellbeing. Some of these homegrown initiatives date back to pre-colonial times, while others are relatively new; all are informed by Rwandan traditional ways of addressing issues and celebrating gains.

In general, there was agreement among Rwandans to build a state based on fundamental principles, and the Senate was created to oversee the implementation of these principles in areas of national interest. It is important to point out here that the fundamental principles are, in part, expected to be implemented using homegrown solutions rather than classical-conventional reconciliation strategies that have delayed the realization of sustainable peace in Africa (Mugenzi, 2018). This is emphasized by the Rwandan constitution of 2003 (revised in 2015), which requires the government to promote the enhancement of national unity and reconciliation and provides for the creation of institutions that have been successful in helping mend the social fragmentation, economic failure, and related harms like mistrust that are often left unaddressed after formal peacebuilding efforts are completed. The sections that follow examine the role of listening in peacebuilding in post-genocide Rwanda, focusing on three homegrown approaches – *Gacaca*, *Umuganda*, and *Umugoroba w'Imiryango*.

Gacaca courts: community-based justice

Following the 1994 genocide against the Tutsis, approximately 120,000 genocide suspects were incarcerated (National Service of Gacaca Courts, 2012). It was estimated that if genocide-related cases were handled exclusively through ordinary courts, it would take Rwanda over 100 years to try that number of suspects under preventive detention, without mentioning those suspects that were still at large. Apart from Rwanda's insistence on prosecution instead of amnesty, it was also preoccupied with finding ways to achieve unity and reconciliation (Muleefu, 2016). The Uruwiro discussions recommended the adoption of *Gacaca* courts that were to be adapted to the specific situation of dealing with genocide-related acts.

Organic Law No. 40/2000 of 26 January 2001 created *Gacaca* courts for several reasons.[1] First, the *Gacaca* courts were established to prosecute and try the perpetrators of the genocide and other crimes against humanity, especially those committed between 1 October 1990 and 31 December 1994. By 2001, formal attempts to prosecute and convict potential perpetrators, by both the Rwandan government and the International Criminal Tribunal for Rwanda (ICTR), were largely ineffective. Indeed, a key reason the *Gacaca* system was initiated was as a means of dealing with prison overcrowding and rendering justice to both genocide victims and perpetrators. In addition, the courts provided a mechanism to establish the truth of what happened and punish the perpetrators of the genocide. In this role, *Gacaca* courts supplied a means of ending impunity and enhanced reconciliation in the country through a process of truth-telling.

In general, the promise of *Gacaca* courts lies in a reflection of what it means to be Rwandan. The law and the *Gacaca* courts emphasized the idea that because genocide crimes were perpetrated publicly, the public had a moral obligation to tell the truth about what happened as witnesses, victims, or offenders. Although *Gacaca* is, in principle, a wholly participatory and democratic system, in practice, it was politicized (e.g., it was built like a typical government institution rather than how it was employed in earlier times). For instance, there were levels and government-imposed limitations including the categories of genocide suspects. Those in the first genocide suspect category were outside the *Gacaca's* trial jurisdiction and were left to civil courts in the country and/or by the ICTR. Among perpetrators in this first category were those who planned and executed genocide, and their cases were not expected to be heard in *Gacaca* sessions. Indeed, *Gacaca* sessions necessarily involved significant listening by not only the Judges and community members but also the genocide perpetrators.

The role of listening in Gacaca courts

In traditional Rwanda, when someone did harm to another member of the community, elders gathered in the "short grass" to listen to what happened and resolve conflicts. This process functioned as restitution, allowing the perpetrator to return to the community, perhaps after facing some form of retribution. This community-based justice system involved listening with the aim of peaceful coexistence of formerly conflicting parties. In essence, this system aimed to build peace within a community from the bottom up.

Similarly, in post-genocide Rwanda, the objective of *Gacaca* was to bring together local communities to witness, identify, corroborate, and deliver justice. The *Gacaca* courts consisted of a local system of participatory and restorative justice in which people, especially community elders, sat together in the *Gacaca* to settle their disputes with the objective of reconciling conflicting parties. Notably, Rwandan adults were required to participate in the weekly *Gacaca* court sessions, and court sessions were presided over by judges, more than 160,000 of whom were elected by Inyangamugayo (citizens of integrity).

Listening has been key to each phase of *Gacaca*. Initially, information gathering sessions were held in each of the communities affected by the genocide to document "those affected by the genocide, the testimonies of witnesses, and those accused of crimes" (Haberstock, 2014, p. 8). Using listening as a form of information gathering seems to have been designed to get to what the South African Truth and Reconciliation Commission (TRC) labeled *forensic truth*, "answers to the basic questions of who, where, when, how, and against whom and possibly the context, causes, and patterns of violations" (Ingelaere, 2020, p. 1). As a tool for information gathering, listening in this phase was likely marked by a motivation to capture as many details as possible without necessarily evaluating the veracity or otherwise interpreting the meaning of collected information. Although little is known about the kinds of training these listeners were provided, if following standard practice, they were likely taught to ask open-ended questions, to use minimal encouragers to signal interest and attention, and follow up their conversations by reflecting back what they heard and checking their understanding of stories (i.e., "active" listening; Bodie et al., 2015).

During the court phase itself, listening would also have been at least partially forensic in nature. But information provided during the *Gacaca* court sessions was, compared to the information gathering phase, much more about making judgments that would serve to provide justice to both genocide victims and perpetrators. In this stage of *Gacaca*, victims and their families shared a space inviting them to give voice to their experiences with perpetrators and their families who were also asked to share theirs. As such, it stands to reason that some called on to share their genocide story were likely facing different kinds of pressure than if simply recounting details to an interviewer in an information gathering exercise. Thus, although there are many examples of justice served in *Gacaca* rulings leading to unity and reconciliation (e.g., learning details about a loved one's death; Longman, 2009), so too are there reports of increased vulnerability and psychological trauma (e.g., Brounéus, 2008). And, like survivors, genocide perpetrators were faced with listening to how their actions affected and continue to affect survivors and their families, thus creating opportunities for both negative self-reflection and genuine understanding; they were also provided opportunities to ask for forgiveness.

In relation to the role of *Gacaca* in providing successful pathways to sustained peace in post-genocide Rwanda, Haberstock (2014) pointed out that this homegrown approach did more than the ICTR to connect the Rwandan people with the justice they deserved. The result of this, as pointed out by Ingelaere (2011), is that Rwandan people much prefer the *Gacaca* system to the ICTR or even the national court system. For the victims, listening was essential because they got to know what happened to their loved ones during the genocide, including how they were killed and by whom. Such information was an ultimate good because it led to confessions by perpetrators and an opportunity for forgiveness by the genocide survivors. Listening and testifying by different actors during the *Gacaca* court sessions lead to forgiveness, contributed to national unity, and created the conditions for reconciliation in post-genocide Rwanda. This also contributed to genocide prevention at a tertiary level and the overall peacebuilding process.

Gacaca courts have also been criticized on several grounds, including the process by which judges were selected. For instance, knowledge of or experience with the legal system were not prerequisites to becoming a judge. Instead, the populace elected the judges based upon reputation (Haberstock, 2014; Rettig, 2008). Another criticism of *Gacaca* is that the judges were not paid for the service rendered, which created a greater propensity for accepting bribes which also undermine the authority of *Gacaca* proceedings. *Gacaca* was also criticized on the basis of safety issues and psychological side effects associated with witnessing in a *Gacaca* trial (e.g., Brounéus, 2008). This weakness affected the process of *Gacaca* because some witnesses were barred from telling their story after intimidation or coercion from the perpetrator's family (see Corey & Joireman, 2004). Apart from the intimidation of survivors by the perpetrators, some genocide survivors were also killed, and their properties destroyed as a way of intimidating them. Some of the *Gacaca* judges were also intimidated, and others were killed. This created a state of suspicion that affected reconciliation in one way or another. Fake confessions by perpetrators because they expected to get pardons, and fear from the victims who felt vulnerable to intimidation and less protected by the government, plagued the *Gacaca* system.

As we admit the seriousness and importance of these criticisms, we also point to the immense promise of the *Gacaca* system for creating peace from the ground up. The approach is grounded in traditional Rwandan culture, and among its foundations is a willingness to listen to and attempt reconciliation of diverse and often deeply held beliefs and convictions. For all affected by traumatic experiences, being heard and feeling safe to share experiences and perspectives is essential, and the *Gacaca* court system was established to allow that type of healing to occur.

Community work, "Umuganda:" a strategy to engage community in development and peacebuilding

Umuganda was a traditional practice and cultural value of working together to solve social and economic problems for mutual benefit rooted in Rwandan culture (Uwimbabazi, 2012). Translated as "coming together in common purpose to achieve an outcome," *Umuganda* is a homegrown solution in which people in Rwanda convene regularly to carry out communal work – specifically related to sanitation, in addition to discussing issues that affect their communities (Kuteesa, 2021). According to Guichaoua (1991), *Umuganda* is rooted in the existing traditional practice of mutual aid that took place during major family and social crises like losing a family member, the destruction of a house, or difficult tasks that required family or neighbors' help. *Umuganda* was instituted as a national holiday and mandate in 2009 (Tasamba, 2019).

In post-genocide Rwanda, the government has emphasized *Umuganda* as a common development and national rebuilding strategy to reduce poverty and promote reconciliation (Uwimbabazi, 2012). As a practice rooted in the Rwandan culture of self-help and cooperation, *Umuganda* was formalized through establishing its legal framework to enhance the development of local infrastructure in addition to strengthening friendship and conviviality among Rwandans (Rwanda Governance Board, 2017). In Rwanda, *Umuganda* is held every last Saturday of the month to allow members of the community to come together and collectively undertake projects of common good and address social and economic challenges (Kuteesa, 2021).

Umuganda has contributed enormously to the physical infrastructure of Rwanda, and the government reports these community engagement activities save the country approximately 20 billion Rwandan Francs a year. In addition, *Umuganda* has led to a considerable improvement in the cleanliness of Rwanda

(Twahirwa, 2018). According to the Rwanda Governance Board (2017), *Umuganda* contributed to environmental protection through erosion control, tree planting, and cleaning and has been used in the implementation of government programs and the socioeconomic development of the community through infrastructure development (i.e., roads, houses for vulnerable people, public offices, health centers, schools, and conservation efforts). More directly relevant to this chapter, *Umuganda* continues to (a) contribute to unity and reconciliation through conflict arbitration between community members, (b) strengthen cohesion between persons of different backgrounds, and (c) provide the community opportunities to articulate their needs and express their opinions on various issues. Indeed, *Umuganda* has succeeded in being the best development framework enabling citizens to participate in the social and economic development of the country and being able to articulate issues patterning development of their communities (Rwanda Governance Board, 2017).

The practice of *Umuganda* is seen by the Rwandan government as an important policy that encourages good governance, proving to be an excellent communication channel between leaders and citizens and between citizens themselves. *Umuganda* constitutes a channel through which norms, customs, and values are discussed, debated, and disseminated, as it motivates citizens to engage in interactions, collaboration, communication, and discussions during and after *Umuganda*. Different programs are discussed during *Umuganda* meetings such as mobilization and sensitization on health insurance subscription and other health issues, security issues, the culture of saving, fighting against corruption, solving for poverty, and much more (Ministry of Local Government, 2016).

Citizens listening to the stories, concerns, perspectives, and experiences of their fellow citizens during mutually beneficial community service functions promote ownership of community peacebuilding processes and is necessary to developing sustainably peaceful communities and societies. For that purpose, community participation and empowerment are needed to help all community members feel part of the efforts to protect their peaceful coexistence and well-being. Indeed, there are specific practices within *Umuganda* that allow community members to handle social conflicts during joint activity. Our focus here is on one primary aspect of listening in *Umuganda* meetings, the listening done by local community leaders and members when handling conflicts.

Listening in Umuganda

The village is the smallest politico-administrative entity of the country and, hence, closest to the people.[2] Therefore, this is the entity through which the problems, priorities, and needs of the people at a grassroots level are identified and addressed. It is also the most basic unit for the mobilization and interaction of the public. Thus, the village is entrusted with many responsibilities including ensuring security by resolving conflicts and reconciling people's differences.

Within the village, there is another small administrative structure called ISIBO, comprised of the ten closest households. Once there is a problem between individuals or household members, those living in ISIBO sit together and listen to the individuals in disagreement. ISIBO members make clear the problem to the parties in conflicts and try to encourage the acknowledgment of mistakes and inappropriate behavior. They encourage requests for forgiveness and reconciliation between people. If people accept the advice, they reconcile. In some cases, the parties are encouraged to share a drink as a sign of forgiveness and reconciliation. If this step does not succeed, or if the conflict persists, the ISIBO gives the victim permission to bring the complaint to the village leader who attempts to reconcile them. If the village leader fails to handle the conflict, then the problem may be brought in the *Umuganda* gathering of the village to be handled in a public hearing where all participants contribute to the resolution of the problem. Thus, community participation and listening are central to the *Umuganda* meeting, convened for the purpose of providing opportunities for people to solve citizens' complaints and address mutual conflicts. These opportunities pass through four distinct phases: Description of the problem, clarification and questioning, brainstorming possible solutions, and negotiating a solution.

In the first phase, *description of the problem*, the village leader moderates a conversation between the parties in conflict. That conversation begins with giving those directly involved in the disagreement the opportunity to describe their situations. At the same time, other meeting participants listen to the parties in conflict with an ear toward providing emotional and tangible aid.

After hearing the problem, the second phase, *clarification and questioning*, involves community members asking questions to clarify parts of the story that remain unclear. According to Weaver and Farrel (1997), "*clarification* consists of questions that aim to clear ambiguities and bring further understanding of the other side's motives and concerns. *Clarifiers* seek to make the meaning of the message explicit" (p. 138). In addition to questioning, community members may participate by providing missing information as witnesses to events, especially those who are neighbors. Likewise, using paraphrasing, they seek to help others understand the role of each party, pointing out the positive and negative approaches used by each. For example, as the community is comprised of people from various backgrounds, some may intervene to provide information related to the danger and consequences of the behavior described, while others may address the law that defends the rights of the victim or outline the punishment of the perpetrator in the case of violence.

Phase three consists of the *brainstorming of possible solutions*. In this phase, community members may react to what others have said, judge the behavior of the parties in conflicts (good or bad), or suggest what to do to end the conflict. In traditional models of listening comprehension, this phase seems closest to "evaluation" or "interpretation" (see Worthington, 2018).

Finally, phase four, *negotiating a solution*, occurs after collecting different views from *Umuganda* participants. At this time, the village leader makes a summary of the key points shared by the many participants. Quite often, the interventions of community members help the parties in the conflict understand their experience from a neutral perspective and prepare them to accept the advice and conclusions of different people. Basically, the decision is based on the consensus of the majority.

In essence, various types of listening behaviors happen regularly within *Umuganda* sessions, including (a) active attempts to fully understand the problem under question, (b) asking clarification questions to fill in missing information or otherwise assist in understanding, (c) applying different perspectives or frames of reference in an effort to understand the situation from multiple vantage points, (d) practicing empathy and compassion toward all parties in the conflict, and (e) paraphrasing and summarizing main points and arguments presented, while (f) checking those understandings against how others are understanding the situation. Looking at the listening practice in the Rwandan community, the Rwandan community promotes an active, reflective listening model, whereby community members actively listen and seek to understand what parties in conflicts are saying to support them in understanding their own thoughts and feelings about the destructive conflict in which they are involved. In this context, active listening is a way to hear and respond to another person that will increase shared understanding (Chastain, 2013). This model involves different skills of:

- Non-judgmental listening to hear what people say from their perspective without trying to interpret it;
- Reflection, or using people's key words and phrases to ensure that they have understood what has been said;
- Clarifying, or questioning to find out missing or unclear information;
- Summarizing what has been said by people and their behaviors;
- Exploring, or getting the parties to start thinking about solutions that each of them could live with;
- Testing, which involves, once you have some clear potential solutions, working with the parties to understand how it might work and who needs to do what and when.

Like with *Gacaca*, active listening is the core skill used to support effective conflict resolution. In particular, *Umuganda* seems to require the type of listening that enables people to "stand back from" their situation, review it so that they can decide whether a different response might improve their situation, and/or start to perceive or experience their situation in a less distressing way (Sharland, 2008). Although listening without giving advice, taking sides, or (dis)agreeing is an empowering activity (Sharland, 2008), this technique of listening is not commonly used in *Umuganda* conflict resolution. Instead, people may return multiple times as they seek to find solutions following a failed resolution. Further, many of the meeting participants are not professional counselors. Hence, potential solutions are suggested to parties in conflict after learning what they tried before.

Like *Gacaca* courts, there are certain types of conflict, like property violations or robbery, that require specific punishments based on the value of what was destroyed, or at least the return of stolen items. If the involved parties are not satisfied, they are allowed to consult higher levels of authority, such as cell and sector leaders who may decide to orient the parties to the local justice court if necessary. The cases are also handled by local community mediators, known as Abunzi.

Umuganda exists, in part, because this method of community conflict resolution has distinct advantages in resolving community problems. In a village, people are used to discussing conflict with their leaders. When their problems are discussed publicly, they are less likely to feel that the leader is biased. In addition, when the misunderstanding is between an individual and their leaders, it is better to use a community approach to resolve problems. In general, Rwandans hold the belief that the many are smarter than the few. Thus, bringing the problem to a large group invites discussion of many possible solutions that may convince individuals to accept a resolution, especially when experts in the discussed problem's domain participate. In addition, inviting the community to reflect on their own problems constitutes a way of empowering each other and promotes the effective use of community human resources for sustainable development. Hence, the ownership of and commitment to community members to local development increases.

To be sure, some individual conflicts need to be resolved by close people who know very well the context and the day-to-day relations between them. At the same time, listening to people's conflicts often requires a neutral stance that help individuals remain fair when resolving others' conflicts. Resolving a conflict in public can be more convincing than providing a stand-alone solution and can thus sustain the community ownership and solidarity towards peaceful cohabitation. Promoting a culture of fairness and integrity is necessary to sustaining community innovative listening activities that promote sustainable peacebuilding.

There are times, however, when the village leader is neither flexible nor humble or may try to influence key people to decide in the direction of their view. When this occurs, it often leads to the dissatisfaction of parties in conflict who may then take their dispute to a higher authority. Purdy (1991) described such co-dependent communities "speaker-oriented" because of a tendency to defer to powerful (real or imagined) speakers; that is, listening is largly in deference to a small number of speakers. He compared such dependency to a more co-creative listener-orientation whereby co-dependency is replaced with interdependency; that is, listening becomes formative to the kind of community building that assumes all voices should be heard. In the same context, Chastain (2013) pointed out that "If we improve our personal listening and communication skills, we will better understand other's perspectives, emotions, and needs" (Para. 1).

Umugoroba w'Imiryango – *facilitating dialogue among community members*

The last of our three homegrown initiatives that has gained popularity in post-conflict Rwanda is *"Umugoroba w'Imiryango,"* which translates to "Families' Evening," but more commonly referred to as the *"Families' Evening Forum."* This forum has evolved from a much smaller women's group known as *"Akagoroba k'Abagore"* (Women's Evening) to forums that were expected to be more gender inclusive and later to broader and even more inclusive community gatherings. Hence, out of the original single-sex (women) forum, *Umugoroba w'Ababyeyi* (Parents' Evening Forum) was born with the aim of encouraging male participation.

The Parents' Evening Forum (*Umugoroba w'Ababyeyi*) relied on the long-standing Rwandan practice and culture of collective action and mutual support to take advantage of existing local potentialities and opportunities to solve problems within a community. One of the social expectations from *Umugoroba w'Ababyeyi* was to improve family relationships and living conditions through resolving family conflicts, preventing and fighting against gender-based violence (GBV) (Mukabera, 2017). Although Ababyeyi refers, in Kinyarwanda, to "parents" in general, the term tends to resonate more with female parents than with male parents. As a result, the initiative largely drew more female citizens and was criticized for lack of effective engagement with more men. Nonetheless, despite the gender gap, the Parents' Evening Forum was officially launched three years after it started its operations (National Women's Council, 2013). Among the Forum's key responsibilities were 1) to *bring together* male and female parents to discuss strategies to improve their relationships and welfare, 2) *listen to and provide advice* to parents or children and victims of violence or other conflicts, and 3) *share experiences and testimonies* and learn from others how they went about settling issues in the family, among many other duties. In 2020, the Forum was further renamed *"Umugoroba w'Imiryango"* (Families' Evening Forum). The name change came as way of broadening participation and being more inclusive (Kagina, 2021), expanding beyond parents to also include voices of other members of households such as young people.

Despite some valid criticism that the evening forums do not "do enough," studies have reported successes. Recent reports have revealed that the community and family-centered forums have made a noteworthy impact in helping parents share ideas on issues faced within and beyond families, ways to improve child education, and handling challenges to resolving family conflicts (Mukabikino, 2020; Nsabimana & Rutsibuka, 2022; Uwizeyimana, 2021). They have done this largely through "allowing them to freely talk; building their ability to listen and critically analyze problems; providing opportunity of self-evaluation and adopting new behavior" (Nsabimana & Rutsibuka, 2022, p. 82). Moreover, it has been observed that the former Parents' Evening Forum played an important role in not only peacefully resolving conflicts within households but also preventing GBV within them (Care International Rwanda, 2018).

More relevant to this chapter, these community forums have continually played a crucial role in building "positive peace" among Rwandan communities. According to Galtung (1996), peace does not simply mean the absence of violence or war (i.e., negative peace). Rather, peace becomes more meaningful when it is "a cooperative system beyond 'passive peaceful coexistence,' one that can bring forth positively synergistic fruits of the harmony ... [that] leads to a continuum from total separation, dissociation, to total association, union" (p. 61). For peace to be even more meaningful, it should be "peace achieved through peaceful means" (p. 56). Undeniably, the framework under which these Rwandan community forums operate are well aligned with the principle of peace underpinned by Galtung's notion of positive peace. The forums contribute to peacebuilding by addressing community issues through non-judicial peaceful means and by striving to build trust and empathy among community members.

These village-based forums have also been credited with playing a vital role in crime prevention and creating a strong bond in security and development. The community gatherings, which mainly bring together parents and elders, have also been advantageous in reuniting families and discussing security issues that require immediate attention (Rwanda National Police, 2018). It is indeed evident that in post-conflict Rwanda, the majority of applied restorative transitional justice mechanisms have heavily relied on community dialogue, which involves talking/confessing, listening, accepting accountability, asking for forgiveness, and forging unity and reconciliation as the end result. While the Forums, *Umugoroba w'Ababyeyi/Imiryango*, may not be seen as transitional justice mechanisms, they do contribute to sustainable peaceful coexistence among community members through dialogue and conflict mitigation; they also tend to complement other existing mechanisms directly concerned with post-conflict peacebuilding (See also Sotelo Castro, chapter 10).

As evident in the discussion above, it is not easy to discuss current Families' Evening Forums separate from the former Parents' Evening Forums given that one is a recently revised version of the other. Other than the name change, the two platforms have the same main objective, namely to create harmonious environments for community members through peaceful means. Thus, as effective spaces to facilitate community dialogue, both forums highlight strongly embedded listening practices that enable community members to come up with concrete solutions to common issues.

For instance, a study conducted on citizen participation in Imihigo (District performance contracts) revealed, at the time, that *Umugoroba w'Ababyeyi* (Parents' Evening Forum) was the most commended citizen participation mechanism among those studied. Moreover, this study noted that through this forum, women have been playing a key role in creating an environment where citizens feel free to express themselves (Care International Rwanda, 2018). For example, one expert observed, "Parents' evening meetings are not used for planning purposes, but rather to discuss problems that affect them, mainly conflicts in families (p. 60)," while a participant stated, "As members of parents' evening meeting, we identify problems that we face as a village, then the committee makes a report which is transmitted to cell and sector authorities" (p. 60).

Similarly, it has been observed that homegrown and grassroots approaches to social policy formulation and implementation in Rwanda have contributed to improving the living standards of Rwandans – especially among the poor and vulnerable in the areas. The fact that Rwandans, even with little formal education, can easily understand and actively participate in making decisions for their welfare and wellbeing has contributed immensely to the success of social interventions in this previously war-torn East African nation (Ezeanya-esiobu, 2017). Hence, the community forums discussed in this section, namely the Women's Evening, Parents' Evening Forums, and Families' Evening Forums, present a tangible example of promoting peaceful community through providing all-inclusive spaces where community members can collectively discuss issues, which involves active talking, listening, and devising appropriate solutions through homegrown and traditional practices.

Conclusion

Peacebuilding requires a radical approach of going to the root of issues, challenging assumptions, and proposing and embodying alternative futures (Montuori & Donnelly, 2017). Rwanda is a unique, complex case where horrendous, genocide-related crimes took place as a result of centuries of animosity and division between Hutus and Tutsi (Sentama, 2022). Just as Rwanda's complicated history is shaping the country's future, its present has also been shaped by the past. The government believes that peacebuilding in the post-genocide context is shaped by citizen participation through various homegrown approaches rooted in Rwandan culture and values.

Common to all Rwandan homegrown initiatives aimed at building and preserving peaceful coexistence in a post-conflict nation is the importance of listening as the actual basis for healing, forgiveness, reconciliation, and social cohesion. Moreover, like other societies emerging from conflict, TRCs are good examples of the important role played by victims listening to confessions and testimonies in ways that lead to healing, forgiveness, and reconciliation. In the same vein, listening has been a vital component of *Gacaca* Courts, *Umuganda*, and *Umugoroba w'Imiryango*. Solutions to conflicts and other issues important to diverse people living in solidarity within community heavily rely on both public participation and having conversations across difference.

We noted that listening has been key in Rwanda's traditional justice approaches including *Gacaca* courts where the citizens have been judges, victims, perpetrators, and witnesses. Listening in *Gacaca* court sessions, especially to conflicting parties, led to sustainable decisions, which can be a basis for peace-building. This phenomenon is more evident in post-genocide contexts like the Rwandan case indicates. It shows that some truth has been said during the *Gacaca* court sessions. Such truth is needed for the unity and reconciliation of the fractured relationships among Rwandans. This truth has helped people start to trust each other again.

The case of *Umuganda* (community work) also illustrates that listening has contributed to peacebuilding in post-genocide Rwanda through the identification of citizens' issues and seeking solutions together. Economic and resource-based issues have been identified and addressed through community work. Family conflicts have been resolved through community participation with their leaders. Such issues have been considered by some to be contributing factors to conflict. With the *Umuganda* approach, some issues that have previously derailed peace-building in Rwanda have been addressed in pursuit of peacebuilding in the country.

Finally, *Umugoroba w'Imiryango/Ababyeyi*, or Families'/Parents' Evening Forums, are highly valued and credited with playing vital roles in promoting social cohesion and peaceful coexistence among community members. They provide spaces where people can be listened to and helped. Not only are they easily accessible, they are also trusted because the members are usually people of integrity chosen by the community members themselves. Besides, there is no better starting point to nurture peace than from close to home. In the words of St. Augustine of Hippo, "Peace in society depends on peace in the family."

Notes

1 A full description of the law and its articles can be found at: https://www.refworld.org/cgi-bin/texis/vtx/rwmain/opendocpdf.pdf?reldoc=y&docid=52f2349c4
2 As a backdrop, it is important to note that Rwanda is currently composed of two layers of government (central and local). The country is divided into four provinces (which are also further divided into 30 districts each) and the City of Kigali. The districts are further divided into 416 sectors, which are themselves divided into 2,148 cells. Lastly, these cells are divided into 14,837 villages (Ministry of Local Government, 2022).

References

Bideri, D. (2009). *Le Massacre des Bagogwe*: Un prélude au génocide des Tutsi Rwanda (1990–1993). [The Massacre of the Bagogwe: A prelude to the genocide of the Tutsi Rwanda, 1990–1993]. L'Harmattan.

Bodie, G. D., Vickery, A. J., Cannava, K., & Jones, S. M. (2015). The role of "active listening" in informal helping conversations: Impact on perceptions of listener helpfulness, sensitivity, and supportiveness and discloser emotional improvement. *Western Journal of Communication, 79*, 151–173. 10.1080/10570314.2014.943429

Boudreaux, K. (2009). Land conflict and genocide in Rwanda. *The Electronic Journal of Sustainable Development, 1*, 86–95. https://www.researchgate.net/publication/42766070_Land_Conflict_and_Genocide_in_Rwanda

Brounéus, K. (2008). Truth-telling as talking cure? Insecurity and retraumatization in the Rwandan Gacaca courts. *Security Dialogue, 39*(1), 55–76. 10.1177/0967010607086823

Care International Rwanda. (2018). *Consultancy to conduct a study on women participation in decision making for Imihigo and GBV related issues: Successes and challenges.* https://www.careevaluations.org/wp-content/uploads/Final-report-V4_CareWPP_05092018-2.pdf

Chastain, A. (2013). Use active listening skills to effectively deal with conflict. Michigan State University Extension. https://www.canr.msu.edu/news/use_active_listening_skills_to_effectively_deal_with_conflict

Chrétien, J-P. (2006). *The great lakes of Africa: Two thousand years of history.* Cambridge, MA: MIT Press.

Clark, P. (2012). *The legacy of Rwanda's Gacaca courts.* Think Africa Press.

Corey, A., & Joireman, S. F. (2004). Retributive justice: The Gacaca courts in Rwanda. *African Affairs, 103*, 73–89. http://www.jstor.org/stable/3518421

Eriksson, J. (1996). *The international response to conflict and genocide: Lessons from the Rwanda experience. Synthesis report 1996.* The Swedish International Development Cooperation Agency. https://cdn.sida.se/publications/files/sida61343en-the-international-response-to-conflict-and-genocide-lessons-from-the-rwanda-experience-synthesis-report-1996.pdf

Ezeanya-Esiobu, C. (2017). The rise of homegrown ideas and grassroots voices: New directions in social policy in Rwanda, UNRISD Working Paper, No. 2017-6, United Nations Research Institute for Social Development (UNRISD). Geneva. http://hdl.handle.net/10419/186097

Galtung, J. (1996). *Peace by peaceful means: Peace and conflict, development and civilization.* Sage.

Guichaoua, A. (1991). *Tiers-Monde. Les travaux communautaires en Afrique centale. [Third world. Community work in Central Africa].* Programme National Persée. https://www.persee.fr/doc/tiers_0040-7356_1991_num_32_127_4651

Haberstock, L. (2014) An analysis of the effectiveness of the Gacaca court system in post-genocide Rwanda. *Global Tides, 8.* https://digitalcommons.pepperdine.edu/globaltides/vol8/iss1/4

Ingelaere, B. (2011). *The rise of meta-conflicts during Rwanda's Gacaca process.* (pp. 303–318). *L'Afrique des Grands Lacs, Annuaire,* 2010–2011. https://www.uantwerpen.be/en/projects/great-lakes-africa-centre/publications/annuaire/

Ingelaere, B. (2020). Assembling styles of truth in Rwanda's Gacaca process. *Journal of Humanitarian Affairs, 2,* 22–30. https://www.manchesteropenhive.com/view/journals/jha/2/2/article-p22.xml#container-26660-item-26661

Kagina, A. (2021, September 24). Gender ministry calls for greater men's engagement in tackling community issues. *The New Times.* https://www.newtimes.co.rw/article/189676/News/gender-ministry-calls-for-greater-mens-engagement-in-tackling-community-issues

Karimunda, A. M. (2019). Gacaca courts and the Abunzi Mediation committees: The journey to justice and peace consolidation in post genocide Rwanda. In T. Gatwa & D. Mbonyinkebe (Eds.), *Home-grown solutions legacy to generations in Africa: Drawing resources from the Rwandan way of life* (Vol. 1, pp. 132–164). Globethics.net Focus. https://www.globethics.net/news/2019/-/asset_publisher/iinr/content/home-grown-solutions-legacy-to-generations-in-africa-vol.1

Kuteesa, H. (2021, November 28). Rwandans launch Umuganda in Ghana. *The New Times.* https://www.newtimes.co.rw/news/rwandans-launch-umuganda-ghana

Lemarchand, R. (1970). *Rwanda and Burundi.* Praeger.

Longman, T. (2009). An assessment of Rwanda's Gacaca courts. *Peace Review, 21*, 304–312. 10.1080/10402650903099369

Mamdani, M. (2001). Beyond settler and native as political identities: Overcoming the political legacy of colonialism. *Comparative Studies in Society and History, 43*, 651–664. DOI: 10.1017/S0010417501004285

Melvern, L. (2006). *Conspiracy to murder: The Rwandan genocide.* London: Verso.

Ministry of Local Government. (2016). *National policy against delinquency.* Republic of Rwanda. https://www.minaloc.gov.rw/index.php?eID=dumpFile&t=f&f=57722&token=de3f921cf24d4de7c4277b370d3123e53eacc2c4

Ministry of Local Government. (2022). *National decentralization policy.* Republic of Rwanda. https://www.minaloc.gov.rw/index.php?eID=dumpFile&t=f&f=36377&token=bb5fe53e14a215bb74cb9ac01b864363f2942e98

Mission of NURC. (n.d.). National Unity and Reconciliation Commission. https://www.nurc.gov.rw/index.php?id=84

Montuori, A., & Donnelly, G. (2017). Transformative leadership. In J. Neal (Ed.), *Handbook of personal and organizational transformation* (pp. 319–350). Springer.

Mugenzi, M. W. (2018). *Girinka reconciliation approach and sustainable peace in Kamonyi district, Rwanda.* [Doctoral dissertation, Masinde Muliro University of Science and Technology]. MMUST Institutional Repository. http://r-library.mmust.ac.ke/123456789/1254

Mukabikino, J. H. (2020). *Parents evening forums and the transformation of domestic conflicts in Rwanda: A case study of Kimisagara sector in Nyarugenge district 2015–2018.* [Doctoral dissertation, University of Rwanda]. UR Campus Repository. http://hdl.handle.net/123456789/1135

Mukabera, J. (2017). *Women's status and gender relations in post-genocide Rwanda: Focusing on the local and everyday life level.* Globethics.net, Series 24. https://www.globethics.net/documents/10131/26882166/GE_theses_24_isbn9782889311934.pdf

Muleefu, A. (2016). Transitioning legal and justice systems in post-conflict/transitional societies. In *Towards a people centered human rights state in South Sudan: A collection of papers presented at the symposium on Human Rights in South Sudan* (pp. 36–48). International Development Law Organization and the University of Juba, College of Law. https://land.igad.int/index.php/documents-1/countries/south-sudan/gender-5/988-idlo-col-towards-a-people-centered-human-rights-state-in-south-sudan-2016/file

National Service of Gacaca Courts. (2012). *Summary of the report presented at the closing of Gacaca Courts activities.* Rwanda Ministry of Justice.

National Women's Council. (2013, March). *Umugoroba w'Abagore' (Evening for Mothers).* http://197.243.22.137/migeprof/fileadmin/user_upload/Umugoroba_w_ababyeyi.pdf

Ndahinda, M. F., & Muleefu A. (2012). Revisiting the legal, socio-political foundations and (Western) criticisms of Gacaca courts. In T. Bennett, E. Brems, G. Corradi, L. Nijzink, & M. Schotsmans (Eds.), *African perspectives on tradition and justice* (pp. 149–173). Intersentia.

Newbury, C. (1995). Background to genocide in Rwanda. *Issue: A Journal of Opinion, 23*, 12–17. 10.2307/1166500

Nsabimana, T., & Rutsibuka, I. (2022). Contribution of "Umugoroba w'Ababyeyi" programme (UAP) or parents' sunset meeting to the reduction of family conflicts in Rwanda: Case study of Cyanika sector, Nyamagabe district (2016–2019). *International Journal of English Literature and Social Sciences, 7*, 76–85. 10.22161/ijels.72.10

NURC (National Unity and Reconciliation Commission). (2012, January). *Citizen's charter.* https://www.nurc.gov.rw/fileadmin/user_upload/CITIZEN_CHARTER_NURC.pdf

Nyseth Brehm, H., Uggen, C., & Gasanabo, J.-D. (2014). Genocide, justice, and Rwanda's Gacaca courts. *Journal of Contemporary Criminal Justice, 30*, 333–352. 10.11 77/1043986214536660

Peacebuilding Support Office. (2010). *UN peacebuilding: An orientation.* https://www.un. org/peacebuilding/sites/www.un.org.peacebuilding/files/documents/peacebuilding_ orientation.pdf

Prunier, G. (1995). *The Rwanda crisis: History of a genocide.* Colombia University Press.

Purdy, M. (1991). Listening and community: The role of listening in community formation. *International Journal of Listening, 5*, 51–67. 10.1207/s1932586xijl0501_4

Republic of Rwanda. (2022). *The government of Rwanda.* https://www.gov.rw/overview

Rettig, M. (2008). Gacaca: Truth, justice, and reconciliation in postconflict Rwanda? *African Studies Review, 51*, 25–50. https://www.jstor.org/stable/27667378

Reyntjens, F. (2013). *Political governance in post-genocide Rwanda.* Cambridge: Cambridge University Press.

Rwanda Governance Board. (2017). *Impact assessment of Umuganda, 2007–2016.* https:// www.rgb.rw/fileadmin/user_upload/RGB/Publications/HOME_GROWN_SOLU-TIONS/Impact_Assessment_of_Umuganda_2007-2016.pdf.

Rwanda National Police. (2018, April 8). *Kamonyi: Umugoroba w'Ababyeyi creating impact.* https://www.police.gov.rw/media-archives/news-detail/?tx_news_pi1%5Bnews %5D=7782&tx_news_pi1%5Bcontroller%5D=News&tx_news_pi1%5Baction%5D= detail&cHash=cb41c2f6a0720ef4c5b993a489847e34

Sentama, E. (2022, February 28). *National reconciliation in Rwanda: Experiences and lesson learnt.* European University Institute. http://hdl.handle.net/1814/74338

Sezibera, R. (2012). *Peacebuilding in Rwanda: The journey so far.* African Peacebuilding Network. APN Lecture Series No. 3. https://www.ssrc.org/publications/peacebuilding-in-rwanda-the-journey-so-far

Sharland, A. (2008). *Promoting mindful communication, growth through conflict.* https://www. communicationandconflict.com/listening.html

Tasamba, J. (2019, December 29). Hundreds join end-of-year community work in Rwanda. Anadolu Agency. https://www.aa.com.tr/en/africa/hundreds-join-end-of-year-community-work-in-rwanda/1686813

Twahirwa, A. (2018, April 21). Cleanest city in Africa? Kigali scrubs up. Thomson Reuters Foundation. https://news.trust.org/item/20180420154930-0yfjv/?view=quickview

Uwihangana, C., Hakizamungu, A., Ritikanga, C., Bangwanubusa, T., & Kalinganire, C. (2020). *Social work practice in Rwanda: Indigenous and innovative models of problem solving.* Fountain.

Uwimbabazi, P. (2012). An analysis of Umuganda: The policy and practice of community work in Rwanda. http://hdl.handle.net/10413/8964

Uwizeyimana, O. (2021). *The contribution of parents' evening forum (Umugoroba w'Ababyeyi) to social welfare of households: Case study of Nyanza district (2017–2019), in the southern province of Rwanda.* [Doctoral dissertation, University of Rwanda]. UR Campus Repository. http://dr.ur.ac.rw/handle/123456789/1269

Weaver, R. G., & Farrel, J. D. (1997). *Managers as facilitators: A practical guide to getting work done in a changing workplace.* Berrett-Koehler.

Worthington, D. L. (2018). Modeling and measuring cognitive components of listening. In D. L. Worthington & G. D. Bodie (Eds.), *The sourcebook of listening research: Methodology and measures* (pp. 70–96). John Wiley & Sons.

13

THE MORAL AND INTELLECTUAL VIRTUE(S) OF LISTENING

Henrik Syse

PRIO (PEACE RESEARCH INSTITUTE OSLO) AND OSLO NEW UNIVERSITY COLLEGE

The rich contributions to this volume teach us in manifold and fascinating ways about the practices and results of true listening. We can only conclude that listening between human beings – and I would add, listening between human beings and non-human nature – is a key *ethical* requirement for achieving understanding, resolution of conflict, environmental and social sustainability, restoring harmony, and lasting peace. But what does listening as an *ethical* requirement actually entail? In my closing remarks to this remarkable book, I will, humbly, delineate what I believe to be a fruitful way to think about the ethics of listening.

Approaches to ethics

The field of ethics is crowded with approaches and theories. The three primary approaches we come across in the literature are deontology, consequentialism, and virtue ethics (Baron et al., 1997).

Deontology

Deontology (from Greek *deon* = duty, necessity, obligation), or simply *duty ethics*, is an approach to ethics that concentrates ethical reflection and practice around the need for baseline *rules* or *duties*, according to which human beings should always strive to act (Alexander & Moore, 2020; Kant, 1785 [2012]). It is worth noting that these duties in many cases correlate with rights. Thus, if we say that listening to someone who has a story to tell – or wants to share something – is a *duty*, then the other party has a *right* to tell that story, and to "be heard" (Bruneau & Saxe, 2012).

DOI: 10.4324/9781003214465-13

Consequentialism

Consequentialism is a variant of ethical thought that does not primarily pay attention to the *rules* to be followed, but rather to the *results* to be produced (Sinnott-Armstrong, 2019). In a famous dictum dating back to British philosopher Jeremy Bentham (1748–1832), "the greatest good for the greatest number" sums up the most efficient of all consequentialist philosophies, namely, utilitarianism. We should try always to produce as much utility and goodness as possible, for as many people as possible. Whereas a deontological approach would advise against lying, for example, because it violates a basic human rule, a utilitarian approach would first ask whether lying could benefit more people than telling the truth, at least in the specific case under consideration. The same calculus would apply to all kinds of cases and questions, including that of listening (e.g., is "listening to" this person in this context "useful"?).

Virtue ethics

Virtue ethics is an approach that focuses not primarily on the *actions* to be performed, as deontology and consequentialism typically do, but rather on the *qualities* of the agent performing them (Hursthouse, 2016). The core ethical question in traditional virtue ethics, with roots in the Greek philosophies of Plato (427–347 BC) and Aristotle (384–322 BC), is therefore not "What should I do?" – as important as that question is – but rather "Who should I be?" or "What characterizes a good person?" Virtue ethics is sometimes seen as a contender to and at other times as a useful complement to the more action-centered ethics approaches of deontology and consequentialism. It reminds us not least of the importance of identifying desirable character traits, habits, or virtues, both generally and related to specific tasks and activities. Applied to listening, virtue ethics would encourage us to identify virtuous character traits that encourage attention, understanding, and openness (e.g., intellectual humility; Leary, 2018).

Intellectual and moral virtues

We could analyze the ethical aspects of individual as well as community listening from all three of these ethical approaches. I believe, however, that the latter – virtue ethics – is especially apt, because it distances us from a kind of rules- and results-oriented thinking in which we easily end up formalizing and even quantifying something that, at its core, is not primarily about formulae or quantifiable consequences, but rather about attitudes and the building and safeguarding of human qualities and relations. In other words, virtue ethics helps us make ethics relevant to the lives we actually live, rather than to a more hypothetical or stylized world that easily comes across as more academic than real.

Going back to Aristotle, virtues are often – and usefully – divided into *intellectual* virtues, dealing with reason and thinking, and *moral* virtues, dealing with character traits and ethically sound attitudes. Examples of the former would be prudence (which is also partly a moral virtue, dealing with right action) and proper scientific thinking, while examples of the latter would be temperance, courage, and justice.

So, what is "listening" in the context of the intellectual and moral virtues? I would hold that listening is a virtue that should be delineated and explained in terms of four other virtues, two intellectual and two moral. I will attempt to draw on them to delineate a complex and fascinating whole.

Studiositas

Firstly, a core intellectual virtue highly relevant to our subject matter is the willingness to know and the accompanying interest in learning. Thomas Aquinas (1225–1274) designates this virtue as *studiositas*, which is contrasted with *curiositas*: the vain, self-centered, and greedy amassing of knowledge, at the expense of true insight and communal responsibility (see Thomas Aquinas, *Summa Theologiae*, II-II, questions 166 & 167, in Thomas Aquinas, 2017).

"Listening in" on something you are not supposed to, perhaps because you want to reveal someone else's weaknesses by picking up on the latest gossip, would be a prime example of *curiositas*. *Studiositas*, on the other hand, the curious search for knowledge and enrichment that characterizes an open and inquisitive mind, lies at the heart of real, constructive listening of the kind we learn about in this book. The virtue of *studiositas* is, in turn, closely associated with the classical Socratic frame of mind, namely, a deep-seated acknowledgment of what one does *not* know. Socrates (470–399 BC), Plato's teacher, held that the key to wisdom is an acknowledgment of one's own limitations and lack of knowledge. Combining that attitude with Socrates's well-known insistence on the primacy of oral, dialogical communication and dialectical thinking (as, for instance, in the dialogue *Phaedrus*), we come to associate true insight with the dialectical movement back and forth between at once inquisitive, sharing, and listening participants in conversation.

If we take peacebuilding as an instance, mediators, facilitators, or negotiators who believe that they already know the whole story, and therefore simply do not have to listen to the stories or self-understanding of the other party or parties, will most likely fail (See Argo & Brown, Chapter 8). One will be seen as self-important and unwilling to learn, even if it may be true that one is already quite knowledgeable about the other. The point is this: *Studiositas* is a habit of character more than an act. It is a way of thinking about oneself or others that manifests itself in an attitude and indeed a willingness to hear the other party out (see Bodie, 2019, for a similar – and enlightening – understanding of listening). That, in turn, instills trust and an increased willingness to share, even between parties in conflict.

Understanding the context

Secondly, the intellectual virtue I choose to call *context understanding* plays a key role in all listening, as it does for both intellectual and relational pursuits more generally. Imagine that you are trying to solve a math problem, but you simply have too little information to understand the way to do it. You need more numbers and more input to solve it – in short, you need *context*. Or if someone asks you to do a guided tour of a city, but you do not know for whom, or maybe not even which city, you obviously lack the necessary context.

For all of us, the initial context for understanding human statements or acts is quite naturally our own background and experience. But if that is all we have, we easily fall short, because it turns out that we have too little context. (This is related to filters and biases in listening, see Bodie & Jones, 2021). In such cases, we will typically not have spent enough time exploring the context in which the other relevant parties find themselves; that is, we have not spent enough time attempting to understand others' positions. This could be due to a lack of cultural knowledge or a lack of insight into the experiences and capacities of the conversation partner. Without such contextual knowledge, the art of listening changes from one marked by empathy and interest to one marked by difference – or maybe even indifference – and distance.

The intellectual virtue of being open to acknowledging and appreciating the context in which other people find themselves lies at the heart of all cross-cultural understanding. It is worth emphasizing, however, that such understanding is not the same as an uncritical acceptance of whatever the cultural context might contain and entail. Knowing that you are speaking with – and listening to – someone with Nazi sympathies, for example, provides context and insight. It does not mean, however, that you morally embrace or in any way accept the points of view in question. What it means, rather, is that you are open and eager to empathize with (which is not equivalent to sympathizing with) the conversation partner, and that you let the context inform your understanding of the contents of the message.

Robert McNamara (1916–2009), US Secretary of Defense during the Vietnam War, famously said, looking back upon his life, that one of his main mistakes was misunderstanding the *context* of the statements of his adversary in Southeast Asia. "Empathize with your enemy," he would insist (Morris, 2003). Try to understand what the "enemy" is actually after, what they are trying to achieve, and what their true intentions are. The Americans took it for granted that they understood North Vietnamese ambitions in Southeast Asia, and thus everything they heard and every message they listened to was filtered through that understanding. They turned out to be wrong. On a brighter historical note, on the brink of the nuclear disaster in 1962, McNamara helped the United States go down another path, succeeding in empathizing with Secretary General of the USSR Nikita Krustschow just enough to formulate a message of peace that was received and understood – and eventually averted nuclear war.

Temperance

This, thirdly, brings us to a *moral* virtue (even though the intellectual virtues above obviously have moral importance): temperance or moderation. In many ways, this is the most crucial virtue related to listening, with its focus on giving space and time to the other party or person. *Temperantia* in Latin is, etymologically speaking, related to the word for time: *tempus*. In a moral sense, both words turn our attention to the fact that too little time, too little focus, and not enough patience can be lethal to any true listening and dialogue process. To be temperate or moderate also means limiting one's *own* need for space and attention, thereby leading – as Socrates would emphasize – to self-knowledge and an acknowledgment of one's own limitations. (Plato's dialogue on temperance, the *Charmides*, is instructive here as well.)

Temperance is often seen as a somewhat dull and restrained virtue; it restrains rather than gives; it hinders rather than facilitates. There is some truth to that; restraint lies at the heart of true temperance. But that impression is nonetheless too facile and simple-minded; it makes us think about temperance or moderation as a virtue without ambitions, or as something downright boring, which is deeply misleading. If temperance as a virtue can provide space and time for that which we need to learn, know, and understand, and for those from whom we can learn, temperance can and should rather be the most open and even exciting of virtues.

Courage

Fourthly, and finally, I list *courage* as an essential virtue of listening. To take aboard the stories of others means that you open yourself to correction, maybe even to blame and shame. As some scholars have noted, it is an openness to being wrong, or what is called intellectual humility (see Leary, 2018, for review). It is easier *not* to check what may be out there, *not* to listen, and to instead comfortably maintain pre-existing illusions and prejudices, akin to what we know from psychology as confirmation bias (see, e.g., Baron, 2008, pp. 172, 176, 191) or what Peirce (1877) called tenacity.

Furthermore, courageous listening sets an example. If I can dare listen to you, it is more likely you feel that you should dare listen to me. If I am willing to open up to your message, then, arguably, you should be willing to open up to mine. Most virtues have reciprocal elements in them, but maybe none as much as courage, as courage at its best both impresses and inspires.

Courage is often associated with physical endeavors, and not least military affairs; and fearlessness remains a strong corollary to courage. However, as Plato famously portrayed in his dialogue about courage, the *Laches*, courage without temperance and courage without prudence can be more of a vice than a virtue. Barging forth, or refusing to retreat, because one wants to display courage and "machismo" can lead to tragedy, if not accompanied by a willingness to be moderate, prudent, and open to advice. This is true as much in civil or political affairs as in military matters.

Plato's reflections also remind us that the different virtues are closely connected. In that light, what I am arguing for in this essay, seeing the virtue of listening as a conglomerate of other virtues, makes much sense.

Concluding remarks

By choosing to close this book with a meditation on the virtues involved in listening – and indeed, seeing listening itself as a virtue – we are also issuing a challenge. Virtues, whether intellectual or moral, are not merely about learning something and then simply doing it. Realizing and manifesting virtues takes time and training. To make something into a virtue, in the sense of being a lasting basis for reliable and morally good practices, we must take the time to turn it into a habit. This is a habit we will never manage to perfect. This is a habit we will spend a lifetime attempting, but never manage, to perfect. New challenges face us all the time. That is why the virtue-ethical tradition insists that true moral virtues are built through habituation and constant practice, and not, or at least not primarily, through intellectual study. A generous person learns by being generous; a courageous person becomes courageous by performing courageous acts. Thereby, we also open ourselves to being corrected and to changing course, and, even more importantly, the virtues – the intellectual as well as the moral virtues – become part of our identity and who we want to be. As I indicated in my introduction, this approach can be applied also to how we face and respect non-human nature, and how we take aboard the needs of, for instance, fully sentient animals.

Homo sapiens is a species with the ability to *listen*, which goes way beyond the physical use of our ears (i.e., hearing; see Bodie & Wolvin, 2020). Even if we cannot hear physically, we can still listen deeply, as evidenced by examples like Scottish musician Evelyn Glennie. Even if our eyesight is impaired, we can still see, as evidenced by research showing that sight-challenged adults have similarly robust implicit theories of color when compared to sighted adults (see Kim et al., 2021). The ability to listen is thus not only a bodily one; as a *virtue* it becomes part of the way we *are* (see Lipari, 2014, for a similar argument). If the current book teaches us one thing, it is the fact that we all need to be listeners, and that we constantly should exercise our ability and willingness to listen and to learn. The key to peace and understanding arguably lies right there, in understanding proper and true listening as a crucial human virtue.

References

Alexander, L., & Moore, M. (2020). Deontological ethics. In E. N. Zalta (Ed.), *Stanford encyclopedia of philosophy* (Winter 2021 ed.). https://plato.stanford.edu/entries/ethics-deontological/

Aquinas, T. (2017). *The Summa Theologiae of Thomas Aquinas*, 2nd part of the 2nd part (II–II). (Fathers of the Dominican Province, Trans.; K. Knight, Online edition. (Original work 1265–1273). https://www.newadvent.org/summa/3.htm.

Baron, J. (2008). *Thinking and deciding* (4th ed). Cambridge University Press.

Baron, M., Pettit, P., & Slote, M. (1997). *Three methods of ethics.* Blackwell.

Bodie, G. D. (2019). Listening. In O. Hargie (Ed.), *Handbook of communication skills* (4th ed., pp. 259–286). Routledge.

Bodie, G. D., & Jones S. M. (2021). Listening fast and slow. In L. Shedletsky (Ed.), *Rationalist bias in communications theory* (pp. 172–188). IGI Global.

Bodie, G. D., & Wolvin, A. D. (2020). The psychobiology of listening: Why listening is more than meets the ear. In L. S. Aloia, A. Denes, & J. Crowley (Eds.), *The Oxford handbook of the physiology of interpersonal communication* (pp. 288–307). Oxford University Press.

Bruneau, E. G., & Saxe, R. (2012). The power of being heard: The benefits of 'perspective-giving' in the context of intergroup conflict. *Journal of Experimental Social Psychology, 48*(4), 855–866. 10.1016/j.esp.2012.02.017

Hursthouse, R. (2016). Virtue ethics. In E. N. Zalta (Ed.), *Stanford encyclopedia of philosophy* (Winter 2021 ed.). https://plato.stanford.edu/entries/ethics-virtue

Kant, I. (2012). *Cambridge texts in the history of philosophy: Kant: Groundwork of the metaphysics of morals* (M. Gregor & J. Timmermann, Trans.; 2nd ed.). Cambridge University Press.

Kim, J. S., Aheimer, B., Montane Manrara, V., & Bedny, M. (2021, August 12). Shared understanding of color among congenitally blind and sighted adults. *Proceedings of the National Academy of Sciences of the United States of America, 118*(33). 10.1073/pnas. 2020192118

Leary, M. R. (2018, September). *The psychology of intellectual humility.* John Templeton Foundation. https://www.templeton.org/wp-content/uploads/2020/08/JTF_Intellectual_Humility_final.pdf

Lipari, L. (2014). *Listening, thinking, being: Toward an ethics of attunement.* Penn State University Press

Morris, E. (Dir.). (2003). *Fog of War* [film]. Radical Media/SenArt Films.

Peirce, C. S. (1877, November). The fixation of belief. *Popular Science Monthly, 12,* 1–15. https://archive.org/details/1877-peirce-fixation-of-belief

Sinnott-Armstrong, W. (2019). Consequentialism. In E. N. Zalta (Ed.), *Stanford encyclopedia of philosophy* (Winter 2021 ed.). https://plato.stanford.edu/entries/consequentialism/.

INDEX